GW01005374

Lone Mothers in European Welfare Regimes

of related interest

Unemployment and Social Exclusion
Landscapes of Labour Inequality
Edited by Paul Lawless, Ron Martin and Sally Hardy
ISBN 1 85302 341 8

The Participation Rights of the Child
Rights and Responsibilities in Family and Society
Målfrid Grude Flekkøy and Natalie Hevener Kaufman
ISBN 1 85302 489 9 hb
ISBN 1 85302 490 2 pb

Lone Mothers in European Welfare Regimes
Shifting Policy Logics

Edited by Jane Lewis

Jessica Kingsley Publishers
London and Philadelphia

All rights reserved. No paragraph of this publication may be reproduced, copied or transmitted save with written permission or in accordance with the provisions of the Copyright Act 1956 (as amended), or under the terms of any licence permitting limited copying issued by the Copyright Licensing Agency, 33–34 Alfred Place, London WC1E 7DP. Any person who does any unauthorised act in relation to this publication may be liable to criminal prosecution and civil claims for damages.

The right of the contributors to be identified as authors of this work has been asserted by them in accordance with the Copyright, Designs and Patents Act 1988.

First published in the United Kingdom in 1997 by
Jessica Kingsley Publishers Ltd
116 Pentonville Road
London N1 9JB, England
and
1900 Frost Road, Suite 101
Bristol, PA 19007, U S A

Copyright © 1997 Jessica Kingsley Publishers

Parliamentary copyright material is reproduced with the permission of the Controller of Her Majesty's Stationery Office on behalf of Parliament

Library of Congress Cataloguing in Publication Data
A CIP catalogue record for this book is available from the Library of Congress

British Library Cataloguing in Publication Data
A CIP catalogue record for this book is available from the British Library

ISBN 1-85302 448-1 hardback
ISBN 1-85302 461-9 paperback

Printed and Bound in Great Britain by
Athenaeum Press, Gateshead, Tyne & Wear

Contents

List of Tables

List of Figures

Acknowledgements

This book represents the culmination of a long-standing cooperation between most of the contributors. Five of us contributed to *Women and Social Policies in Europe: Work Family and the State*, published in 1993 (Edward Elgar). We were enabled to continue working together through the generosity of the European Commission, which gave us a 'Human Capital and Mobility Grant'. This allowed us to employ researchers and to meet three times between 1994 and 1996. During that period several other networks of researchers working on 'women and welfare' formed, which resulted in Barbara Hobson and Trudie Knijn joining the project.

We would like to thank the researchers on the project – Sabine Rivier, Miri Song, Simonetta Simoni, Pauline Stoltz, Nicola Yates, and Monica Zulauf – all of whom worked on their own papers, for sharing their ideas with us. The sincere thanks of the editor also go to the Research and Consultancy Office of the LSE, for help in administering the EC grant, and to Sara Campbell and Diana Sibbick in Oxford, whose administrative expertise in dealing with various aspects of the research and with the preparation of the manuscript has been invaluable.

Introduction

Jane Lewis with Barbara Hobson

Lone mothers have reached the top of the political agenda in many western countries during the 1990s. In the UK, their maintenance has been the subject of specific legislation and they have frequently been discussed at the Annual Conferences of the Conservative Party. In the United States, where the backlash against lone mothers has been stronger than in any European country, 1996 legislation in the form of the Personal Responsibility and Work Opportunity Act ended lone mothers' entitlements to welfare payments (Waldfogel 1996).

The main reasons for the attention focused on lone mothers in the 1990s are twofold: (1) the visibility of this group of women has increased markedly as both their numbers have increased and their composition has changed from a group that comprised mainly widows early this century to one that in most countries is composed mainly of never-married and divorced women. In the USA in particular, but also in the Netherlands and the UK, the issue of visibility has been linked to that of race and the number of black unmarried mothers, although in the UK there is in fact little evidence that Afro–Caribbean women are more likely to become young, unmarried mothers (Phoenix 1993). (2) Lone mothers' dependence on state benefits has become a live political issue as all western governments seek to reduce the amount of welfare provided by the state and to pass more responsibility for social provision to the market, the family and the voluntary sector. That said, the essays in this book show wide variation in the extent to which lone mothers are publicly identified as a social problem. In countries as different as Italy, Germany and Denmark lone mothers are not much singled out (despite their large numbers in the last of these countries), nor are they a controversial political issue. However, while lone mothers themselves are not identified as the problem, as they are in English-speaking countries, issues to do with their maintenance and the care of their children are nevertheless on the political agenda, often as part of an expression of more general concern about changes in the labour market and the provision of child care than as a separate issue. It may be that in the English-speaking countries, as McLanahan and Booth (1989) have suggested, lone mothers have become the touchstone for wider struggles around women's roles, the relationship between the state and the family, race and class.

Lone mothers are an interesting 'border case' in the sense that they focus some of the most difficult issues faced by modern welfare states in respect of the recognition that is (or, more often, is not) accorded the unpaid work of caring, the ways in which unpaid and paid work are combined, and the responsibilities of the state as opposed to the individual and the family. The issues are complicated further by the fact that historically the problem of lone motherhood has been defined in moral as well as social terms, something that persists to this day particularly in the English-speaking countries. This has meant that never-married mothers have tended to be more heavily stigmatised than other types of lone mothers.

Lone mothers have emerged as a significant category in the discourse on social citizenship. Among feminist researchers, there has been a recognition of the need to construct alternative theories and typologies that incorporate a range of policy dimensions sensitive to gender (Lewis 1993; Sainsbury 1994). They have challenged the gender bias in both the empirical measures based on an average male worker or male head of household, as well as the frameworks that do not take into account the division of paid and unpaid work between husbands and wives. Within the dominant paradigm of policy regimes, variations in welfare states are interpreted as reflections of policy logics that revolve around a paid worker's dependence or independence of the market, which Esping Andersen (1990) referred to as 'decommodification' in his influential study of welfare regimes. However, the current wave of feminist research has revealed the weakness of this approach for understanding gender differences and has proposed alternative frameworks that reveal gendered policy logics (for example; Lewis 1992, Lewis and Ostner 1994). In seeking a dimension of social citizenship that goes beyond decommodification, feminist scholars have framed gendered social rights around the category of lone mothers, that is the right to form an independent household without the risk of poverty and marginalisation. Hobson (1994) has maintained that policy logics that permit women the right to live independently from a husband's income form the basis of a theory of gendered social citizenship, while Orloff (1993) has suggested that we develop a more generic concept of independence that would encompass 'individuals freedom from compulsion to enter potentially oppressive relationships'. Lister (1994) has employed the concept of 'defamilialism' to express the same dimension of social citizenship: the right to form one's own household.

The authors who have contributed to this book have tried to understand policy formation in respect of lone mother families since the Second World

War. We have not attempted to deal systematically with outcomes for lone mothers and their children. We have concentrated instead on the need to contextualise our understanding of the development of policies in the different countries. The importance of doing this has been acknowledged by Esping Andersen (1990):

> It is analytically difficult to confront detailed historiography with a table of regression coefficients. The former paints a dense portrait of how myriads of events impinged upon social policy formation; the latter seeks economy of explanation, and reduces reality to a minimum of variables. From the former, it is difficult to generalize beyond any particular case, in the latter, we have no history. (p.106)

We have a long way to go in coming to a more complete understanding of the fabric of welfare regimes. For example, in the case of Southern European welfare states in addition to considerable fragmentation and the persistence of clientilism (Ferrera 1996) it is important to appreciate the role of the family in channelling income from different sources and acting as a crucial buffer against poverty. Only then can the very different assumptions that have been made by policy makers about the roles of men and women be understood (Lewis forthcoming).

Policy logics and differences in the way lone mothers package income[1]

Lone mothers are potentially the sole carers and sole supporters of their children. This becomes extremely significant in the light of McLanahan, Caspar and Sorensen's (1995, p.18) conclusion that 'marriage and work reduce the risk of poverty for women in all countries, whereas motherhood increases the chances of being poor'. The huge difficulty for women in combining full-time work and care has historically been recognised by governments in the context of the widespread belief in the desirability of the male-breadwinner model family, in which men were assumed to provide income for women and children and women to provide care. In the case of the relatively small number of lone fathers, governments have expected fathers to work and to hire a housekeeper if necessary to care for any children. This expectation reflected both the idea that men should provide as breadwinners and the reality that they are paid more than women and are more strongly attached to the labour force. However, recent trends in the UK indicate that in response to changes in the labour market, increasing numbers of lone fathers are in part-time work and are drawing benefit.

---

1 We use illustrations from the country case studies in the book to make our case in this chapter. The points we refer to are elaborated in the chapters that follow.

In the case of lone mothers, there are three main possible sources of income: the labour market, the absent father and the state. During the twentieth century, in Northern European countries, lone mothers have been able to reduce their dependence on men and to increase the amount of income they obtain from the labour market and the state. However, in Southern Europe, in Italy for example, kin continue to represent an important source of support. In respect of the labour market, participation may be full time or part time and patterns vary markedly across the countries (Table 0.1).

Table 0.1 Percentage employed full-time and part-time (less than 30 hours per week) for lone mothers

	Full-time	Part-time	All employed	% of employed who are full-time
Denmark	59	16	69	86
Germany (reunited) (1992)	28 (36+ hours)	12	40	70
Ireland (1993)	-	-	23	-
Italy (1993)	58	11	69	84
Netherlands (1994)	16	24	40	40
Sweden (1994)	41	29	70	59
United Kingdom (1990/2)	17	24	41	41

Source: J. Bradshaw *et al.* (1996), p.13.

Contributions from fathers are in all countries the least important source of income for lone mothers, but countries vary widely in terms of the importance that is attached to making fathers pay, the kind of legislation that is in place to force them to do so, and whether the state guarantees maintenance payments from fathers. Finally, state benefits, which are an important source of income for lone mothers in all countries also vary widely (Figure 0.1).

Lone mothers may claim insurance based benefits if they are insured as workers or as the widows of insured men. The vast majority of divorced and unmarried mothers, however, must claim social assistance benefits as either mothers or as citizens. In other words, in some countries benefits are categorical, attaching to lone mothers *qua* lone mothers, while in others lone mothers may be part of a much broader group of people who are eligible for the same assistance-based benefits. Similarly, the children of lone mothers may be eligible for particular benefits, or qualify alongside all other children for child benefits. Nor is the separation between categorical and non-categorical benefits always complete. Sometimes, as in the UK until very recently, lone mothers claim

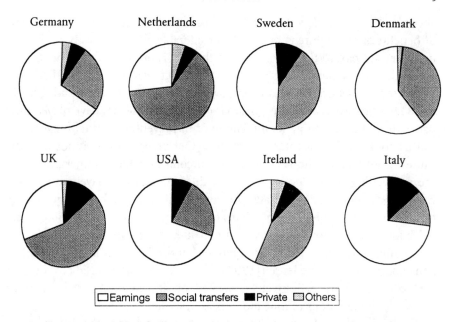

Germany	Netherlands	Sweden	Denmark

UK	USA	Ireland	Italy

☐Earnings ▨Social transfers ■Private ☐Others

Note: Social transfers include child or family allowances, unemployment compensation, parental leave pay, means tested cash benefits, near cash benefits and other social insurance. Private transfers include alimony or child support, other private income.

Source: Data for this figure are from Luxemburg Income Study. The years included are; USA 1991; Germany 1984; UK 1986; Netherlands 1991; Sweden 1992; Denmark 1992; Ireland 1987; Italy 1991.

Figure 0.1: Income packages of lone mothers, aged 20–55.

assistance-based benefits alongside other adult claimants, but also receive small premiums or top-ups in recognition of their special needs.

Thus lone mothers 'package' income from different sources, but the way in which they do so varies considerably from one country to another. It should be noted that married mothers also package income over the lifecourse, using in the main the labour market and husbands. In Britain the proportion of household income contributed by women increased from 20 to 28 per cent between 1975 and 1979, following the introduction of the Equal Pay and Sex Discrimination Acts. However, during the whole of the 1980s it increased only a further 2 per cent, to 30 per cent (Land 1995), despite the continued increase in married women's labour market participation.

Competing explanations for the heavy reliance of lone mothers on state welfare have emphasised the extent to which such support is a 'rational choice' in the light of the available options; the extent to which welfare systems shape the recipient's self-confidence and willingness/capacity to leave the welfare system; and the extent to which it is lone mothers' values that are an important factor (Bane and Ellwood 1994). Given the nature of the debate in the USA about 'welfare dependency' (a term often used to describe long-term recipients of benefits and therefore perjorative), considerable attention has been focused on the moral hazard that may attach to the provision of welfare benefits, that is, whether the availability of state support is in fact a cause of lone motherhood. Respected academics (Bane and Jargowsky 1988; Furstenberg and Cherlin 1991) have concluded for the USA that government policies have played little part either in encouraging family failure or in preventing marital breakdown. In this book we do not enter this territory. Our preoccupation is not with the causes of lone motherhood or with the outcomes for lone mothers, but with the unravelling of the 'policy logics' of different European welfare regimes. Even if social policies do not 'cause' or 'cure' family change, they can ameliorate to very different degrees the problems of lone mothers and in so doing affect behaviour. In addition, they may play an important part in promoting and sanctioning a particular view of lone motherhood, which may in turn also affect behaviour. As Mason and Jensen (1995) have stressed, it is important to consider the part played by collectively generated or agreed norms and sanctions alongside the decisions of lone mothers as individual actors.

Explaining the differences between countries in regard to the way in which lone mothers package income is complicated, but we suggest that they are strongly related to the policy logic, by which we mean the assumptions, principles and premises of welfare regimes. In the first book in which many of the contributors to this volume came together (Lewis 1993), we used the male-breadwinner model to examine the nature of assumptions underpinning social policies towards women. The model was derived from the empirical investigation of the history of women's relationship to welfare regimes, first in Britain, France and Ireland, with the German case being added later (Lewis 1992; Lewis and Ostner 1994). In its pure form, we would expect to find married women excluded from the labour market, firmly subordinated to their husbands for the purposes of social security entitlements and tax, and expected to undertake the work of caring (for children and other dependants) at home without public support. No country has ever matched such a model completely, but some have come much closer than others. Previous work also found that some countries, especially Scandinavian countries, had moved much further away from such a model in the late twentieth century, towards an assumption that all adults would be breadwinners. Thus, policy logics have shifted as assumptions regarding women's role have shifted. Policies based on the assumption that adult women would be wives have given way in varying degrees to assumptions that they will be engaged in the labour market. Furthermore, as the pace of family change has quickened, policy has focused more on the obligations of mothers and fathers than on those of wives and husbands. In this book we began our work by examining the policy logics operating in respect of policies towards lone mothers.

Historically, under the logic of the male-breadwinner model, lone mothers became a social problem because they lacked a male breadwinner and yet had children to support. The terminology used to describe lone mothers has often reflected this way of thinking about lone mothers (as well as the level of stigma that lone mothers have faced). Thus in Britain in the late 1960s the term 'fatherless families' was often used and in the Netherlands, 'incomplete families'. This kind of terminology contrasts with that used in Sweden, where the term 'solo mother' indicated a measure of support for the idea that lone mothers should be self-supporting.

Governments were faced with a decision as to whether and how far to step in to replace the male earner, in other words, how far to treat lone mothers as mothers and how far to treat them as workers. Historically, countries in which the male-breadwinner logic has been strong have tended to make a dichotomous choice in this respect. Thus in Britain under the poor law (which was finally abolished in 1948), lone mothers tended to be treated as *workers* and were told to keep as many of their children as they could by wage-earning. The rest would be cared for by the state. Widows were treated most leniently, and shortfalls in income were often made up by 'outdoor relief' in the form of cash or kind. Unmarried mothers were treated the most harshly because of their moral taint, a tendency that was stronger still in Ireland and which has come to the fore most recently in Italy (*see* Chapter 7). In Britain, relief was usually given to them and/or their children only inside the workhouse. Separated women (divorce was relatively rare until after World War II) would often be refused help for a period of time, to make sure that there was no collusion between husband and wife to defraud the authorities.

In Britain, as in the USA, women campaigned for mothers' pensions or mothers endowment, renamed in Britain during the inter-war years children's endowment or allowances. In the USA, as Theda Skocpol (1992) has traced, they were conspicuously successful. However, in Britain, governments fought shy of allowing claims on the basis of motherhood and in 1925 finally agreed to mothers' pensions only for widows, paying them on an insurance basis to the wives of men who had been insured (Pedersen 1993; Lewis 1995). The claims of lone mothers as mothers were recognised explicitly in Britain after World War II, when under the National Assistance Act of 1948 they were not required to register for work if they had dependent children under 16. Indeed, lone mothers on benefit who have wished to go out to work have been penalised by very low earnings disregards. The reasons for this had to do with the increased importance attached to mothering as a result of the influential work carried out by Bowlby (1951) on 'maternal deprivation' and the persistence of male- breadwinner ideology. William Beveridge's 1942 blueprint for post-war welfare reform insisted on the 'vital importance' of the work that women did at home.

Thus the USA and the UK, both strong male-breadwinner regimes, made provision by mid-century for treating lone mothers as *mothers*. However, while it is possible to argue that the policy logic associated with the idea of a male-breadwinner model family has continued to influence the way in which the 'problem' of lone motherhood is conceptualised, particularly in terms of the dichotomous choice that tends to be made between regarding lone mothers as workers or as mothers, there were and are important differences between strong male breadwinner countries in terms of lone mothers' sources of income.[2] Labour market participation differs widely between the UK, the USA, Germany, the Netherlands and Ireland, all countries in which adherence to the male breadwinner model has persisted into the late twentieth century. Furthermore, lone mothers' labour participation rates in these strong male-breadwinner countries often differ significantly from those of married mothers. The reasons for lone mothers' labour market behaviour has to do largely with the nature and generosity of their other sources of income, particularly state benefits, and also with the nature of the sources of care for their children. However, it may also be related in complicated ways to culture and identity. For example, in the Netherlands, the labour market participation rates of both married and lone mothers are low and Chapter Four refers to data that indicates the extent to which mothers attach importance to spending time at home with children. In Britain, Hakim (1996) has argued (very controversially) that the large number of women working part-time do so out of choice rather than because there are impediments to their full-time employment.

If we pursue explanations for differences between strong male-breadwinner states, we find that in the case of the USA Orloff (1994) has stressed the importance of the market as a decisive determinant of the welfare regime. Mishra (1993) has also insisted on the importance of differentiating market liberal from welfare liberal regimes. In the USA the only market liberal regime in his view, state provision for lone mothers has been stigmatised as a categorical assistance-based benefit and is mean in terms of amount, with the result that lone mothers have been pushed into the labour market. The state provision of child care provision in the USA is also poor, although there is more state support for childcare (largely through the tax system, which favours those in better paid jobs) than in Britain.

In Germany, the state benefit system is insurance based. Lone mothers who have to resort to state support must rely on second class social assistance benefits and their position is very unfavourable compared to that of wives who have not entered the labour market, and who rely on insurance-based benefits derived from their husbands. In addition, the jobs secured by lone mothers in

---

2   Scheiwe (1994) has also stressed the importance of differentiating between male-breadwinner regimes.

Germany tend to pay better than those held by lone mothers in Britain. Thus in Germany also there is a substantial incentive for lone mothers to work, notwithstanding the relatively lower state provision of childcare. In the Netherlands and in Britain the position is somewhat different. Lone mothers draw social assistance, but in the post-war period this has been a nationally determined benefit, which is drawn by men as well as women. The stigma attaching to such benefits has lessened substantially in Britain since the 1970s. The Netherlands has historically paid generous benefits, sufficient to replace a male breadwinner's earnings. In these countries lone mothers have not been pushed into the labour market. Nor have they been in Ireland, where assumptions about female dependence on a male wage have been most explicitly embedded in the categorical benefits that are available to lone mothers, which classify them in terms of their relationships, past or present, to men.

However, it must be remembered that policy logics based on assumptions about male breadwinning tend to treat lone mothers as *either* workers *or* mothers. In the USA, the recent trend towards implementing 'workfare' programmes, under which claimants must work or train in return for benefit, has also been applied to lone mothers. In the UK, Ireland and the Netherlands, the pendulum has, in the 1990s, begun to swing in the direction of treating lone mothers more as workers. Thus in the UK earnings disregards for lone mothers have been increased and the eligibility criteria for benefits paid to those in work have been extended. In the Netherlands, similar moves have also been accompanied by measures to increase local discretion over the rate of assistance-based benefits.

Indeed, the swing to treating lone mothers as workers is more pronounced in the Netherlands and Ireland than in the UK, where, as in Germany, more attention has been paid to the role of fathers as providers. If lone mothers continue to be treated mainly as mothers and it is decided (for reasons that have much to do with Conservative ideology in the UK and with traditional attachment to the principle of subsidiarity in Germany) that the state should play a minor role, then biological fathers represent virtually the only other possibility for support. In Germany, which operates a guaranteed maintenance scheme and where maintenance payments from fathers are deducted by employers, very few fathers avoid payment. However, in the UK it has proved very difficult to implement the new policy of extracting more money from fathers. The 1991 Child Support Act moved child support from the sphere of private law into the sphere of public administration and aimed to make men support all their biological children. The Act places an obligation on women to identify the father of their children, something that was abolished in Sweden in the 1970s at the same time as it was also rejected in the UK as illiberal. Protests from mainly middle-class fathers and their second wives has resulted in substantial modifications to the formula governing payment by fathers. This contrasts with Sweden, where proposed legislation to increase fathers' contributions has been broadly accepted. The Swedish two-earner model is also a two-parent model and it is assumed that fathers will provide care as well as cash. Similar legislation to the British Child Support Act was enacted during the 1980s in the USA and in Australia, although the form the legislation took was substantially different. In Australia the main aim was to do something about child poverty, whereas in the USA and the UK the aim was largely to bring down public expenditure. In other words, lone mothers should depend on the labour market and on absent fathers for income rather than the state.

In other policy regimes the way in which lone mothers are treated is substantially different. The Scandinavian countries have moved furthest away from the male breadwinner model towards an assumption that all adults, male and female, will be in the labour market, which means that lone mothers *per se* are not conceptualised as a problem. Rather, it is assumed that adult women will have different employment profiles and needs for child care over the life-cycle. The fault line is drawn not between one- and two- parent families, but between single earner and dual earner families, which means that the issue of achieving equity between one- and two-parent families which has troubled policy makers in strong male-breadwinner countries is absent. The state provision of child care is high, and lone mothers' labour market participation is, like that of married mothers, high. But they also have substantial call on citizenship-based state benefits and also on insurance-based benefits, such as parental leave, which operates in Denmark as a tax-based benefit and in Sweden via the labour market and the insurance system. As Sainsbury (1996) has stressed, mothers' entitlements to benefits and to care services have been universalised in Sweden (and indeed in Denmark), which has proved enormously important for the welfare of lone mothers. Thus the Danish and Swedish welfare regimes (the Norwegian is somewhat different (*see* Leira 1989)) can be interpreted as being based on a combination of principles that are in a hierarchical relationship one to the other. First comes the dual earner principle, indicating that all citizens must work; second comes the worker citizen's right to social services (provided at the local level); and third comes an official commitment to sharing unpaid work which, however, is not enforced legally. It is interesting too that while there are current debates about the role of fathers in the Scandinavian countries, these focus on the father's responsibility to care rather than to provide.

Italy has been categorised as a 'Latin Rim' welfare state (Leibfried 1991), although Trefiletti (1995) has argued strongly that it in fact constitutes a separate welfare regime model. As Chapter Seven shows, dependence is primarily an intergenerational matter in Italy, with children remaining economically dependent on parents longer than is usual in most Northern European countries and lone mothers resorting to their family of origin for support. What is interesting from our point of view is the fact that lone mothers are not perceived as a problem in this country either, although for entirely different reasons from the Scandinavian countries. The labour market participation of lone mothers is high and it is largely child care provided by the extended family that permits them to work, a state of affairs that was common in the UK until the 1970s. The majority of lone mothers are in fact widows and these women have entitlements to state benefits. Divorced and unmarried mothers, however, must depend entirely on the labour market and on kin. They are thus largely invisible to the state.

The policy logics that operate within welfare regimes are helpful in determining how a choice is made in deciding whether a lone mother is to be treated as a worker or as a mother, or whether both kinds of work are recognised. They are, therefore, helpful in predicting the way in which lone mothers package income. These logics, however, are far from stable. In countries where the male-breadwinner model has been strong, the choice for governments has been dichotomised: lone mothers are to be treated predominantly as either mothers or workers. There has been some movement in all four strong male-breadwinner countries – Ireland, the UK, the Netherlands and Germany – towards treating lone mothers as workers, but in the UK and Germany there is considerable ambivalence about the proper role of women with young children which has resulted in a renewed emphasis on the role of men as providers, albeit as biological fathers, rather than as husband–breadwinners. In countries that have moved furthest away from the male-breadwinner model, we would expect there to be, as indeed there is, high labour market participation on the part of all mothers, supported by citizen-based entitlements to cash and to child care. However, as Chapters Five and Six show, rising unemployment has had a disproportionately detrimental effect on Danish and Swedish lone mothers. In Italy, there is some evidence of moves towards a more explicit set of male-breadwinner assumptions in the most recent legislation, reflecting the inflexibility of the labour market and the economic dualism between north and south.

There is some evidence of convergence between the countries in that there is now no country where lone mothers are not expected to work. Even in the Netherlands, where relatively generous benefits to mothers who stayed at home stopped the emergence of a poverty problem associated with lone motherhood, there has been a move towards treating lone mothers as workers. However, it is difficult to be sure of policy directions in the 1990s which are proving to be a period of considerable change; the number of countries in which a 'commission' on the family has been set up bears witness to this. Equally, we can as easily stress diversity as convergence. For example, the Netherlands shares a commitment to the ideology of motherhood with Germany and Ireland, its social assistance system with the UK, and its tolerance of family diversity with Sweden.

It would in any case be a mistake to claim too much for a framework based on the policy logics attaching to the male-breadwinner model. All principles are subject to enormous modification in the process of implementation. The mechanisms for delivering social welfare are also an important factor affecting the income packaging behaviour of lone mothers. The fact that the UK social security system relies primarily on nationally determined, non-categorical, means-tested assistance based benefits and that in Germany on social insurance based benefits means that lone mothers in Germany have to choose between lower social assistance benefits and reasonably good jobs, while their counter-parts in the UK are treated the same – albeit meanly – as other adults, male and female, who draw benefit. With low earnings disregards in the benefits system, low earnings and high child costs, it is not surprising that labour participation rates are lower in Britain than in Germany and that British lone mothers spend relatively long periods of time on benefit (on the effects of means-tested benefits *see* Wong, Garfinkel an McLanahan 1993). Mechanisms may also affect the treatment of lone mothers. For example, decentralised benefits and services have produced favourable outcomes for lone mothers in Denmark, where minimum levels of provision are set nationally and active local participation decides whether these will be topped-up. However, a move to decentralisation in the Netherlands and in Sweden has had the reverse effect because local powers of discretion are much greater and the policy has succeeded in puncturing nationally agreed levels of provision.

There are also variables that cross-cut policy logics. The studies in this book show that politial ideology in respect of family policy is one of the most important. Martin (1995) has stressed the importance of a commitment to explicit family policies in France in lowering the poverty rate among lone mother families. In the UK in the 1960s and early 1970s, it was considered important to strive for the equal treatment of children in two-parent and in one-parent families, just as it has been in Germany in the more recent past. However, during the 1980s and 1990s in Britain commitment to investing in families and in children has faded. While the UN Convention on the Rights of the Child was influential in Germany, it was not in the UK, where child poverty increased dramatically in the 1980s. Research has also suggested that the lack of investment in children in the UK is crucial to explaining the high rate of teenage motherhood (Kiernan 1996). There is a similar lack of any commitment to explicit family policies in Ireland, where the rhetoric of motherhood and family values has not resulted in extensive investment in children. Despite their very different policy regimes, Germany and the Scandinavian countries share a political commitment to investing in children. Furthermore, it is this commit-ment that helps to explain the difference in the way that German policy in respect of father/providers works out compared with the UK. In Germany, the commitment was to further the best interests of the child, whereas in the UK the primary aim was to reduce public expenditure.

Policy trends and future prospects

In the countries considered in this book, lone mothers have only been labelled a severe social problem only in the UK. It is possible that an increase in their numbers in either Italy or Germany might change the situation in this respect in those countries, while changes in other variables such as unemployment rates, have begun to have some effect on the perceptions of lone motherhood in Sweden, if not in Denmark.

Though the essays in this book do not address explicitly the outcomes for lone mothers in terms of poverty and social exclusion, embedded in the policy logics of welfare states are policy formulas that help to shape outcomes. Looking at the European data, it seems that where lone mothers' labour market participation rates are high they are likely to be better off. However, Deborah Mitchell (1993) has pointed out that were a hypothetical Australian lone mother to be transported to the USA or Sweden they would be more likely to be employed, but in the USA their poverty rate would increase whereas in Sweden it would decrease. In other words, income from employment is only part of the story.[3] In Sweden transfers are also generous, as well as the jobs lone mothers are likely to get being generally better paid than in the USA. Bradshaw et al.'s (1993) study of child benefit packages in Organisation for Economic Cooperation and Development (OECD) countries reached the same conclusion as Kahn and Kamerman (1983) in the early 1980s: that lone mothers are likely to do best where benefits for children generally are generous. Sainsbury (1996) has also pointed out that they do best where benefits and care services for mothers are universalised. Thus it seems that lone mothers' welfare is greatest where they are allowed to package income: that is where there is income from employment and from transfers; where benefits are universal for mothers and for children rather than categorical for either lone mothers or their children; and where the 'social wage' is high, especially in respect of child care provision. It is the UK's relatively generous child benefit package that helps to lift lone mothers in that country far above USA poverty rates; whereas in the Netherlands it is the relative generosity of assistance based benefits. But it is in the Scandinavian countries that most of the criteria for well-being are met.

A key policy issue that emerges in respect of lone mothers is thus the degree and kinds of recognition that are given to care work, such as child care, care allowances, child benefit, and parental leave. Variations in the recognition accorded care work, both in the level and conditions of entitlement, reflect

---

3 Mitchell's findings are based on coefficients derived from a regression equation based on a range of variables and not on actual people.

different policy logics around male breadwinning. Thus in the Scandinavian countries, the incentives for women to enter the labour market go hand in hand with extensive public daycare services and parental leave benefits linked to labour market activity. In contrast, means-tested benefits in the UK have acted as a constraint to labour market activity among lone mothers because of low earnings disregards. Yet the value of carework has been awarded some recognition in the British welfare state[4], which has meant that until 1988 lone mothers received relatively higher means-tested benefits than couples (Lewis, Land and Kiernan, forthcoming).

As the majority of lone mothers are the primary carers in their families, lone mothers in welfare states with meager provision for women's unpaid care work tend to have the worst outcomes (Figure 0.2).

%

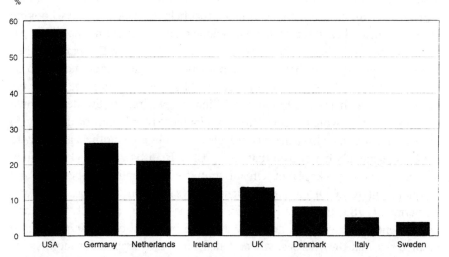

Source: Data for this figure are from Luxemburg Income Study. The years included are; USA 1991; Germany 1984; UK 1986; Netherlands 1991; Sweden 1992; Denmark 1992; Ireland 1987; Italy 1991.

Figure 0.2: Poverty rates of lone mothers, aged 20–55

From this perspective, one can interpret the very high rates of poverty among lone mothers in the United States and Australia in terms of the failure to acknowledge care work as a legitimate area of societal responsibility. In both countries widows are treated generously for their service to male breadwinners, but unmarried mothers and divorcees lie outside the policy logic of provisioning based upon the contributions of breadwinners.

---

4   The UK is one of the few countries to provide an allowance for the carers of elderly and disabled people. This benefit, the invalid care allowance, was introduced in order to compensate those carers who had to leave the workforce.

The position of lone mothers thus begs questions to do with the relationship between caring and social citizenship. Fraser (1994) has proposed two equity models that reflect different forms of support for women's carework: the Universal Caregiving Parity Model and the Universal Breadwinner Employment Model. The former would promote equity through support for women's informal work of caring. The latter would provide daycare and services that permit women to become equal participants to men in the labour market. Fraser put these models forward in order to guide feminist strategies. We have modified them in order to propose a framework for Care Regimes, based on the sources available to reward lone mothers for their carework: the Parent–Worker Model and the Caregiver Social Wage Model. These represent two alternatives for recognising caring and both reveal coherent strategies for the organisation of paid and unpaid work. Two countries featured in this volume have exemplified these two models: Sweden (*see* Chapter 6) may be held to represent the paradigm case of the parent–worker model and the Netherlands (*see* Chapter 4) comes closest to approximating the caregiver social wage model.

Table 0.2 outlines the basic characteristics of societies that express these two types of care regimes. The caregiver social wage model assumes that all mothers will be carers and that lone mothers are entitled to care benefits equivalent to an adequate wage for the duration of the childrearing years. Unlike social benefits that require recipients of state benefits to seek employment, the caregiver benefit assumes that mothers will not be in paid work. The parent–worker model assumes all mothers will be active labour force participants and that care services are available and affordable for working parents. It also

Table 0.2 Care regimes: ideal types

Characteristics of Caregiving Model	Characteristics of Parent/ Worker Model
High rates of economic dependency among married women	Low rates of economic dependency among married women
Strong male breadwinner ideology	Weak male breadwinner ideology
Low rates of labour force participation	High rates of labour force participation
Mothers would be full-time carers	Mothers would be full-time earners
Main source of income, social transfers	Main source of income, earnings
Low rates of poverty for solo mothers	Low rates of poverty for solo mothers
The ability to form one's household	The ability to form one's household
No stigmatisation	No stigmatisation

Source: Hobson and Takahashi 1996.

provides recognition of care in the form of parental leave benefits and benefits to care for sick children that are dependent upon employment status. The parent–worker model thus offers lone mothers inclusion in the labour market and a social wage to make labour market participation possible. Both models reflect different policy logics around the organisation of unpaid caring work, as can be seen from the top half of Table 0.2, but both recognise the importance of care and offer coherent policy solutions that have enabled lone mothers to form autonomous households with a low risk of poverty an marginalisation. This is shown in the same outcomes at the bottom of the table.

These possible models for rewarding all women's carework effectively encapsulate the feminist dilemma over equality versus difference, that is, whether to treat women like men or to recognise gender differences. Governments, for example in the Netherlands and the UK, are moving away from supporting a lone mother-as-carer model but there is always the danger in historically strong male breadwinner states such as these, that policy makers will treat lone mothers dichotomously as either mothers or workers and ignore the social wage that is necessary to make their labour market participation possible.

The relatively scant evidence that is available on what lone mothers themselves want seems to indicate an interesting similarity between women in different countries. Chapter Five (on Denmark) refers to the fact that women would like to work part-time, a similar finding to that of the Dutch and British contributors from a small scale, comparative study of divorced mothers in the two countries (Knijn and Lewis, forthcoming). In other words, lone mothers would seem to want to package income, rather than be treated solely as mothers or as workers. This is due as much to the priority they give to their work of child care, which most would list as their prime responsibility, and to the acute time-poverty suffered by lone mothers who work full time as to concern about material well-being.

There can be little doubt that lone mothers also want to live autonomously in the sense of being able to form their own households. As soon as they were able never-married mothers in all countries voted with their feet to quit the mother and baby homes that were usually run by religious orders. It is a fundamental ambiguity of most modern welfare states[5] that while they have held to assumptions as to the rightness of the traditional two-parent family, they have, by providing benefits and social housing, also permitted family transformation.

---

5   Sweden has since the 1970s been officially neutral in respect of the desirability of any one family form. The same is true of Denmark in practice, although there is no clear legislative basis for the policy.

There remains the issue as to whether the autonomy of lone mothers is being eroded by current policy trends. In the English-speaking countries, particularly in the UK and the USA, there has been a singular backlash against the autonomy of lone mother families. This has been provoked in part by fear of the behaviour of unattached young men, 'the yob culture' to use the British term, and in part by the effects on the socialisation of children measured mainly in terms of educational achievement. While the welfare of children has also been a priority in the German debate, lone mothers have not been made the focus of blame as they have in the USA and the UK. In the USA the situation is clear: the abolition of eligibility for welfare benefits in the form of Aid to Families with Dependent Children is bound to have an adverse effect on the autonomy of lone mothers. Curtailing lone mothers' access to social housing has been high on the policy agenda in Britain for some years and benefits for lone mothers have been cut. In Ireland autonomy is severely restricted in a social security system that is so far from individualising benefits. In Germany, the focus on children rather than on lone mothers *per se* enables that country to avoid the worst excesses of the USA and the UK, but means that the special needs of lone mothers may go unrecognised. In Italy, the needs of all lone mothers except widows remain largely hidden.

What is clear from the experience of the Netherlands and the Scandinavian countries is the extent to which the existence of a social wage is crucial to securing the autonomy of lone mothers. Any expectation that an increase in labour market participation alone will be enough substantially to improve their position is doomed to disappointment. The social wage, however, is most effective where it works in concert with high labour market participation, as in the Scandinavian countries. Our findings are in line with those of McFate, Smeeding and Rainwater (1995), who conclude that lone mothers do best in countries where they both work and receive state benefits, or where government is generous in supporting all mothers who stay at home. The threat of higher unemployment and attempts to roll back the support of the state in the form of cash and care to lone mother families is bound to erode their autonomy.

Outcomes for lone mothers in terms of low poverty levels are also best in the Scandinavian countries, although they are also good in Germany, where the emphasis is placed on securing the welfare of children, and in the Netherlands, where the stress has been on adequate support for all mothers who stay at home to care for children. Indeed, it is not clear that an emphasis on lone mothers *per se* serves them well. In Ireland the focus of attention is lone mothers, but the system does not secure their social integration. Nevertheless, there is a difficult balancing act to be performed. Lone mothers want to be full participants in their societies; they want inclusion but they also want recognition of their special needs. While the Scandinavian countries have gone furthest in terms of inclusion, Chapter Five warns of the risk that their needs may be obscured.

Nevertheless, it is impossible to ignore the importance of a commitment to integration and inclusion on the part of governments in determining the welfare of lone mothers, whose welfare depends on there being universal, citizenship-based entitlements to benefits and services. The key to achieving that is a commitment to a welfare state that amounts to more than merely the provision of social provision to the destitute. It is the absence of such a commitment to social inclusion and integration that makes the UK the exceptional case and gives rise to the circumstances in which polarisation increases and the gulf between rich and poor continues to widen. The policy logics of the UK and the Netherlands in respect of lone mothers were very similar until very recently in that they both treated lone mothers with dependent children as mothers and did not require them to register for work while on benefit. However, in terms of the wider social policy context, it is possible to argue that the UK has been closer to the USA in its determination to free the rich from high taxation and to limit its expenditure on the poor. Thus benefits were far less generous in the UK than in the Netherlands. Pressures are mounting in other European countries to be more market driven and to spend less on policies designed to secure social inclusion, but thus far no country other than Britain has eagerly embraced policies that result in social polarisation. The viciousness of the attack on lone mothers in Britain is deplored by many, but is nevertheless understood as part and parcel of the way in which social policy has developed in the 1980s and 1990s, and it is this that is incomprehensible to those from other European countries.

References

Bane, M. and Jargowsky P.A. (1988) 'The links between government policy and family structure: what matters and what doesn't.' In A. Cherlin (ed) *The Changing American Family and Public Policy.* Washington DC: Urban Institute Press.

Bane, M. and Ellwood, D. (1994) *Welfare Realities. From Rhetoric to Reform.* Cambridge: Harvard University Press.

Beveridge, W. (1942) *Report on Social Insurance and Allied Services.* Cmd. 6404. London: HMSO.

Bowlby, J. (1951) *Maternal Care and Maternal Health.* Geneva: Geneva World Health Organisation, Switzerland.

Bradshaw, J., Ditch, J., Holmes, H., Whiteford, P. (1993) *Support for Children. A Comparison of Arrangements in Fifteen Countries: Department of Social Security Research Report No.1.* London: HMSO.

Bradshaw, J., Corden, A., Eardley, T., Holmes, H., Hutton, S., Kennedy, S., Kilkey, M. and Neale, J. (1996) *The Employment of Lone Parents.* London: Family Policies Study Centre, T.I.3.

Esping Andersen, G. (1990) *The Three Worlds of Welfare Capitalism.* Cambridge: Polity.

Ferrera, M. (1996) 'The "southern model" of welfare in social Europe.' *Journal of European Social Policy 6*, 1, 17–37.

Fraser, N. (1994) 'After the family wage: gender equity and the welfare state.' Paper given at the 'Crossing Borders' Conference, Stockholm, May 27–29.

Furstenberg, F. Jr. and Cherlin, A. (1991) *Divided Families. What Happens to Children when Parents Part.* Cambridge: Harvard University Press.

Hakim, C. (1996) *Key Issues in Women's Work. Female Heterogeneity and the Polarisation of Women's Employment.* London: Athlone.

Hobson, B. (1994) 'Solo mothers, social policy regimes, and the logics of gender.' In Sainsbury, D., *Gendering Welfare States.* London: Sage.

Hobson, B. and Takahashi, M. (1996) 'Care Regimes, Solo Mothers, and the Recasting of Social Citizenship Rights.' In *Engendering Citizenship, Work and Care,* Seminar 1 of EC Programme, 'Gender and Citizenship: social integration and social inclusion in European welfare states. Aaborg.

Kahn, A. and Kamerman, S. (1983) *Income Transfers for Families with Children: An Eight Country Study.* Philadelphia: Temple Press.

Kiernan, K. (1996) 'Family change: parenthood, partnership and policy.' In D. Halpern, S. Wood, S. White and G. Cameron *et al.* (eds) *Options for Britain.* Aldershot: Dartmouth Press.

Knijn, T. and Lewis, J. (typescript 1997) 'Divorced mothers in the Netherlands and the UK: realities and preferences.'

Land, H. (1995) 'Rewarding care. A challenge for welfare states.' Unpublished paper.

Leifried (1991) 'Towards a European welfare state? On the integration potentials of poverty regimes in the EC.' Bremen University Working Paper.

Leira, A. (1989) *Models of Motherhood. Welfare State Policies and Everyday Practices. The Scandinavian Experience.* Oslo: Institute for Social Research.

Lewis, J. (1992) 'Gender and the development of welfare regimes.' *Journal of European Social Policy 3,* 159–73.

Lewis, J. (ed) (1993) *Women and Social Policies in Europe. Work, Family and the State.* Aldershot: Edward Elgar.

Lewis, J. (1995) 'The problem of lone-mother families in twentieth century Britain.' WSP/114 STICERD Welfare State Programme, LSE.

Lewis, J. (forthcoming) 'Further thoughts on gender and welfare regimes.' *Social Politics.*

Lewis, J. and Ostner, I. (1994) 'Gender and the evolution of European social policies.' Working Paper no. 4/94 Centre for Social Policy Research, University of Bremen.

Lewis, J., Land, H. and Kiernan, K. (forthcoming) *Lone Mothers in Twentieth Century Britain.* Oxford: Oxford University Press.

Lister, R. (1994) 'The child support act: shifting family financial obligations in the United Kingdom.' *Social Politics 1,* 2, 211–22.

McFate, K., Smeeding, T. and Rainwater, L. (1995) 'Markets and states: poverty trends and transfer system effectiveness in the 1980s.' In K. McFate, R. Lawson and W.J. Wilson (eds) *Poverty, Inequality and the Future of Social Policy.* New York: Russell Sage Foundation.

McLanahan, S. and Booth, K. (1989) 'Mother-only families: problems, prospects, and politics.' *Journal of Marriage and the Family 51,* (August), 557–580.

McLanahan, S., Casper, L. and Sorensen, A. (1995) 'Women's roles and women's poverty in eight industrialized countries.' In K.O. Mason and A.M. Jensen (eds) *Gender and Family Change in Industrialized Countries.* Oxford: Oxford University Press.

Mason, K.O. and Jensen, A.M. (eds) (1995) *Gender and Family Change in Industrialized Countries.* Oxford: Oxford University Press.

Martin, C. (1995) 'Father, mother and the welfare state. Family and social transfers after marital breakdown.' *Journal of European Social Policy 5,* 1, 43–63.

Mishra, R. (1993) 'Typologies of the welfare state and comparative analysis: the "liberal welfare state".' Paper given at RC 19 Conference on Comparative Research of Welfare States in Transition, Oxford, 9–12 September.

Mitchell, D. (1993) 'Sole parents, work and welfare: evidence from the Luxembourg income study.' In S. Shaver (ed) *Comparative Perspectives on Sole Parents' Policy: Work and Welfare.* University of New South Wales Social Policy Research Centre Reports and Proceedings no. 106.

Orloff, A. (1993) 'Gender and the social rights of citizenship: state policies and gender relations in comparative research.' *American Sociological Review 58,* 3, 303–28.

Orloff, A. (1994) 'Restructuring welfare: gender, work and inequality in Australia, Canada, the UK and the USA.' Paper given at 'Crossing Borders' Conference, Stockholm, May 27–29.

Pedersen, S. (1993) *Family, Dependence and the Origins of the Welfare State: Britain and France, 1914–1945.* Cambridge: Cambridge University Press.

Phoenix, A. (1993) 'The social construction of teenage motherhood: a black and white issue?' In A. Lawson and D.L. Rhode (eds) *The Politics of Pregnancy.* New Haven: Yale University Press.

Sainsbury, D. (ed) (1994) *Gendering Welfare States.* London: Sage.

Sainsbury, D. (1996) *Gender, Equality and Welfare States.* Cambridge: Cambridge University Press.

Scheiwe, K. (1994) 'Labour market, welfare state and family institutions: the links to mothers' poverty risks. A comparison between Belgium, Germany and the UK.' *Journal of European Social Policy 4,* 3, 201–24.

Skocpol, T. (1992) *Protecting Soldiers and Mothers. The Political Origins of Social Policy in the United States.* The Belknap Press of Harvard University Press.

Trefiletti, R. (1995) 'The gendered "rationalisation" of Italian social policies in the nineties.' Paper given at the Second ESA Conference, 'European Societies: Fusion or Fission?', 30 August–2 September.

Waldfogel, J. (1996) *What Do We Expect Lone Mothers to Do? Competing Agendas for Welfare Reform in the United States.* London: London School of Economics, Sticerd, WSP/124.

Wong, Y-L., Garfinkel, I. and McLanahan, S. (1993) 'Single-mother families in eight countries: economic status and social policy.' *Social Service Review 67,* June, 177–197.

CHAPTER ONE

Lone Mothers in Germany Before and After Unification[1]

Ilona Ostner

Introduction

Family issues like other value laden subjects were highly contested in the old Federal Republic and have remained so. Controversies revolve around the degree and nature of family changes, although reliable statistical and other data have existed for the last ten years (Burkart 1995). Despite the remarkable body of empirical evidence, social scientists and politicians either trumpet the tenacity of marriage and the family or proclaim their imminent end. The majority of women have caught up with or even overtaken their male counterparts in educational attainment; a growing number have gained economic independence. Therefore, as the prevalent argument goes, the gains of marriage are on the wane.

Married women's rising employment, which has resulted from better education, is widely regarded as the single most crucial factor for transforming the German and the American family system alike. To those critical of this 'independence argument', educational and occupational attainment explain why women delay – not forego – marriage and motherhood. Any postponement inevitably promotes non-marriage and childlessness, since the pool of marriageable men and female fertility sharply deteriorate with age (Blossfeld 1995; Oppenheimer, Blossfeld and Wackerow 1995, p.152). A discourse which closely links family changes to women's market position gives little or no space for singling out lone mothers as a group of special concern. Germany does not view lone motherhood as a single trend *per se*, but as a temporary effect within more general complex developments.

---

1   I am grateful to Mary Daly and Jane Lewis for their helpful comments and correcting my Germanic English.

The following first assesses lone mothers' status in public discourses. Lone mothers have not become an independent issue or a focus of public policy and legislation. The term 'lone-mother' or 'lone-mother-family' does not exist in Germany. It did not exist in the GDR either. There are one-parent families (*Einelternfamilien*) or 'lone carers' (*Alleinerziehende*). Both terms are gender-neutral. In this article in order to avoid confusion, I have used the terms 'out-of-wedlock' or 'non-marital' for children born to unmarried mothers; the German language uses 'extra-marital' to mean the births that result from the extra-marital relationships of married persons. It further prefers 'unmarried' mothers to 'never-married' mothers, since the vast majority of them either cohabit and/or marry sooner or later, or are divorced.

This section summarises trends in lone motherhood and offers some explanations. Principles of West and former East German family policies and how these affected lone mothers are outlined. The GDR and the old FRG clearly belonged to two different welfare and family policy regimes: a strong male-breadwinner norm and equally strong family obligations on the one side, and barely existing policy regime, on the other. Unification revealed the extent to which West German family laws ignored basic rights like equal treatment of all children whether born to a married couple or extra-maritally, and women's equal rights. So, unification became the catalyst of reforms that had been discussed for a long time.

However, changes have been moderated by policies based on the principle of children's best interest (*Kindeswohl*). The shift of focus towards children's rights has not led to equal treatment of all family forms. Indeed, lone mother families have been increasingly questioned in terms of the extent to which they deprive children of the kind of economic and social resources that cannot be compensated for by society. The traditional notion of *parental* responsibility which has been weakened since the 1970s has been re-established and together with it the male-breadwinner norm which underlies the German welfare regime. Stress has been put on parents' responsibility whether married or not, and on the father's right and obligation to provide for his children and their mother while the children depend on her. The husband–breadwinner has been recast as 'father–provider'.

Women in Germany are now also expected to contribute to the household income and compensate, if only by part-time work, for lower male wages and employment prospects, and they do so, especially East German women. As recent panel data shows (Holst 1996, p.466), full-time working women (a stable 21% of West German couple households, and 43% in the East, declining from 60% prior to Unification) have steadily increased their contribution to net household income from 44 to 47 per cent between 1990 and 1995. Part-time working women who make up roughly 30 per cent in the West and one fifth in the East of married couple households contribute a stable 20 per cent in the West compared to 30 per cent in the East to collective net income. Overall, married East German women's total contribution to household net income was 46 per cent in 1994. The East/West differences are mainly due to lower male incomes and job prospects in the East, and correspondingly higher male wages and prospects in the West.

Germany has finally said goodbye to the 'specialisation model' of a small nuclear family system based on a strong male breadwinner and a homebound wife and mother. Relying on one specialist and solely on his/her resources is a risky strategy. It makes 'the family's welfare vulnerable to the temporary or permanent loss of one of the two major specialists' and their resources insecure in times of growing socio-economic uncertainty (Oppenheimer 1995, p.238).

Increasingly temporary or contingent employment, joblessness and long term unemployment are hitting Germany's welfare system which has been built around the standard of lifelong, full-time, and skilled male employment, which has in turn strengthened the male-breadwinner norm. Nowadays, very few men and, correspondingly women, can expect or afford to live according to these norms. The new focus on parents and their shared responsibility, regardless of marital status, answers this challenge.

Lone mothers – why not an independent issue in Germany?

Like other western societies, Germany, too, has experienced what demographers call the 'second demographic transition' marked by a decline of the birth rate to 1.3 children per woman, decreasing marriage and increasing divorce rates, a significant drop in the number of standard two-parent families and a steady growth of diverse family forms, among them one-parent, step-families and childless couples. At present, 12 per cent of West and 40 per cent of East German children are born out of wedlock. Twenty per cent of first births in West Germany are now to unmarried or lone parents, again with a much higher rate of 60 per cent in the East. Equally 12 per cent of the children in the old Länder (up to 1990) compared to 20 per cent in the former GDR experience their parents' divorce (Schwarz 1995, p.291).

However, the majority of West German adolescents who come of age have still lived their lives with their two natural parents, 73 per cent in the West (compared to 40% in the East). This might be one reason why, despite increasing numbers since the 1970s, lone mothers have not reached the public agenda as a separate and single issue, let alone a moral one, in either pre- or post-unification Germany (Schwarz 1995).

Brave mothers

There are many other reasons for this scant attention. First, assessment of family change depends on the bench mark used (Oppenheimer et al. 1995, p.154–5).

A rate of about 10 per cent of children born out of wedlock appears to be quite normal to demographers. In their view, the low non-marital birth rates of the 1950s and 1960s deviated from the standard which had prevailed before 1933 in Germany. Taking that exceptional period as a bench mark logically exaggerates family change (Schwarz 1995, p.278). Second, teenage pregnancy hardly exists (*see* Table 1.1 below), and where it does research on how these very young women fare and are treated is missing.

Table 1.1 Out-of-wedlock births and age of mother (per 1000 women of respective age)*

Age of unmarried mothers	1961	1992
15–19	7.7	6.2
20–24	20.2	12.7
25–29	23.0	19.6
30–34	15.7	23.5
35–39	8.8	12.4
40–44	3.9	3.1

* Cohabiting mothers included (the Microcensus does not differentiate between unmarried non-cohabiting and cohabiting mothers/fathers).

Source: Schwarz 1995 on the basis of the 1994 Microcensus.

The majority of Germany's lone mothers are divorcees and to a lesser extent widows, not unmarried mothers (*see* Table 1.2). The German Microcensus does not differentiate between unmarried 'unpartnered' mothers on the one hand, and those cohabiting with the child's father or a partner, on the other.

The extent of 'single' lone motherhood is therefore regularly overestimated. Never-married motherhood is rare, unmarried, 'partnered' or 'unpartnered' motherhood low and/or temporary. As will be shown later, East Germans more regularly than West Germans start having their first child before being married, but they get married more quickly than West Germans after the child's birth (*see* Tables 1.3 and 1.4). Thus, it is more a question of couples deferring marriage.

Table 1.2 Lone-parent families

Year	total in 1000	% of all families	male*			female*			
			% of all	un-married** %	widowed	in 1000	of which un-married** %	divorced %	widowed
Old FRG									
1971	1488	8.9	11.2	-	70.0	1322	10.2	22.4	61.3
1981	1613	9.6	15.9	3.9	50.0	1357	9.8	31.8	48.2
1991	1858	10.7	16.5	11.1	36.6	1552	17.7	36.7	35.1
1992	1904	10.8	16.0	11.8	37.0	1599	18.6	36.5	34.0
1993	1949	10.9	16.8	14.1	35.2	1623	18.8	36.0	32.7
1994	1982	11.1	16.8	15.7	33.4	1650	19.6	36.4	32.1
Unified FRG									
1991	2540	11.5	15.5	15.2	34.5	2146	22.3	39.0	30.4
1992	2585	11.6	15.2	16.3	35.0	2192	23.0	38.1	29.8
1993	2647	11.8	15.9	18.1	34.0	2228	24.8	37.3	28.8
1994	2696	12.0	15.5	17.0	33.1	2279	24.0	37.6	28.1

* Married but separated parents excluded.

** Cohabiting parents included.

Source: Calculation on the basis of the 1994 Microcensus.

Table 1.3 Out-of-wedlock birth rate* (%)

year	old Länder	new länder
1950	9.7	12.8
1960	6.3	11.6
1970	5.5	13.3
1980	7.6	22.8
1990	10.5	35.0
1993	11.9	41.1

* Cohabiting mothers included.

Source: Schwarz 1995 on the basis of the 1994 Microcensus.

Table 1.4 Children legitimised through the subsequent marriage of parents*

year	old Länder	new Länder
1979	34.1	38.5
1989	34.7	55.9
1992	35.0	35.0
1993	21.4	70.3

* As a percentage of those born out-of-wedlock (average of year and previous year).

Source: Schwarz 1995 on the basis of the 1994 Microcensus.

Third, lone motherhood has not attracted much attention because most lone mothers earn their own living (*see* Table 1.5), and therefore do not, or only temporarily, depend on social assistance (Voges and Ostner 1995)[2]. Moreover, lone mothers, especially divorcees, have always done more full-time work than married mothers. Some consider this unfair in a society which expects mothers personally to take care of their younger children, when lone mothers do not or in the case of divorce, no longer profit from the marriage-based provisions offered by the German welfare state.

The German welfare system is based on social insurance (*Sozialversicherung*). Entitlements are predominantly employment-centred and largely follow the

---

2   Due to their relatively high educational attainment employed women earn decent wages; this is especially true for women in the public sector (Meyer 1994). In contrast, women on social assistance are much worse off financially, because of – by international standards – relatively low social assistance benefits (Daly 1996). Duncan *et al.* (1992) and Duncan and Voges (1993) compare relatively generous German social assistance levels and generous eligibility rules to the mean levels and rules of the American Aid for Families with Dependent Children (AFDC) system; they investigate why German lone mothers have spells of welfare receipt similar to those of AFDC recipients and why lone mothers in the UK have the longest spell of the countries compared.

Table 1.5 Mothers' employment – weekly working hours (%)

family size	employment rate		working hours								
			less than 20 h			21 h – 35 h			more than 36 h		
	married mothers	lone mothers	all mothers	married mothers	lone mothers*	all mothers	married mothers	lone mothers*	all mothers	married mothers	lone mothers*
all working mothers	55.2	62.0	30.5	33.3	17.4	19.5	19.5	19.0	50.0	47.0	64.0
one child	57.4	64.0	26.0	29.4	15.7	19.4	19.7	18.6	54.0	51.0	65.7
two children	56.8	62.2	34.0	35.8	20.0	19.9	19.8	20.0	46.0	44.0	59.9
three children	45.7	47.0	39.7	40.1	26.5	18.0	17.9	20.0	42.2	51.0	53.0

* Cohabiting mothers included.

Source: Calculation on the basis of the 1994 Microcensus.

principle of equivalence (provisions match contributions); old age and, to some extent, unemployment insurance entitlements mirror citizens' employment efforts and their earning power over the life course. These principles have advantaged the continuously employed, skilled and well-paid worker, in short the typically German strong male breadwinner. Little redistribution has been built into the system. However, the welfare state has been redistributive in favour of the male breadwinner marriage, especially, of his non-working wife. She has been entitled to a 'contribution-free' pension in old age which is derived from her husband's employment record and his social insurance contributions and – like her children – she has access to equally 'free' health services paid from insurance funds. Due to married women's discontinuous employment and hence much lower old age insurance contribution, many women can claim higher pensions in respect of their marital status than of their own employment record.

Unmarried mothers and women who divorce have to make do without these marriage-based benefits and to rely on their own earning power and social insurance record under conditions which favour full-time male employment. Divorce legislation gives divorced women the right to half of their former husbands' pensions for the years of their marriage, however few divorced women have a marriage long enough to provide a decent widow's pension. Most lone mothers work to earn a living, but lacking a husband's pension, also in order to contribute to old age insurance. Occupational skills help them to do so. Almost all German women invest on average in three years vocational training after secondary school. As qualified workers they find decent jobs, provided that they have acquired work experience and did not interrupt employment, or stayed at home only for a couple of months to look after children.

Lone mothers' invisibility in public debates can also be explained by cultural norms which expect women with children below the age of three to stay and personally take care of the child rather than go out and earn a living. Hence, being on social assistance during the first three years after the child's birth, if the father has left or offers insufficient means to support the child, carries little or no stigma. Child support laws and the 1986 Parental Leave Legislation are based on norms which promote a home-based role for the mother of small children regardless of marital status. In this sense, motherhood is universalised irrespective of marital status. Consequently, the 1996 welfare reforms which tightened eligibility rules for both social assistance and unemployment benefits, and enforced workfare programmes for those who have been dependent long-term on benefits, do not apply to mothers on welfare. They are explicitly exempted from these measures. The significantly higher numbers of East German lone mothers on social assistance and their longer spells in welfare have not attracted public attention either. Instead, welfare dependency has been perceived – also by East Germans themselves – as the product of structural shortcomings in the course of socio-economic transformation. Moral panic in Germany, where it exists, targets male shirking and free-riding within the social security and welfare system, not lone mothers.

Finally, it has now been realised that men, regardless of educational attainment, contribute a great deal to the postponement of marriage and fatherhood. As in the USA and Britain, attention has slowly but visibly shifted to the socio-economic status and well-being of men, rather than women (Huinink 1995, Tölke 1995).

The impact of poverty research

Poverty research was traditionally marginalised in a society proud of its socio-economic achievements. It has of late acquired higher prestige through more sophisticated panel studies. These have offered detailed analysis of the driving factors behind spells of welfare dependency and their changes over time. These insight have been widely used for 'de-dramatising' poverty levels in Germany.

Social assistance payments roughly match the EU wide poverty threshold of 50 per cent of median equivalent household income. Using this measure, 22.2 per cent of children in West German lone mother households and 34.6 per cent of East German ones were poor in 1994 according to data from the Socio–economic Panel. Table 1.6 indicates that children below the age of six who live in families with low incomes are more often to be found in lone mother households[3]. Researchers and politicians however are quick to stress that between 1984 (West Germany) and 1994 (unified Germany) overall child poverty rates have declined from 6 to 5 per cent. Poverty among children within lone-mother households decreased from 34.6 per cent (West) to 25 per cent (unified Germany). Weick (1996, p.3) explains the decline of poverty in lone-parent families to a growing use by lone mothers of social assistance and additional benefits.[4] In contrast, poor working families, or families affected by unemployment, claimed social assistance benefits to a lesser extent both in 1984 and 1994. Thus, about two-thirds of children below the poverty threshold have not benefited from social assistance payments (Weick 1996). In sharp contrast to the USA and Britain (Morgan 1995, McLanahan and Sandefur 1994) and typical for Germany, Weick does not comment on different attitudes towards welfare dependency among different types of families. Lone mothers' poverty has reached the public agenda under the heading of *children's poverty*,

---

3   Social assistance for a lone parent with one child plus housing benefit amounts to roughly DM 1600 which corresponds to the net income of many full-time employed sales assistants.

4   Poverty rates depend in the first instance on the chosen measure. In Germany, it is publicly agreed that social assistance successfully fights poverty.

Table 1.6 Children in families
children* and family income** (%)

Income** [DM]	<1000	1000–1800	1800–2500	2500–3000	3000–3500	3500–4000	4000–5000	5000–6000	6000–7500	>7500
children of married couple families	0.3	2.3	7.3	10.7	13.1	12.4	20.3	13.2	10.8	9.6
of which under 6 years	0.2	4.3	11.2	16.7	18.3	14.7	17.4	8.5	5.0	3.9
children of lone parent families	9.2	21.3	22.7	12.2	9.6	7.1	/	4.3	2.7	2.1
of which under 6 years	26.8	38.2	25.5	7.1	2.3	-	/	/	/	/

* Children regardless of age who live with their families, step or lone parent families.

** Income after tax including transfers (salaried and wage workers only).

Source: Calculation on the basis of the 1994 Microcensus.

and the latter is considered as an indicator of German *families'* socio-economic status and welfare *in general.*[5]

From mothers' to children's best interests

According to the Family Report (1994, p.100, *see* footnote 5) the instability of couples' relationships and, consequently, of those between natural parents and their children has contributed to shifting the focus of political concern to children and their *'best interest'* regardless of their parents' legal (family) status. Concern, even on the part of the Social Democrats, has shifted from married women and mothers' vulnerability to that of children in general, and children in non-standard family forms in particular. Unlike feminist and Green Party demands, the switch has not led to special anti-poverty measures for non-standard families. Instead, a newly strengthened 'parentalism' has emerged (Lessenich and Ostner 1995): the idea that a child is naturally born to two parents who are responsible for her well-being in the manner that has traditionally underpinned family legislation and policies in Germany.

The 1989 UN Convention on Children's Rights, *First Call for Children*, which explicitly states the child's right to both parents, influenced various decisions of the German Constitutional Court in outlawing the practice of automatically giving divorced mothers custody rights, and other forms of discrimination against 'legitimate' and 'illegitimate' fathers, which were considered to deprive children of important social and economic resources (Family Report 1994, p.100, Ebert 1995, p.69).

The legalistic legacy shaping social relations

Germany is renowned for its normative, legalistic or institutionalist treatment of public policy issues (Schultheis 1995, p.771). German law and legislation play an important role in shaping social relations. In the continental European tradition, law has always served as a remarkable means of governing change. Sometimes legislation tries to catch up with changed norms and a changing reality as in the case of the diversification of family forms; sometimes it promotes new norms to become reality. Parental legislation and policies, however, combine both reaction and innovation.[6] According to the Family Report (1994 author's translation):

---

5   This logic runs through the influential Fifth German Family Report 1994, commissioned by The Federal Ministry of Family Affairs (in the following cited as 'Family Report'). The Report generally focuses on strengths and shortcomings of current family structures.

6   Therborn (1993) elaborates as to how legal cultures together with gender or 'patriarchal' orders and religious traditions have contributed to the emergence of the concept of children's rights.

by stressing the child's right to both parents, the UN Convention discloses an essential legal concept. The underlying idea suggests that the couple's freedom as to the relationship they want to have corresponds to their increased responsibility as a father and a mother, that is, as parents… (p.100)

To some, like Margot von Renesse (1996, p.58)[7], German family reform proposals, which follow lines similar to those quoted, indicate a paradigm shift: from unduly privileging the mother–child dyad and lone mothers where fathers are absent, to acknowledging fathers' rights and, thereby, the child's rights and interests. Others, like Jutta Limbach (1988, p.232), also a family lawyer and currently president of the German Constitutional Court, hold that reference to parents and parental authority and responsibility was in fact already built into the first version of the German Civil Code (BGB) in 1900, although it was not implemented. Both positions are agreed that children have two parents and the right to both a mother and a father. From this point of view Nazi state-centred pronatalist policies which deprived both parents of their right to decide on family matters (e.g. by promoting the birth of 'healthy' German children regardless of family status), as well as the 1980 custody legislation which turned children into 'orphans by divorce' after their parents' separation, represent deviations from established norms.

The term 'orphan by divorce' was constructed by therapists and legislators in analogy with war orphans who had lost one parent, usually, the father. Now it is argued, for instance by Renesse, that this analogy as well as therapeutic and legal interventions in divorce cases have supported both the idea and the reality of 'absent fathers' and have made it hard for the latter to keep in touch with their children. As will be shown later, the politics of children's best interests in lone-parent families and legislation have thus shifted focus from the child who lost a father through divorce to the child's right to two parents.

A trend towards lone motherhood?

Demographic research points to the apparent prevalence of marriage in Germany. According to the 1994 Microcensus, 61 per cent of people older than 18 have been married and one third of them live with children. The proportion of married persons even rises to 75–80 per cent for the 35 to 55 age bracket. About 18 per cent live solo, 3.4 per cent are lone parents, and roughly 5 per cent cohabit (Dorbritz and Gärtner 1995). The following summarises demographic trends in post-war West and East Germany.

---

7   Margot von Renesse has been a family judge for many years and serves at present as a SPD (Social Democratic Party) member of the Federal Parliament (*Bundestag*).

Three major demographic changes

Due to war casualities, the number of lone mothers was large during the first post-war years. The surplus of women led to the acceptance of a diversity of family forms and to the tolerance of pre- and extra-marital sex, unwed motherhood, abortion and divorce. Such phenomena, however, were viewed as natural responses to exceptional, abnormal or chaotic times, and therefore as temporary. Unsurprisingly, in 1961, 92 per cent of children under 18 lived with two parents, just as they had in the 1920s. This rate remained stable for the following twenty years (1980: 91%) in West Germany.[8] Significant changes have developed since then (Schwarz 1995, p.273).

Three major changes in the marriage system have occurred in West Germany. The first involves a steady deferral of marriage and family formation by both sexes despite earlier sexual experience. In turn, more West German women have remained childless and more will be so. Second, divorce rates have increased. Lone motherhood in Germany mainly results from divorce. The third trend points to gender specific contributions to these patterns. Women spend more years in education and thereby defer having a family. Men, irrespective of educational enrolment and attainment, hesitate to start a family. Birth cohort analysis suggests that the 1975–1980 male cohort with secondary school education will have their first child on average at the age of 32, five years later than previous cohorts. Highly educated men, such as university graduates, will delay having a family even further (Tölke 1995, p.495).

Early sexual experience – delayed family formation

Young people in West Germany have started to have sex earlier, due to changing norms and the availability of contraceptives, beginning on average at the age of 16 compared to 18 in the 1950s. They have a greater number of sexual relationships than their parents before forming a stable relationship and eventually marrying. Both sexes have contributed equally to this trend during the last twenty years regardless of educational attainment. During the 1950s, grammar school graduates had their first stable relationship in their early twenties, an average of three years later than secondary school leavers (Tölke 1995, p.491).[9]

The delaying effect of education and the East/West divide

In contrast to the UK or USA, earlier sexual experience has not led to an increase in lone motherhood in West Germany. On the contrary, the out-of-wedlock birth rate declined for younger women between 15–29; falling for unmarried

---

8   No comparable data available for East Germany.
9   No comparable data available for East Germany.

women aged 15–19 from 7.7 children (per thousand unmarried women) in 1961 to 6.2 in 1992, from 20.2 for women aged 20–24 to 12.7, and from 23.0 to 19.6 for those between 25–29 years old. In contrast, out-of-wedlock births have significantly increased for women aged 30–39 years between 1961 and 1992 (Schwarz 1995, p.279 and Table 1.1).[10]

According to West German norms, and in contrast to the former East Germany, young women who are in training or otherwise enrolled in education are not considered ready to have a child (Blossfeld and Rohwer 1995, p.73). Since the late 1960s, West German adolescents, especially young women, have continuously increased their number of years in the educational system. Educational aspirations, enrolment, occupational training and promising job prospects have apparently 'diverted' young women from having children. Blossfeld and Rohwer (1995) suggest that extending education is just another way for many to defer adulthood. The 'delayed adulthood' assumption is further supported by the fact that nearly two thirds of young people between 18 and 25 still live with their parents, often by preference rather than need. The majority leave their family of origin in order to marry or form a stable relationship (Sozialpolitische Umschau 1995/33, p.13). As they see it, time spent in education accounts indirectly for the decline in the number of out-of-wedlock births among younger women, and their increase among older ones, as well as accounting for the postponement of marriage.[11] Their data show that more well-educated women marry and/or have their first child later (Sozialpolitische Umschau 1995/33, p.75). In contrast, East German women, irrespective of educational enrolment and attainment and with the support of public childcare facilities, have their children significantly earlier and often while still in training or university. By the time they enter regular full-time employment, their children are of school age.

While West German out-of-wedlock births amounted to only 5 per cent between 1960 and 1975, the rate never fell below 10 per cent in post-war East Germany (Schwarz 1995, p.278 and Table 1.5). East German lone mothers used to be younger and tended to remain unmarried more often than their West German counterparts. In the 1980s, half of firstborn children were born to unmarried women in East Germany compared to 20 per cent of West German firstborn children (1976: 10% in FRG; 19% in GDR).[12] About one-third of these first-born children will be legitimised through their parents' marriage, on average within two years (50% during the first year). Schwarz (1995, p.282) also mentions the many good reasons embedded in the German welfare regime for marrying: access to widows' pensions; maintenance and pension rights

---

10 No comparable data available for East Germany.

11 No comparable data available for East Germany.

12 Meanwhile, the total birth rate per woman has fallen to 0.8 children in the East compared to 1.3 in the West.

against a former husband; exemption of non-employed family members from health insurance contributions; higher unemployment insurance benefits for the breadwinner; and marriage friendly taxation (*Ehegattensplitting*).

The marginal role of cohabitation

Data on consensual unions and information about their long-term development are rare (Blossfeld and Rohwer 1995, p.63). Since the 1970s consensual unions have become an accepted phenomenon. They tripled in number in West Germany from 348,000 to 1.2 million in 1993.[13] There are 362,000 cohabiting couples in the East at present (Sozialpolitische Umschau 1995/33, p.14). These couples forego the many social and economic advantages which marriage offers. According to Microcensus data, in 1993 only 2.8 per cent of West German consensual unions and 8.4 per cent of those in the East had children (Peschel-Gutzeit and Jenckel 1996, p.129). This reveals the extent to which family formation coincides with marriage in today's Germany.

Blossfeld and Rohwer (1995, p.63) provide some birth cohort data on the frequency and duration of consensual unions.[14] Living together without being married is a relatively new phenomenon in (West) Germany, and is a feature of the younger age cohorts. Only 11 per cent of people born between 1954 and 1963 had lived in consensual unions in 1984. The youngest birth cohort (1964–1968) does so habitually and for some years, and feels the least pressure to legalise cohabitation. The increase in consensual unions for the younger cohorts is closely connected to educational enrolment and the prevailing norm of not marrying or having children whilst in education.

The majority of these unions are relatively short-lived (median duration: about three years): either the partners marry within a few years or they split. The propensity to short-lived unions is greatest among the relatively young. As outlined above, the birth of a child is closely connected to entry to marriage. However, a failed marriage 'reduces the desire to marry again' (Blossfeld and Rohwer 1995, p.64), explaining why many divorced women or men live in consensual unions.

Divorce – prime cause of lone motherhood

Since the 1960s divorce rates have steadily increased in West Germany and even more so in the East. After unification the number of divorces fell in the East. Since then, they have slowly risen without reaching their pre-unification peak. Part of the growth can be explained by the increased number of marriages

---

13 No comparable trend data available for East Germany.
14 No comparable data available for East Germany.

during the 1980s. Very young couples and very young marriages fall apart more frequently than older ones. Divorce rates for marriages of longer than 25 years have also increased, but have not made a significant impact on the finding that young marriages are the ones primarily at risk of divorce.

Nearly 40 per cent of all lone-parent families were divorced, about 30 per cent lost the father or the mother through death (Microcensus 1994).[15] A hundred years ago, in 1890, there were only seven divorces per ten thousand marriages compared to eighty in the West in 1992 and 123 in East Germany in 1989 per ten thousand. In 1993, 120,000 German children were affected by divorce. Children are increasingly at risk of becoming 'orphans by divorce' rather than by the death of a parent. As mentioned before, the widely used concept of 'orphans by divorce' assumes that a parent (a father) who no longer lives in the same household is *absent* and of little or no relevance for the child. That idea was built into the 1979 Custody Law (*Sorgerechtsgesetz*) which automatically granted sole custody to the child's mother after a divorce. The recent family law reform proposal challenges the assumption of the ever-absent father.

The demographers Dorbritz and Gärtner (1995) as well as some sociologists, for instance Burkart (1995), suggest that the change in family forms and living arrangements should be described as a process of polarisation rather than of pluralisation. This analysis deviates from the mainstream discourse on family change. However, the trend towards polarisation is supported by empirical data. Living arrangements increasingly fall into dichotomous categories: the unmarried versus the married; those with children versus childless individuals versus couples. These 'bipolar' trends, as Dorbritz and Gärtner term them, have started to attract policymakers' attention as they worry about how to finance old age pensions and a 'pay-as-you-go' welfare state in general. In their view consensual unions are morally hazardous since they lack obvious signs of mutuality and put the economically weaker partner at risk of poverty in case of separation. Childless people, many argue, are 'freeriders' on the welfare state who do not care about how old age and frailty are to be supported (Family Report 1994, p.271, 296). Hence the demographers' concern with childlessness and the opportunity costs of having children has merged with the demand of family lawyers for shifting policies in the direction of the child's best interest. Little or no room is left for policies addressing the needs of lone mothers.

---

15 Note that the Microcensus uses a broad definition of 'children' and 'family'. 'Children' are those regardless of age who live with two parents, or in step or lone parent families, a definition which contributes statistically to broadening the meaning of the 'family'. It also reflects the strength of German family obligations which never end: children regardless of age have to support their needy parents and vice versa.

Policies towards lone mothers in the Federal Republic (FRG) before and after unification

In any case, policies towards lone mothers have existed thus far as an implicit and incoherent element within the explicit family policies of West and unified Germany. In former East Germany, policies for lone mothers were an implicit part of socialist child policies. Some discussion of German family policy is therefore necessary. The recent shift towards children's best interests has strengthened the role of the law in determining lone mothers' position. The second part of this section concentrates on changes in family law and recent reform proposals which will fundamentally affect lone mothers. Law and policy rest upon a particular concept of the family. Hence, it is necessary to ask what a 'family' is.

Family rhetorics – from couples to parents, from 'husband–breadwinners' to 'father–providers'

Neither the recent Fifth Family Report nor the Government's official comment on the Report make any mention of marriage as the basis of a family. This marks a radical change. The Family Reports were usually co-authored by social scientists and political advisers who worked within different 'paradigms'. Each report has to be read as a compromise. Nevertheless, the reports presented the official reading of what was to be seen as 'family'. The First Family Report, published in the mid-1960s under a solely Christian Democrat government, stressed that the institution of marriage should precede family formation. The following Family Reports all issued under coalition governments before unification struggled with the idea of marriage and family taking place in the right order (Walter 1995). The recent Fifth Family Report states that the father–mother–child relationship, and no longer marriage, constitutes a family, thereby also reflecting the 'deviant' reality of East German family life. It goes even further by distinguishing between the 'family', the parental relationship, and the 'household' defined as people who share accommodation and other resources (Family Report 1994, p.24). Obviously, a family does not have to share a household in order to be a 'family'.

The Family Report's efforts at definition do not simply represent the Germanic obsession with concepts. Rather, they attempt to launch a 'family rhetoric' (Lüscher, Wehrspaun and Lange 1989) capable of justifying the forthcoming policy focus on *parents*, irrespective of their marital status and living arrangements. The rhetoric obviously breaks with the traditional marriage-based male-breadwinner model, although it acknowledges that in reality most 'nuclear families' (*Kernfamilien*) consist of *married* couple households with children alongside various other family forms (Family Report 1994, p.24). The new rhetoric transforms the 'husband–breadwinner' into a 'father–provider' who normally lives in his family's household but does not have to do so in order to be legally treated as a responsible father.

It thus becomes clear that the new family rhetoric further marginalises lone mothers. In a strict sense it even questions their 'family' status. One-parent units are not families. They cannot claim preferential treatment and do not *per se* deserve special support. Quite the reverse, for as the present Christian Democrat Family Minister Claudia Nolte[16] argues, preferential treatment – for instance, giving lone mothers the full amount of the tax exemption instead of one half (the other half goes to the father) – flies in the face of the constitution. She claims that a non-co-resident father has comparable expenses for his child (Nolte 1996, p.86). However, the Constitutional Court has not yet ruled out the controversial Civil Code (BGB) article 1705, which grants the unmarried mother (unlike divorced mothers) sole custody rights. As we will see later Nolte is in tune with recent legal judgements which have increasingly disregarded article 1705 and its 'slanderous treatment of unmarried fathers' custody rights' (Meixner 1996, p.15).[17]

In contrast to the Family Minister's outspokenness, the Family Report dodges any clarification of its position towards the status of lone mother 'units'. It even erodes the term 'family' when it states that our concept of the family has become diffuse, such that some people claim that diverse family forms should be treated equitably, that is according to their specific needs. Having said this, the Report immediately insists that

> Every society has a vital interest preferentially to honour, protect, and advance those living arrangements which provide services (*Leistungen*) necessary for the society as a whole, not just for the individuals involved… In this sense, Basic Law (*Grundgesetz*) Article 6 commands the protection of the family by the state. What counts as a family depends highly on legal definitions, ethical convictions and pragmatic considerations. (Family Report 1994, p.24–5)

The new family rhetoric, its emphasis on dynamics and diversity, creates an arena for all sorts of fathers as 'father–providers'(albeit predominantly biological), irrespective of their marital status and where they live.

In reality, however, Article 6 still protects marriage and the family. Even short-lived post-unification 'Commission for Constitutional Reform' (*Verfas-*

---

16 The Fifth Family Report was commissioned and issued by the Family Ministry shortly before Nolte came into office. It is argued that Chancellor Kohl acted strategically in calling the 28 year old East German married and working mother of one child into his cabinet to represent both pan-German family centredness and working mothers.

17 Meixner is quoting the authors of a 1994 Family Law Commentary who judge article 1705 BGB as follows: 'The slanderous treatment of paternal custody rights over his non-marital (*nichtehelich*) children (by German law) does not provide for any exceptions and is promulgated with the strictness of an eternal dogma'.

sungskommission)[18] did not succeed either in dropping 'marriage' from Article 6 or in adding 'consensual unions'. Similarly, it failed to get Section 5 of the same article (which commands equal treatment of non-marital (*uneheliche*) children) changed. The Commission had proposed to replace the norm of equal treatment by something that came close to demanding 'equality of results' for all children irrespective of their familial, economic and social status (Commission for Constitutional Reform, quoted in Wichmann 1996, 41). The proposal implicitly alluded to inequalities of income and life chances between East and West German families, especially among lone parents in both parts of Germany, and thereby claimed the state's responsibility for its children. This sort of state familism was, however, not in tune with the new family rhetoric.

German family policy – concepts and peculiarities

As was already evident during the 1950s social state principle debate (*Sozialstaatsprinzip*), (West) Germany and her *social market economy* have promoted Rawlsian 'justice as fairness' principles; equal opportunity but not equality of result. Policies of 'equal results for all children' (*einheitliche Lebensverhältnisse*), as required by the Commission for Constitutional Reform in the early 1990s, contradict the equality as fairness principle. In my view, this is another reason why the Commission proposal failed.[19]

'Material equality' or 'equality of results' has always been viewed as socialism by the West and was in fact laid out in the policy model of the East. The 1949 GDR Constitution outlawed discrimination of against 'non-marital' children. The 1950 Mother and Children Protection Bill stated that being born out-of-wedlock was not stigmatising. These legal reforms were a prelude to comprehensive child-focused policies. When the wall came down, the socialist state paid directly or indirectly for 80 per cent of the costs of children, through all sorts of subsidies, public child care and holiday facilities.

In contrast, West German family policy was deliberately designed as a counterweight to what was seen as natalist intervention of the socialist state into the privacy of marriage and the family. Hence West German family policy focused, albeit moderately, upon horizontal rather than vertical redistribution and on promoting equal opportunities rather than outcomes. Families, irrespective of income, were entitled to flat rate child benefit and tax allowances per child. The Family Report (p.296) and politicians of all parties have reiterated

---

18 The Commission was a post-unification, a bottom-up initiative by intellectuals which aimed at revising and amending the Basic Law so that it better matched both East German concepts and practices and the many challenges of a dynamic and diverse postmodern society.

19 Basic (Constitutional) Law Article 72 demands the 'homogeneity' or 'equalisation of living conditions' (*Vereinheitlichung der Lebensverhältnisse*). In practice, the article has been narrowly interpreted in terms of horizontal redistribution from richer to poorer Länder within the German federal system (*Länderfinanzausgleich*), as a means of easing mobility in an open society.

that redistribution from childless people to families, rather than vertical redistribution from high to low income families, has been the concern of German family policy.

Nevertheless, the Report has proposed a tax reform that is friendly to low-income families, in consideration of their high numbers in East Germany. The existing progressive taxation and the 'splitting' system advantage high-income (one-earner) families. The proposal, the content of which is still unknown, is due at the latest in 1997. The 1996 Family Compensation Bill (*Familienlastenausgleich*) has already abolished the right to claim both child benefit (*Kindergeld*) and the child tax allowance together. These are now alternatives, which means that parents, irrespective of their income, get either a monthly benefit of DM 210 per child, or an allowance which reduces the tax burden. Parents are entitled to choose between the alternatives and take whichever is the most advantageous for them.

In its 40 page official comment attached to the 1994 Family Report, the Federal Government stressed additional concepts and principles of family policy.[20] Above all, however, it drew a clear boundary between public responsibility and the privacy of the family. In doing so, it stressed 'subsidiarity', that is, the priority accorded the smaller unit, comprising parents, mothers and fathers of all sorts over the wider community and the state. It presupposed parents' (not individuals') free agency, rights and responsibilities, and it appealed to a solidarity which respects such principles. The Government also stated that family policy goes beyond giving money. It claimed (Family Report 1994, p.XXXIII–IV– author's translation) that

> ...in a democratic polity, family issues and family policy are prime concerns of the families themselves. These are by no means just targets of family policy, but above all political agents... Family policy originates in families which actively pursue their interests... Hence, family policy is by no means only a state affair, but a genuine concern of the many groups involved: of families and their representatives, churches, welfare associations, the economy, collective bargaining partners and of political parties.

Kaufmann (1993, p.144) distinguishes 'explicit', 'implicit' and 'non-existing' family policies. He defines 'explicit' to mean; first, rhetoric and measures that specifically target families (and not, for instance, mothers or children only) and second, particular political institutions that exist to represent family issues. Drawing upon this definition, East German socialist and pronatalist policies were implicit, since they focused on children and hence on their mothers

---

20 In fact, family policy shares the constitutive principles of a 'stakeholding' social market economy and its public policy in general.

irrespective of marital status, rather than on families *per se*. (West) German family policy, however, has been explicit and institutionalised. A Family Ministry exists, even though it is marginal in terms of both the Ministry's influence and budget, and the provisions made for families.

This is why Schultheis (1995) arrived at a different conclusion when comparing (West) German and French family policy. French, like former East German family policy is, he insists, explicit and coherent, while the West German variant is fragmentary and implicit. The coherence of the former is reinforced by other factors; first, by an open pro-natalism as opposed to the West German rejection of population policy; second, by the ideal of 'la république une et indivisible' which is at the heart of the French (and the former GDR's) centralist 'raison d'état'. The Federal Republic of Germany's (FRG) public policy embeds the principle of subsidiarity in a multi-tiered policy process. Third, while (West) German family policy has been based on a normative and institutionalist concept of the family, French family policies like those of former East Germany, have acknowledged without discrimination the reality of diverse family forms. Fourth, centralism goes together with tax-based provisions for families and vertical redistribution, while the West German social market economy has linked families' welfare to employment-related social insurance and moderate horizontal redistribution. Finally, since children and their mothers have come first in East Germany and France, the state has supported mothers' employment, while (West) Germany supports at best the part-time working mother.

Lone mothers and policy

Germany does not have policies that target lone mothers, although they benefit from some measures designed for purposes unrelated to their special needs. This is true for both East and West Germany.

Family policies mainly include economic and legal measures which affect the status and welfare of family members (Kaufmann 1993, p.145). Family policy has traditionally responded to social inequalities between various types of families, and between families and childless couples. It has thus regularly moderated the effects of social policies and led to some redistribution. For instance, children (and non-employed married partners) are entitled to health insurance through the head of household's contribution. Pension entitlements, albeit meagre, are attached to periods of parental leave. Social assistance rules grant supplements to special categories of families, among them lone-parent families. Kaufmann (1993, p.151) points to the fact that (West) German family policy has so far advantaged low and high income families at the expense of the majority of middle income families. The latter have significantly contributed to the decline of the birth rate.

Family policy also involves parental leave and/or the provision of child care facilities, measures that help to reconcile family and employment. Lone parents have regularly had preferential treatment in the child care centres provided by local authorities.[21] A parent, usually a mother, can take parental leave for three years with each child without losing their job provided that they leave the labour market or works for not more than nineteen hours per week. After parental leave, mothers are expected to seek employment at least on a part-time basis. The new child care policy is designed to enable them to do so. The parental leave benefit (DM 600) has recently become means-tested. Mothers who rely on social assistance can claim the full parental leave benefit.

Social assistance is means-tested. In the case of unmarried mothers this means that, according to the principle of subsidiarity, the child's father is looked to first for maintenance for the mother. He pays according to his income for three years if the mother is entitled to social assistance. The number of years that maintenance should be paid has been constantly debated. Three years matches the parental leave standard, however, divorced women with school-children under the age of twelve are not expected to enter employment, which means that fathers have to maintain the mothers of their children 'appropriately' according to their incomes. Normally, if the child's father has no, or a low, income (below the social assistance level), the mother's parents are looked to next to support their daughter before the state will pay. Unmarried mothers are exempted from this rule. The eligibility rules for social assistance and parental leave benefits deviate from the standard as a result of the Abortion Law compromise. The exemption rules have been designed to prevent unmarried women from having an abortion for economic reasons, or from fear of becoming dependent on their parents. They are also intended to help mothers stay at home and personally take care of their child. These rules have not been devised as special measures for lone mothers. Implicitly, they aim at equalising the status of all mothers of children under three, for the sake of the children rather than their mothers.

Unmarried mothers who qualify for social assistance can thus draw both social assistance and parental leave benefit for three years without any means-testing. In reality, this offers some women, often those with bleak employment prospects, incentives for leaving or staying out of employment and/or not marrying during this period even if there is someone willing to marry them. As Schultheis (1987) maintains, parental leave policies help lone mothers to cope with the first three years after the child's birth on their own at home, but hinder rather than support their re-entry to the labour market.

---

21 From the 1st August 1996 every child of three has had the right to a public child-care place, at least part-time. The local authorities are obliged by law to provide these facilities by whatever means.

The law as upholder of traditional relations

Lone mothers' social status and their entitlements have been largely shaped by Marriage and Family Law, especially by laws which regulate the child's status *vis-à-vis* her parents, both mother and father (*Kindschaftsrecht*). For good and for ill, the child's and her mother's social and economic status have been tightly linked to marriage.

The first version of the Civil Code (*Bürgerliche Gesetzbuch*) in 1900 assumed that out-of-wedlock children were the illegitimate 'extra-marital' offspring (*Kegel*)[22] of men of property, who were married, and who did not want to be encumbered by a child or have their legitimate family involved (Peschel-Gutzeit and Jenckel 1996, p.131). Otherwise, so went the sexist logic of the law, these men would have married the child's mother or not have got involved with her. Therefore, it ruled out any affinity (*Verwandtschaft*) between the putative father and the child, and hence any obligations.

From the legal point of view, the child was fatherless, since born to an unmarried mother. Marriage, not biological origin, established relations of kin. Thus the husband became the father, guardian and provider of his wife's child by law, irrespective of the child's true origin. Once within marriage the child had full rights as well as duties *vis-à-vis* her father, for example, maintenance and inheritance rights. Of course, the father could legally question the status of the child.[23]

Two paths to 'fatherhood' have existed since the time of the first Civil Code: marriage or adoption. Through adoption the child becomes legitimised, irrespective of her origin. Even today, when unmarried couples with children marry, the husband has to adopt his natural children in order to become their father. However, in the rare event of a father adopting his 'illegitimate' child without marrying the mother, the latter ceases to be her child's mother (Wichmann 1996, p.42). Hence, a married couple's children have by law two parents, whereas the 'illegitimate' child has one parent, her mother.

These rules make sense when it is remembered, first, that up to the present, the Civil Code has involved primarily Private (Contract) Law which regulates the exchange of goods and services between equals (equal proprietors) as well as the rights and duties connected to this exchange. Marriage and Family Law,

---

22 *Kegel* is an old German word commonly used up to the turn of the century for the illegitimate children of love, passion, and misused power of the *pater familias*. Its content is neutral, sometimes even positive, compared to 'bastard'. The phrase 'mit Kind und Kegel' alludes to the normalcy of all sorts of natural children living in/or near the traditional household family.

23 Up to very recently, children were not allowed to legally question their origins in the interest of the existing marriage of their parents. However, the turn towards children's rights, which includes the right to know one's natural parent in order to develop a proper identity, has placed the emphasis on biological origin. This together with recent court cases concerning maintenance payments and custody rights for artificially inseminated children are some of the reasons why a *laisser-faire* attitude towards reproductive technologies is highly unlikely in Germany.

as part of Private Law, establishes property rights between husband and wife and parents and their children as well as associated obligations which, as in the case of divorce and death of one or two parents, extend beyond the existing marriage. Second, the rules are meaningful when set in the context of a civil society which emphasises the privacy of marriage and the family and, according to the principle of subsidiarity, reciprocity and solidarity of husband and wife, parents and children. The laws have established the hierarchy of married couples and parents as providers for children before any other individual or institution can be called upon, even in the case of divorce. These entitlements and obligations have made marriage costly, both to get into and to get out of, for all involved. Hence the law protects the institution of marriage and marital status.

The wife's marital status does not end on divorce or the death of the husband. The father has to continue to make monthly maintenance payments on the basis of his income to his divorced family. Such payments should be sufficient to help them retain their former socio-economic status. When he is retired and his divorced wife reaches retirement age she can claim half his pension for the same number of years as their marriage. Their are vice-versa rules, however, in the majority of cases husbands and fathers, rather than wives and mothers, have to pay. Additionally parents, even when divorced, have to maintain their children and pay for their education, normally until the age of twenty-seven, sometimes longer.[24] In turn, however, offspring have to pay for their parents up to a financial threshold, if the parents become dependent on the means-tested safety net (social assistance).

The Youth Office (*Jugendamt*), an institution set up in the 1920s to safeguard children's best interest, advances maintenance payments[25] for 'illegitimate' children or those of divorced parents below the age of twelve for a maximum of 72 months, as long as the mother applies and names the father. Maintenance payments can also be legally deducted from the monthly paycheck.[26] In these cases, the Youth Office acts in collaboration with the court as an authorised

---

24 Kleffmann (1996) has elaborated recent developments in Maintenance Law (*Unterhaltsrecht*) on the basis of court cases. Courts have regularly decided that an additional qualification can be useful if it adds to the first, and thus the parents have to pay, irrespective of the child's age. Other decisions have concerned maintenance payments, for instance, for the divorced partner who left employment to take care of the children, or who starts training or attends university. In each of these cases the former partner (regularly men in the cases surveyed) has to pay.

25 Payments for children vary with the child's age and the father's income, and are thus status maintenance oriented. A quasi official table (*Düsseldorfer Tabelle*) exists which, however, gives only a rough guideline. Small payments are topped up by social assistance.

26 Data only exist for cases where the husbands/fathers do not pay or do not pay the agreed amount and lone mothers or children go to court or to the Youth Office to complain. However, for the many in regular employment and for all legal residents, it is difficult to avoid paying. Unmarried fathers, in general, pay less willingly than divorced ones. Men are also more reluctant to pay for the child's mother than for the child.

agent. Finally, orphans and widows are entitled to pensions related to the breadwinner's income and social insurance contribution.

The return of fathers

The rules of origin (*Abstammungsregeln*) have not much changed since 1900, despite a steady improvement of both the status of the 'illegitimate' child and her mother. They have also lagged behind Article 6 of the Basic Law which outlawed discrimination against 'illegitimate' children.

The 1969 Law on the Legal Status of Illegitimate Children (*Gesetz über die rechtliche Stellung nichtehelicher Kinder*) finally moved towards granting the putative father the status of a 'father'. He assumed a legal relationship with his child, albeit only through obligations, not rights, while the child's mother retained sole custody rights, albeit monitored by the Youth Office which named a guardian for the child as a 'father substitute'.[27] The mother was also authorised by law to decide on the frequency of contacts between the child and her father (*Umgangsrecht*). The child was entitled to monthly maintenance payments and to a limited inheritance[28], and the mother to maintenance payments, if she did not work and personally cared for her baby during the first three years.[29] The 1969 Reform improved the 'illegitimate' child's status significantly and, as many today would argue the mother's status unduly at the expense of the child's father.

The lopsided legal status of the unmarried father was confirmed by a Constitutional Court decision in 1981 which maintained that article 1705 BGB which gave the mother sole custody rights was in accordance with the Basic Constitutional Law and did not contradict Article 6 (Protection of Marriage and the Family). If the father wanted to have custody rights, the Court argued, he had to marry the mother. To rule against sole custody rights, it continued, meant violating adult people's free agency (Meixner 1996). In reality, the Court was still following the traditional interpretation that unmarried fathers were irresponsible and were therefore to be kept from the child in her best interest.

In 1982 the Constitutional Court ruled the opposite in the case of divorced children and their mothers. It outlawed the practice of the family courts which automatically gave the mothers sole custody, ruling that this was against Basic Law and the protection of the family. The practice resulted from the 1979

---

27 The family reform proposal intends to transform guardianship into a service by choice for the lone parent.

28 In the case of inheritance, the 1969 Law did not grant an equal share to 'illegitimate' children, but a set, residual sum that was paid after other claims were met. Both maintenance and inheritance have deviated up to now from the status maintenance principle granted to the children of divorced parents.

29 In 1995, the period was extended from one to three years as a result of the abortion debate. Some argue that unmarried mothers should have the same maintenance rights as divorced ones, that is as long as the children go to school and are considered to need their mother.

Custody Law which had promoted the idea of the child as an 'orphan by divorce'. In 1982, the Court justified its decision as being in the best interest of the child who by nature has two parents and, hence, the right to both.

In 1991 the Court outlawed the denial of custody to unmarried fathers who were living with their families. Equally in 1995 the Court conceded the right to be heard to unmarried fathers if the mother wanted to give the child away for adoption. Meanwhile, the Ministry of Justice has issued a proposal on the reform of the status of children (*Kindschaftsrecht*) which has fully taken account of the various Court rulings. The proposal defines first who is mother and who father and thereby introduces flexibility into the concept of origin: the woman who gives birth to the child, is her mother by law. Her father is the person who is married at the time of the birth to the mother, or who acknowledges paternity, or who has been revealed as the father through testing. According to Wichmann (1996, p.42) while solving old problems this flexible definition creates new ones not tackled by the law, for example, the status of surrogate mothers or maintenance obligations in cases of artificial insemination. Second, the proposal recommends joint custody by the divorced parents as the rule; exceptions need good reasons and an application to the court. Unmarried parents can apply for joint custody, otherwise the mother has sole custody. The proposal also provides the means for the 'illegitimate' child to be in touch with her father and *vice versa*. Although child abuse has finally reached the public agenda in Germany, the various child custody reform proposals omit the issue. Husbands and fathers are not generally treated with suspicion.

Meixner (1996) and Wichmann (1996) emphasise the role which the European and the UN Human Rights Conventions played in bringing forward the concept of children's rights and in particular their right to both parents. German unification was another catalyst. The socialist regime spoke in terms of workers, mothers and children, rarely fathers. It did not differentiate between fathers of different status; nor did it ask much of them. They had hardly any rights in relation to their children and rarely any obligations. The socialist, natalist state was in some ways a 'father surrogate'. West German family law had to be slowly transformed to cushion the adjustment of East German everyday practices. This has been accomplished, however, by steadily strengthening the legal status of divorced and unmarried fathers in the 'best interest of the child'.

Conclusion

There is considerable irony in the ongoing family law reform. By bringing in fathers, often rightly so, the position of many divorced and unmarried mothers will be weakened. Notwithstanding their broken or non-existent relationship to the father, they must remain in touch and grant them access to the child, a not dissimilar situation to that of the UK (*see* Chapter 2). On the one hand, policymakers and researchers stress the new diversity of family forms, the weakening of marriage and related 'blood bonds'. On the other, the new focus on children's rights has moved towards granting children the right to know their biological origin as well as the right to question – against their mother's will – their status at birth. This can easily lead to a biological reductionism which defies the idea of origin as social construct.

Legal reforms and related family policies have slowly promoted the transformation of the 'husband–breadwinner' into a 'father–provider' who maintains his children, and their mother, for as long as necessary. The 'father–provider' normally lives in his family's household but does not have to in order to be responsible for his family. As always the norm is sustained by the negative example. Now, wilfully childless 'husband–breadwinner marriages' with a homemaker wife and a full-time employed man (a tiny minority) are accused of unduly profiting from marriage-friendly tax policies, health insurance rules, and widows' pensions. Germany has turned slightly towards a pronatalist rhetoric. Hence, it is childless individuals, not lone mothers, who have so far got the blame and little evidence exists that this will soon change even if the number of lone mothers increased significantly. Finally, since German norms continue to expect the mothers of young children to personally take care of their family, strong 'father–providers' are needed for their maintenance. Therefore, the 'father–providers' take the place of the male breadwinners. This, however, is a change in name only; the actors remain the same.

References

Blossfeld, H.-P. (1995) 'Changes in the process of family formation and women's growing economic independence: a comparison of nine countries.' In H.P. Blossfeld (ed) *The New Role of Women. Family Formation in Modern Societies*. Boulder: Westview Press, 3–32.

Blossfeld, H.-P. and Rohwer, G. (1995) 'West Germany.' In H.P. Blossfeld (ed) *The New Role of Women. Family Formation in Modern Societies*. Boulder: Westview Press, 56–76.

Burkart, G. (1995) 'Zum Strukturwandel der Familie. Mythen und Fakten.' *Aus Politik und Zeitgeschichte B*, 52–53/95, 3–13.

Daly, M. (1996) *The Gender Dimension of Welfare. The British and the German Welfare States Compared*. Florence: European University Institute. Ph.D. Dissertation.

Dorbritz, J. and Gärtner, K. (1995) 'Bericht 1995 über die demographische Lage in Deutschland.' *Zeitschrift für Bevölkerungswissenschaft 20*, 4, 339–448.

Duncan, G., Voges, W., Hauser, R. *et al.* (1992) 'Armuts- und Sozialhilfedynamiken in Europa und Nordamerika.' *Working Paper 12/92*. Centre for Social Policy Research. Bremen: University of Bremen.

Duncan, G. and Voges, W. (1993) 'Do generous social-assistance programs lead to dependence? A comparative study of lone-parent families in Germany and the

United States.' *Working Paper 11/93*. Centre for Social Policy Research. Bremen: University of Bremen.

Ebert, K. (1995) 'First call for children!' Zur Notwendigkeit einer verfassungs- und völkerrechtskonformen Familienrechtsreform in Österreich. *Juristische Blätter 117*, 2, 69–87.

Family Report (Bundesministerium für Familie und Senioren (1994) *Familien und Familienpolitik im geeinten Deutschland.* Fünfter Familienbericht. (Federal Ministry of the Family and the Elderly). Bonn.

Holst, E. (1996) 'Erwerbstätigkeit von Frauen in Ost- und Westdeutschland weiterhin von steigender Bedeutung.' *DIW-Wochenbericht 63*, 28/96, 461–469.

Huinink, J. (1995) 'Education, work, and family and family patterns of men: the case of West Germany.' In H.P. Blossfeld (ed) *The New Role of Women. Family Formation in Modern Societies.* Boulder: Westview Press, 247–262.

Kaufmann, F.-X. (1993) 'Familienpolitik in Europa.' In Bundesministerium für Familie und Senioren (ed) *40 Jahre Familienpolitik in der BRD – Rückblick/Ausblick.* Neuwied: Luchterhand, 141–167.

Kleffmann, N. (1996) 'Die Entwicklung des Unterhaltsrechts im Jahre 1995.' *Familie und Recht 7*, 1, 22–36.

Lessenich, S. and Ostner, I. (1995) 'Die institutionelle Dynamik 'Dritter Wege' – Zur Entwicklung der Familienpolitik in 'katholischen' Wohlfahrtsstaaten am Beispiel Frankreichs und Deutschlands.' *Zeitschrift für Sozialreform 41*, 11/12, 780–803.

Limbach, J. (1988) 'Die rechtlichen Rahmenbedingungen von Ehe und Elternschaft.' In R. Nave-Herz and M. Markefka (eds) *Handbuch der Familien- und Jugendforschung. Volume 1.* Neuwied and Frankfurt: Luchterhand, 225–240.

Lüscher, K., Wehrspaun, Ch. and Lange, A. (1989) 'Familienrhetorik – über die Schwierigkeit, 'Familie' zu definieren.' *Zeitschrift für Familienforschung 2*, 61–79.

McLanahan, S. and Sandefur, G. (1994) *Growing Up With A Single Parent.* Cambridge: Harvard University Press.

Meixner, F. (1996) 'Gemeinsames Sorgerecht der Eltern für ein nichteheliches Kind?' *Familie und Recht 7*, 1, 14–21.

Meyer, T. (1994) 'The British and German welfare states as employers: patriarchal or emancipatory.' In D. Sainsbury (ed) *Gendering Welfare States.* London: Sage, 62–81.

Morgan, P. (1995) *Farewell to the Family? Public Policy and Family Breakdown in Britain and the USA.* London: The Institute of Economic Affairs (IEA) Health and Welfare Unit.

Nolte, C. (1996) 'Der Familienlastenausgleich 1996.' *Familie und Recht 7*, 2, 81–87.

Oppenheimer, V.K. (1995) 'The role of women's economic independence in marriage formation: A skeptic's response to Annemette Sorensen's Remark.' In H.P. Blossfeld (ed) *The New Role of Women. Family Formation in Modern Societies.* Boulder: Westview Press, 236–243.

Oppenheimer, V.K., Blossfeld, H.-P. and Wackerow, A. (1995) 'United States of America.' In H.P. Blossfeld (ed) *The New Role of Women. Family Formation in Modern Societies.* Boulder: Westview Press, 150–173.

Peschel-Gutzeit, L. and Jenckel, A. (1996) 'Gleichstellung von ehelichen und nichtehelichen Kindern – Altfälle.' *Familie und Recht 7*, 2, 129–137.

Renesse, M. von (1996) 'Warum können Eltern nicht kündigen, Frau Renesse? Ein Interview.' *Frankfurter Allgemeine Zeitung (FAZ-Magazin)*, 846, May 5th 1996, 58–59.

Schultheis, F. (1987) 'Fatale Strategien und ungeplante Konsequenzen.' *Soziale Welt* *38*, 1, 40–56.

Schultheis, F. (1995) 'Die Familie: Eine Kategorie des Sozialrechts? Ein deutsch-französischer Vergleich.' *Zeitschrift für Sozialreform 41*, 11/12, 764–779.

Schwarz, K. (1995) 'In welchen Familien wachsen die Kinder und Jugendlichen in Deutschland auf?' *Zeitschrift für Bevölkerungswissenschaft 20*, 3, 271–292.

Therborn, G. (1993) 'The politics of childhood: the rights of children in modern times.' In F.G. Castles (ed) *Families of Nations. Patterns of Public Policy in Western Democracies*. Aldershot: Dartmouth, 241–291.

Tölke, A. (1995) 'Geschlechtsspezifische Aspekte der Berufs- und Familienentwicklung.' In B. Nauck and C. Onnen-Isemann (eds) *Familie im Brennpunkt von Wissenschaft und Forschung*. Neuwied: Luchterhand, 489–504.

Voges, W. and Ostner, I. (1995) 'Wie arm sind alleinerziehende Frauen?' In K.-J. Bieback and H. Milz (eds) *Neue Armut*. Frankfurt: Campus Verlag, 122–147.

Walter, W. (1995) 'Familienberichterstattung und familienpolitischer Diskurs.' In U. Gerhardt, S. Hradil, D. Lucke *et al.* (eds) *Familie der Zukunft*. Opladen: Leske und Budrich, 81–97.

Weick, S. (1996) 'Zunehmende Kinderarmut in Deutschland? Studie zur Kinderarmut im Vergleich: 1984 und 1994.' *Informationsdienst Soziale Indikatoren [ISI] 15*, January 1996, 1–3.

Wichmann, K. (1996) 'Zum Stand der Reform des Kindschaftsrechts.' *Nachrichtendienst des Deutschen Vereins für öffentliche und private Fürsorge [NDV] 76*, 2, 41–45.

CHAPTER TWO

Lone Mothers: the British Case

Jane Lewis

There has been a dramatic increase in the numbers of lone mothers over the past 25 years in Britain, due first to the rise in the divorce rate and more recently to the growth in never-married motherhood. With this more recent rise in extra-marital childbearing has come a degree of political concern about lone motherhood that is unique within western European countries. From a continental European perspective, the moral panic about lone motherhood with its often lurid imagery[1] seems, to say the least, puzzling. Lone mother families have in the 1990s been characterised as not just a social problem but a social threat, in terms of the amount of public money that is spent on them (*see* for example; Morgan 1995); of the fate of the children in these families (the latest review of the more extensive American evidence shows that they are more likely to drop out of secondary school and more likely to have a child before the age of 20 in their turn (McLanahan and Sandefeur 1994)); and of the dangers posed by the anti-social behaviour of unattached young men (*see* for example; Dennis and Erdos 1992).

Thus the extraordinary backlash against lone mothers spearheaded by politicians and large tracts of the media is founded on anxieties about the end of marriage and the traditional family, the sexual autonomy of women and the irresponsible behaviour of men, which results, it is believed, in the failure adequately to socialise children. However, while continental Europe may to some extent appreciate the impact of very high rates of divorce and extra-marital childbearing on public debate (although the Scandinavian countries have a

---

1. For example, the cover of the *Sunday Times* colour supplement, 28/7/96, which shows three generations of overweight women (the youngest being a baby). The oldest woman looks over the baby's mother's shoulder and both women look adoringly at the the child. The picture invites the interpretation that we are looking at three generations of lone mothers and asks the question: 'Public enemy or backbone of Britain? The truth about single mothers'.

longer experience of similar levels of extra-marital births), what makes the British case incomprehensible is the lack of any positive commitment to family policies that would improve the lot of the children whose position arouses such concern. British policy in respect of achieving a balance between employment and care on the part of adult family members has been neutral, which means that no help has been given to any parent in this respect, unlike most other European countries (Hantrais and L'Etablier 1996). There is a marked reluctance on the part of Government to intervene in the family unless there is evidence of acute dysfunction, for example, child abuse, and then intervention may be sharp and severe. The family has been deemed private in the sense that parents are left to reconcile paid and unpaid caring work as best they can, and children are largely viewed as the private responsibility of their parents.

As in the USA, the trend in policy has been towards trying to force a change in the behaviour of lone mothers by treating them more punitively and by trying to enforce the responsibility of biological fathers to maintain their children, rather than by increasing investment in children. This in turn can only be understood in the context of policies that have resulted in a substantial growth in inequalities during the 1980s and 1990s (Hills 1995). Furthermore, in a country where the aim over the past decade and a half has been to decrease public expenditure and to elicit more by way of contributions to welfare from the family, the voluntary sector and the state, statistics that appear to signal widespread family breakdown are bound to be particularly threatening to politicians.

However, lone mothers have always been regarded as a source of difficulty by policy makers in Britain mostly because of their need for financial support, although within the category of lone mother, widows have always been regarded as inherently more deserving of help because they could not be construed as morally blameworthy. In the absence of a male provider the state must decide how far and under what conditions it will provide for the mother and her children and there have been major changes over time in the views that different governments have taken. Very broadly, under the nineteenth century Poor Law it was assumed that lone mothers would go out to work to support as many children (usually one or two) as possible, with the state supporting the rest in the workhouse. By the mid-twentieth century the emphasis was more on their role as mothers and in the legislation that formed the post-war settlement, lone mothers with children below the school-leaving age of sixteen did not have to make themselves available for work and were eligible for social assistance. At the end of the 1980s, the pendulum began to swing back again (as it did in the United States and in the Netherlands) and more encouragement was given to lone mothers to enter the labour market. However, in Britain, more emphasis still was given to eliciting a contribution for the support of lone mothers and their children from the absent father.

Lone mothers have always 'packaged income' (Rainwater, Rein and Schwartz 1986) from their families (in particular the father of their children), from earnings, and from charity (especially in the early part of the twentieth century). In the post-war period earnings have significantly *decreased* in importance as a proportion of lone mothers' income and the state has become increasingly important as a provider of *cash*, if not of child *care*, for British lone mothers. The reasons for this shift in the balance of support are various: first, the dramatic increase in the numbers of divorced and never-married lone mothers made lone motherhood a more visible problem during the last quarter of a century and the significant changes in sexual morality that accompanied the changes in the marriage system reduced the stigma felt by lone mothers, which in turn made them more ready to claim assistance from the state; second there have been changes in the structure of and opportunities in the labour market; third there have been changes in eligibility for and levels of state benefits; and fourth there have been changes in the availability, location and cost of child care, which have in turn been affected by housing policies which determine where lone mothers live. Most recently Government has sought to reassess its role as provider for lone mothers and their children. More encouragement has been given to lone mothers to enter the labour market, although the strong strand of authoritarian conservatism within the Conservative Party (*see* King 1987) has remained ambivalent about the desirability of full-time work for these mothers. Thus Government has also turned to the only other source of income for lone mothers, insisting that fathers do more to provide, a move that has been bolstered by concern about the irresponsible behaviour of young men in particular.

The increase in lone motherhood in post-war Britain

There have been two major changes in the marriage system in the post-war period. First, there was a widespread separation of sex and marriage. The evidence suggests that significantly more single teenagers began to have sex in the late 1950s and 1960s before the pill became widely available (Bone 1986; Black and Sykes 1971; Moore and Burt 1982). Table 2.1 shows that there was a marked increase in unmarried teenagers with sexual experience, especially in the younger ages, between 1964 and 1974/5. In addition, the gap between girls and boys closed to some extent.

The increase in sexual activity outside marriage resulted in a sharp rise in both the extra-marital and marital birth rates during the 1960s (*see* Table 2.2). This contrasts with the war years, when the extra-marital rate increased because so many marriages were thwarted by war-time disruption and to a lesser extent by death. The pattern for the 1960s also differed from that of the period since the mid-1980s, when the extra-marital birth rate rose dramatically and the marital birth rate fell as a consequence of the movement away from marriage.

Table 2.1 Teenage sexual experiences, 1964 and 1974/5

Percentage of single teenage males with experience of sexual intercourse.			Percentage of single teenage females with experience of sexual intercourse.		
Age	1964	1974/5	Age	1964	1974/5
16	14	32	16	5	21
17	16	50	17	10	37
18	34	65	18	17	47

Source: Bury 1984.

Table 2.2 Marital and extra-marital births per 1000 women aged 15–44, 1940–1992

	Marital birth rate per 1000 married women	Extra-marital birth rate per 1000 single, divorced and widowed women
1940	98.8	5.9
1945	103.9	16.1
1950	108.6	10.2
1955	103.7	10.3
1960	120.8	14.7
1965	126.9	21.2
1970	113.5	21.5
1975	85.5	17.4
1980	92.2	19.6
1985	87.8	26.7
1990	86.7	38.9
1992	82.4	42.4

Source: OPES (Office of Population and Census Statistics, now ONS), *Birth Statistics: Historical series 1837–1983*. Table 3.2b and c, Series FM1 No.13, HMSO, 1987. OPCS, *Birth Statistics*, Table 3.1, Series FM1 No.22, HMSO, 1995.

What happened in the 1960s was that increased sexual activity led to an increase in the pre-marital pregnancy rate, but these women still tended to marry before the birth. A majority of births to women under 20 were conceived outside marriage in the 1960s, but the majority of pre-maritally conceived births took place inside marriage. In 1969, 55 per cent of extra-marital conceptions were legitimised by marriage, 32 per cent resulted in 'illegitimate' births, and 14 per cent were aborted (the Abortion Act was passed in 1967) (OPCS 1987). In addition, small scale studies of illegitimacy carried out during the late 1950s and 1960s showed that between 35 and 40 per cent of illegitimate births were to separated, divorced and widowed women (Registrar General 1971). As a result of his review of a number of these studies, Cyril Greenland, a senior psychiatric social worker in Scotland, concluded that one in three illegitimate births were to women in older age groups and cohabiting in more or less permanent unions (Greenland 1957). It is perhaps, therefore, not so surprising that there was seemingly little panic about what amounted to a significant increase in the separation of sex from marriage. The fact that a majority of premarital conceptions were legitimised and that divorce rates were still low (see Table 2.3) resulted in a series of optimistic statements from social investigators about family stability (see for example; Fletcher 1966).

Table 2.3 Divorce rate per 1000 married population

1950	2.8
1960	2.0
1965	3.1
1970	4.7
1975	9.6
1980	12.0
1985	13.4
1990	13.0
1992	13.7

Source: OPCS (now ONS), *Marriage and Divorce Statistics 1837–1983*. Historical Series, FM2, No.16, Table 5.2; OPCS, *Marriage and Divorce Statistics.* Table 2.1, FM2, No.21, HMSO, 1995.

Since the beginning of the 1970s, there have been marked changes in marriage patterns: substantial declines in marriage rates, less marriage and older marriage; a dramatic rise in divorce rates that levelled off from the 1980s; and the emergence of widespread cohabitation. The rise in extra-marital childbearing evident during the 1960s levelled off for a time during the 1970s as a consequence of the 'contraceptive revolution' and the availability of legal abortion for unwanted pregnancies. Young unmarried women who found themselves pregnant in the 1970s opted for an abortion or an illegitimate child rather than marriage. From the late 1970s the proportion of births outside marriage began to increase slowly at first and then rapidly throughout the 1980s, with signs of stabilisation in the early 1990s at around one in three of all births (*see* Table 2.2).

Declining marriage and increased childbearing outside marriage have been inextricably linked to the growth of cohabitation. Cohabitation was apparently common in the early part of the twentieth century when divorce was rare, particularly among working people (Gillis 1986). When separation allowances were provided for the wives of servicemen during World War I, special provision had to be made for 'unmarried wives' (Parker 1990; Pedersen 1993). Indeed, cohabitation was probably at its nadir during the 1950s and 1960s when marriage was almost universal (Kiernan and Estaugh 1993). Living together as a prelude to marriage began in the 1970s. In the 1990s typically 70 per cent of never-married women who marry have cohabited with their husbands, compared with 58 per cent of those marrying between 1985 and 1988, 33 per cent of those marrying between 1975 and 1979, and six per cent of those marrying between 1965 and 1969. Additionally, in 1993, 25 per cent of divorced women were in cohabiting unions. Cohabitations have tended to be short-lived and childless, but during the 1980s, children were increasingly being born within these unions. The changing patterns of birth registration provide some evidence of this (see Table 2.4). By 1994, 58 per cent were registered by couples living at the same address. Teenage mothers are the least likely to be cohabiting.

Table 2.4 Registration of births outside marriage, 1964–1994

	1964	1971	1981	1994
Sole Registration	60%	55%	42%	26%
Joint registration	40%	45%	58%	75%
Births outside marriage as a % of all births	7%	8%	13%	32%

Source: OPCS (now ONS), *Birth Statistics: Historical Series 1837–1983.* Tables 1.1 and 3.7, Series FM1 No.13, HMSO, 1987 and Population Trends No.81, Table 10, Autumn 1995.

Increases in divorce, cohabitation and childbearing outside marriage have thus all contributed to the second major change in the post-war marriage system: the separation of marriage and parenthood, from which lone parenthood is the outcome. Between 1970 and 1990 the percentage of lone mother families more than doubled (*see* Table 2.5 below).

Table 2.5 Distribution of the different types of lone-mother families with dependent children, 1971–1991

	%* of all families with dependent children			
	1971	1981	1986	1991
Single lone mother	1.2	2.3	3.2	6.4
Separated lone mothers	2.5	2.3	2.6	3.6
Divorced lone mothers	1.9	4.4	5.6	6.3
Widowed lone mothers	1.9	1.7	1.1	1.2
All lone mothers	7.5	10.7	12.5	17.5

* Estimates are based on three year averages, apart from 1991.

Source: Haskey 1993.

This was due in large measure to the rise in the divorce rate (*see* Table 2.3), which increased almost three fold over the same period. Britain also has a much higher teenage fertility rate than other western European countries, and unlike any other European country, the British rate has not declined over the last decade. In 1989, the UK contributed only 20 per cent of the total number of births within the European Union, but contributed 37 per cent of all teenage births (Kiernan 1996). The decline in the number of teenage births since 1988 is largely due to the falling teenage population, rates of births to teenagers have changed little. In 1990 it was 33.3 per 1000 women aged 15–19 compared with a rate of 12.7 for Sweden and 6.4 for the Netherlands (Selman and Glendinning 1996). However, teenage unmarried mothers nevertheless constitute a small proportion of the total number of lone mothers.

Behind these changes in behaviour lay an equally profound set of changes in attitudes towards sexual morality, which resulted in the almost complete erosion of the stigma attaching to divorcees and unmarried mothers, which in turn set new parameters for policy makers. During the 1960s, doctors, churchmen and social investigators began to establish the foundations of a new sexual morality (Lewis, Kiernan and Land forthcoming). Doctors expressed optimism that a new concept of sexual relations that included premarital sex and the use of birth control would make marriage more considerate and sexually satisfying (*see* for example; Carstairs 1962; Comfort 1963). Clergymen did not give their approval to extra-marital sex, but they did reformulate their ideas about morality such that they could be used to justify more radical behaviour. The Christian new moralists of the 1960s stressed that love was the only proper basis for personal relationships and agreed that the morality of sex had nothing to do with marriage, sex could be moral or immoral in or outside marriage. Some felt that the most invidious aspect of the traditional, rule-bound morality that was imposed via an external moral code in respect of marriage was the fact that coercive behaviour inside marriage was not condemned. The Bishop of Woolwich's highly influential contribution to the debate advocated a position based on love, whereby morality came from *within* rather than being imposed from *without* and whereby nothing could be labelled as wrong, not divorce nor premarital sex, unless it lacked love (Robinson 1963).

Such ideas were not new; a radical minority had expressed similar notions during the 1920s and 30s, but during the 1960s they became sufficiently widespread to influence legislative reform. In particular, the 1969 reform of the divorce law moved substantially away from the idea of 'fault-based' divorce. Fault was determined by reference to an externally imposed moral code, which allocated blame (for adultery, unreasonable behaviour and so forth). After 1969 marriage became increasingly a matter for the individuals concerned and the interest of the state in the reasons for ending a marriage receded to 'vanishing point' (Davis and Murch 1988, p.13).

Policies towards lone mothers

The debates about state support for lone mothers during the early part of the twentieth century show clearly the importance that was attached to the male-breadwinner model and how difficult it was, therefore, to include lone mothers in social security schemes as mothers, or as workers.

1900–1945

The years between 1911 and 1925 were marked by a long campaign, mainly on the part of women's groups, to 'endow motherhood' by granting women and children allowances. Prior to World War I, these were usually called 'mothers' pensions', as they were in the much more successful campaigns in the United States, where 30 states introduced such benefits by 1918 (Skocpol 1992). The arguments for mothers' endowment stressed the need to improve the health and welfare of mothers and the dangers inherent in poor mothers taking up work that was 'sweated' in terms of both its pay and conditions. The campaign sought to include all mothers and 'endowment' was conceived of as a payment for the work of caring as well as a form of maintenance for children. During World War I, women within the Ministry of Reconstruction tried to use the separation allowances that were paid to the wives and cohabitants of servicemen as a lever for securing allowances for all mothers. As a practical strategy towards this larger end, they proposed endowing lone mothers first; the vast majority of lone mothers being widows at this point in time. Eventually, in 1925, Government accepted the argument for paying pensions to widows, but explicitly rejected the idea of covering other separated and divorced or unmarried mothers because it would have meant recognising their claim as mothers and setting up a new form of public assistance. Widows were covered as wives under their husbands' insurance contributions. The campaign for endowing mothers proceeded to concentrate on securing family allowances for children from 1925 until these were granted in 1945.

William Beveridge tried to include lone mothers in his scheme of social insurance during the 1940s, but failed (Cd. 6404 1942). Beveridge was keen to recognise the unpaid work performed by wives, not least for eugenic reasons (he was, like many of his contemporaries, very worried about the fall in the birth rate during the 1930s). Lone mothers also performed important caring work, but were very difficult to deal with once the decision had been taken not to treat married women independently for insurance purposes, but rather to insure them via their husbands. In the case of unmarried mothers, there was never any hope of including them within an insurance scheme and they were from the start consigned to social assistance. Beveridge, however, struggled to find a way of insuring against marital breakdown. He swung between making marriage breakdown a risk analogous to industrial accident and seeing it as 'leaving work without just cause'. As it crystallised, the problem in relation to the principles of insurance became three fold: first, the issue of whether it was possible for women to profit from an insurance paid for by their husbands when they were at 'fault' in the process of marriage breakdown, and whether it was possible for men to have insurance cover in respect of their wives if they were at fault; second, the issue of the possibility of double cover for women under the public law of social security and the private law of divorce which secured maintenance; and third, the problem of proving the status of a deserted or separated wife, whom it was feared might collude with her husband to secure benefit. In the end, these practical considerations made Beveridge reject the possibility of including separated and divorced women in his social insurance scheme.

The one hope for lone mothers lay in family allowances, which offered a partial solution to the problem so long as they were set at a high enough rate and covered all children. When these were legislated in 1945, however, the amount paid was only 60 per cent of that recommended by Beveridge and nothing at all was paid in respect of the first child, which effectively excluded most lone mothers. In the post-war world, lone mothers had to depend on social assistance rather than social insurance. However, in Britain they were not alone, because social insurance never became the all-encompassing scheme that Beveridge intended, and large numbers of elderly people in particular found that they had to resort to social assistance, which was a means-tested scheme with nationally determined rates of benefit.

The 1950s and 1960s

In fact relatively few lone mothers depended on the state during the 1950s and early 1960s. The 1949 Annual Report of the National Assistance Board, which administered social assistance, commented:

> Plainly the great majority of separated wives and unmarried mothers succeed in keeping independent of assistance, either because they receive a sufficiency from the person liable [ie., the father] or (probably more often) because they maintain themselves by their own efforts. The Board must be dealing only with the exceptional cases. (Cmd. 8030 1950, p.21)

The demand for women's labour in the service of the welfare state – in the health, welfare and education service – grew substantially in the 1950s and 1960s and large numbers of women entered the labour market. A Ministry of Health Circular (37/38) published in 1968 stated clearly that lone parents took priority for the limited number of day care places that were available from local authorities, something that changed later on as priority was increasingly given to children who were at risk of abuse. It is also likely that child care was provided by their families of origin during the period, because significant numbers of lone mothers were co-resident with kin. A national study of women's employment commissioned by the Government in the mid-1960s commented on the heavy reliance of all women with children on family-based childcare (Hunt 1968). An unmarried mother was likely to have entered a mother and baby home run by a voluntary organisation (9 out of 10 of which were religious) and then to have returned to her family of origin. While lone mothers with dependent children were permitted to draw assistance benefits, there is evidence from contemporary studies that welfare officers pressed many to take paid employment (Marsden 1969). It also seems that these local officers did their best to secure help from voluntary and religious bodies and to minimise the contribution from the state (Cmnd 1730 1961, Appendix 10).

It was part of the responsibility of the National Assistance Board to pursue 'the liable relative', that is the father, and to try and extract maintenance from him which would be set against benefits payable by the state. However, from an early stage the Board acknowledged the difficulties inherent in this task because the husband was either unable to pay, or was paying for a second family. While the Board admitted that respect for the marriage tie suggested that the first wife should be the prior charge on the husband, in practice he was more inclined to support the woman (and children) he was currently living with:

> Extracting money from husbands to maintain wives from whom they are separated is at best an uncertain business; it is easier to enforce the maintenance of those with whom the man is living than of those from whom he is parted, and the man is more likely to exert himself to maintain the former. (Cmd. 9210 1953, pp.17–18)

Thus it was tacitly agreed that the father would support his second family while the state supported the first.

During the 1950s and 1960s the burden on state expenditure was not huge because the number of lone mothers was relatively small. They were also relatively invisible, being often hidden within their families of origin. All this changed during the 1970s and 1980s. Table 2.6 summarises the most striking changes between 1971 and 1991.

Table 2.6 UK lone parents over 20 years

	1971	1991
Number of lone parents	570,000	1,270,000
% of all families with children	8%	20%
% lone mothers employed	52%	41%
% married mothers employed	39%	62%
% lone mothers receiving supplementary benefit	37%	79%

Source: Millar 1996.

The numbers of lone parents increased dramatically and at the same time the percentage in the labour market fell and those drawing state benefits increased. It was also the case that many more lone mothers began to live independently. Between 1974 and 1989 the proportion living alone doubled to 73 per cent. Whereas only 16 per cent of single lone mothers lived alone in 1974, 49 per cent did so by 1989 (Haskey 1989), chiefly as a result of the increased availability of social housing. The move to independent living was accompanied by a flight from the mother and baby homes, the number of homes declined from 172 in 1968 to 65 in 1974 (Nicholson 1968; Cmd. 5629 1974). This change in living patterns and their increasing dependence on state benefits made lone mothers much more visible to policy makers. The decision to live independently and claim benefit from the state was made possible by changing incentive structures in respect of the earnings that could be expected from the labour market as opposed to benefit levels, and changing policies in regard to social housing, but also by the decline of stigma due to changes in sexual morality.

The 1970s

In respect of housing, there is evidence during the 1950s and 1960s that lone mothers were less likely than two-parent families to become tenants of local authority housing departments. Those who could not live with their families of origin were likely to be pushed into the overcrowded private rented sector. Studies of homelessness in the 1960s began to make the connection between it and marital breakdown (see for example; Greve 1964), although at that time it was suggested that homelessness caused marital breakdown. Not until the 1970s and the rediscovery of domestic violence was it suggested that marital breakdown was the cause of homelessness (Land and Lewis 1997). Rent rebate schemes were rationalised during the 1970s and under the 1977 Housing (Homeless Persons) Act local authority housing departments were given the responsibility for housing the unintentionally homeless, which meant that public housing was no longer confined to those on the waiting list. In the first two years of the Act's operation over half of those housed were single parents. By the 1980s, the conflict between the needs of families on the waiting list and homeless families had grown and Margaret Thatcher charged in a 1988 speech that young single women were jumping the housing queue by deliber-ately getting pregnant (Macaskill 1993), a charge that has been repeated by Conservative MPs during the 1990s.

Also during the 1970s, the Matrimonial Proceedings and Property Act 1970 enabled the divorce courts to make decisions concerning the re-ordering and disposition of property. Thus if the wife remained in the matrimonial home, this could be taken into account in determining the level of maintenance for her (unlike Scottish and most continental European law, English law has no concept of community property). Thus while divorced women were increasingly allowed to stay in the matrimonial home, the maintenance paid by their former husbands decreased. Changes in the private law of divorce, therefore, had a major impact on public law as lone parents became increasingly dependent on means-tested assistance to meet the costs of their housing (via housing benefit) as well as for their maintenance.

The Finer Committee on One-Parent Families reported in 1974 that the increasing number of lone parents claiming benefit was due mainly to the fact that it had become 'progressively less worthwhile for a lone woman with children to take up full-time employment and cease to claim supplementary benefits (social assistance), unless they could earn well above the average wage for women in full-time work' (Cmnd. 5629 1974, p.24). In other words, the cost of child care was too high and the wages commanded by women too low to provide any incentive to join the labour market. This position has remained essentially unchanged and largely explains the fall in lone mothers' labour market participation (Joshi 1990). A recent cross national study of the barriers to employment for lone mothers has concluded that it is the cost of child care that distinguishes the British case (Bradshaw *et al.* 1996). Since the 1970s, the percentage of lone parents drawing means-tested benefits has continued inexorably to rise (*see* Table 2.7) while the percentage in the labour market has fallen (*see* Table 2.8). Up to the mid-1970s some 50 per cent of lone mothers were in employment, the fall since has been chiefly in terms of full-time work.

Table 2.7 Numbers and percentages of lone parents in total and receiving benefit by sex

	1978	1973	1983	1988	1993
Total lone mothers (000s)	576	733	848	984	1347
Total lone mothers recipients (000s)	250	325	417	694	989
Female recipients (%)	43	44	49	71	73
Total lone fathers (000s)	82	97	103	95	122
Total lone father recipients	7	15	24	32	59
Male recipients (%)	9	15	23	34	49

Source: DHSS, *Social Security Statistics* (1973, 1980 and 1983); Table 34.82, 1989, Table 37.22 and DSS, *Social Security Statistics*, 1994, Table A2.15, Calculated using DSS grossing factors.

Table 2.8 Economic activity of mothers with children under 16

	Single Lone	Divorced/Separated	Married
1973–5	43.0	51.8	48.1
1981–3	29.7	44.4	48.6
1991–3	29.7	45.0	62.1

Source: General Household Survey, secondary analysis by Dr Kathleen Kiernan.

The Finer Report acknowledged that in a free, democratic society it was impossible to restrict the freedom to divorce, remarry and reproduce, that is fundamentally to change the marriage system which was beginning to redefine the nature of lone motherhood. Given this, it concluded that 'the community has to bear much of the cost of broken homes and unmarried motherhood' (Cmnd. 5629 1974, para 4.224). This point established, the Committee proceeded to review the way in which public and private law could be brought together to secure a more efficient and humane system of support for all types of lone mother families. The Report stressed the need to tackle the problem of poverty among lone-mother families and concluded that their needs were greater than those of two-parent families. Furthermore, the Committee's diagnosis of the problem of lone parenthood made it sensible to treat all lone parents together. The integration of unmarried mothers into a more general consideration of lone motherhood was particularly significant and could not have been accomplished without the accompanying changes in thinking about sexual morality. The pressure group, the National Council for the Unmarried Mother and her Child (formed in 1917), changed its name to the National Council for One-Parent Families in 1973 in an attempt to embrace all types of lone-mother family and in particular to erode the distinction between legitimate and illegitimate children. The Finer Committee considered the possibility of adopting the Scandinavian system of state guarantees for the maintenance payments from fathers agreed in private divorce law, but shied away from the effort necessary to determine paternity and trace fathers, believing that this would prove too intrusive for the British public, an interesting position given the much greater intrusiveness of the child support legislation passed in 1991. Instead, the Committee recommended a non-contributory Guaranteed Main-tenance Allowance payable to all one-parent families after a three month period (to allow for the possibility that the husband might return). The Committee took a neutral position on the issue of employment for lone mothers, suggesting that they should be free to choose whether to go out to work. Being free to choose not to do so involved having an adequate income, hence the proposal for the Guaranteed Maintenance Allowance. Being free to choose to go out to work depended on it being worthwhile to do so. Thus the committee recommended a more generous system of earnings disregards for those drawing state benefits. As Carol Smart (1984) has pointed out, the Committee's idea of choice in respect of paid work amounted to something more than staying neutral in the manner of the non-interventionist stance adopted by Governments since.

The Finer Committee's proposals were not adopted by Governments in the 1970s. The Conservative Government of the early 1970s tried to encourage employment by introducing family income supplement, a means-tested benefit for low wage earners with children, in 1971. By 1974, half the recipients were lone parents. In addition, earnings disregards for those on benefit were doubled in 1975. While the balance of Government measures in the 1970s was towards helping lone parents in employment and encouraging those on benefit to supplement their income by earning, the numbers drawing benefits grew, in part because the numbers of lone mothers increased rapidly, but also because it was not realised the extent to which the labour market participation of lone mothers in the 1950s and 1960s had depended on the provision of childcare by co-resident kin. Publicly provided child care in Britain has been among the lowest in Europe (*see* Table 2.9) and child care costs have therefore been extremely high.

Table 2.9 Number of places in day nurseries, playgroups, childminders and nursery education in England

	1984	1994
Day nursery places provided by local authorities[1,2]	28,872	22,300
Playgroup places run by local authorities[1,2]	2692	1600
Registered day nursery places[1,3]	23,124	124,000
Registered playgroup places[1,2,3]	384,523	407,600
Registered childminder places[1,2,3,4]	116,331	357,500
Pupils in nursery schools (in January) Full-time Part-time	 12,367 37,260	 9140 43,474

[1] Prior to 1992, where a local authority had not submitted a return, the latest available data for that authority was substituted. Figures since 1992 are estimates which have been rounded.

[2] Including facilities provided by voluntary organisations under agency arrangements under Section 22 of the National Health Service Act 1946.

[3] From October 1991, registered under the Children Act 1989 and prior to that date registered under the Nurseries and Child Minders Regulation Act 1948 (as amended by Section 60 of the health services and Public Health Act 1968).

[4] From 1992 figures for childminders relates to registration for children aged under 8. In 1994, 19,700 places were registered specifically for children aged 5–7.

Source: Barker 1995.

As Gustaffson (1994) has pointed out, the effect of child care subsidies on women's labour market participation depends very much on the policy logic of the welfare regime. In the UK, it is the cost of child care above all that deters lone mothers from entering the labour market (Bradshaw *et al.* 1996)

It was also the case that lone parents continued to do reasonably well under social assistance. When a tax-free child benefit replaced family allowances and personal tax allowances for children in 1975, it was paid in respect of the first child of all lone parents. As Daly (1996) has pointed out, while Britain's social security system secures a vastly inferior standard of living to that provided by Germany, whose system is much more heavily insurance based, lone mothers in Britain do rather better than their German equivalents and do better relative to men. Under the 1978 review of social security, one parent families did a little better than two parent families (Millar, 1989). Even in the 1985 review of social security, which was prompted by the Thatcher Government's determination to reduce social security expenditure, lone mothers were not singled out for special attention, indeed it was accepted that lone parents on benefit should get a premium in addition to that received by all families with children.

The 1980s and 1990s

Instead, the attention of policy makers in the 1980s began to focus on men as a source of income for lone mothers. The Finer Committee had accepted that fathers should be liable to maintain, although it also accepted the long-established practice that they would in fact support their second rather than their first families. During the 1970s the 'cohabitation rule' caused considerable controversy. By this rule the Supplementary Benefits Commission (which administered social assistance at that time) insisted, in accordance with the male-breadwinner model, that if a woman was living with a man then that man must be supporting her and so ceased to pay benefit. The Commission stressed that it was concern about equity between one- and two-parent families rather than concern about morality that informed its judgement:

> It is not the business of the Supplementary Benefits Scheme either to penalise or to favour those who are not legally married... It has also been argued that the cohabitation rule is out of tune with modern trends of life... In our view it would be wrong in principle to treat the women who have the support of a partner both as if they had not such support and better than if they were married. It would not be right, and we believe public opinion would not accept, that the unmarried 'wife' should be able to claim benefit denied to a married woman because her husband was in full-time work. We express no opinion about whether this would be an encouragement to immorality. (Supplementary Benefits Commission 1971, p.2–3)

Feminists strongly attacked the presumption that women should be dependent on men. During the 1980s, however, the cohabitation rule ceased to be an issue, not least because the number of benefit officers had been cut and the intrusive home visits necessary to establish the presence of a 'man-in-the-house' ceased (National Audit Office 1991).

However, the issue of the support provided by men as fathers, rather than as cohabitees, gathered force. Academic studies showed that both the levels and regularity of payment on the part of men to be low (Eekelaar and Maclean 1986; Bradshaw and Millar 1991; Davis *et al.* 1992). At the end of the 1980s on average maintenance accounted for only 7 per cent of lone mothers' income. This was hardly new. Even in the 1930s no persisting obligation to maintain was placed on men, but by the late 1980s only one out of three lone mothers received regular maintenance and a majority were receiving state benefits. Sixty per cent of the children in families receiving income support were members of one-parent families. It was this situation that the 1991 Child Support Act set out to change by forcing a shift in the balance of support for lone mothers and their children towards biological fathers.

There were arguably two sets of anxieties prompting this change of direction. The first was expressed most loudly by Conservative politicians and Right wing think tanks and focused on the extent of 'welfare dependency' among lone mother families and the cost to the public purse. The second was concerned more about the effect of lone motherhood on children and has been more widely shared across the political spectrum and among academic researchers. The emphasis on the common material needs of all lone mother families during the 1970s blurred the historical divisions between the widowed, the divorced and the unmarried mothers in terms of debate (although widows continued to be better provided for under national insurance), but the huge increase in first divorced and then unmarried mothers made Conservative politicians in particular fear the 'breakdown of the family'. The possibility of independent living for unmarried mothers additionally raised the spectre that women might be choosing unmarried motherhood, while others feared that divorce, the majority of which is initiated by women, might be too easy.

The profound shift in the political culture during the 1980s in Britain resulted in lone mothers once more being categorised as a special problem. In Britain and the United States, the moral became entwined with the social and lone mothers became not just a social problem but a social threat. In the mid-1980s in the USA, Charles Murray (1984) advocated a draconian withdrawal of benefits, which he believed would force a change in behaviour. He wanted to reverse the process by which social assistance had become treated more as a citizen right in the late twentieth century income maintenance systems, and to return to the poor law conception of assistance, with its ideas of less eligibility and the concomitant loss of political citizenship. He stressed the extent to which in a society where birth control techniques were advanced, unmarried motherhood was a question of choice. In his view, the moral hazard of providing welfare benefits was too great. Perhaps more influential still in terms of policy was Lawrence Mead's (1986) analysis of welfare dependency. He too advocated remoralising the poor, but by bringing them into employment. Stressing the importance of citizen obligations rather than citizen rights, Mead favoured the idea that people should work (defined in terms of paid employment rather than unpaid work such as child care) in return for benefits. This argument also became tied to the future of children in lone-mother families. Still other theorists of the New Right in the United States suggested that it was better for a child to have the example of a breadwinner mother than none at all (Novak *et al.* 1987). In the United States a majority of States introduced 'workfare' programmes, which have resulted in lone mothers being treated the same as men – as workers rather than as mothers.

However, Conservatives have been traditionally ambivalent about whether to encourage mothers to work outside the home. In the United States, George Gilder (1987) deplored the idea of more mothers entering the labour market. In his view, the problem was the lack of paid work for young men; more women working could only exacerbate the problem. In Britain, as late as 1990, the National Audit Office reiterated the Government's official policy of neutrality regarding lone mothers' employment, although changes to the social security regulations introduced alongside the child support legislation contained some additional incentives for lone mothers to enter the labour market. However, lone mothers' labour market participation continued to fall, while that of married mothers rose, chiefly because of the difficulty they experienced in finding affordable childcare. Bradshaw and Millar (1991) reported that if all the lone mothers in their large sample survey who said they wanted to work had been able to do so, the proportion in the labour market would have been similar to that of married mothers. Commentators in Britain, however, have tended to follow the more traditionally conservative American literature. Patricia Morgan (1995, p.75) for example, has argued that policies to encourage lone mothers to enter the labour market are 'the solution to the wrong problem'. Given the determination to reduce the role of the state and ambivalence about the desirability of women with young children entering the labour market, attention was not surprisingly drawn towards the third main option for support: men. Nor was Britain alone in this, child support legislation was also passed in both the United States and Australia.

Another important strand in the shift in focus towards men as a source of support was the new attention paid to the importance of the role of fathers. For writers such as Morgan, but also for those on the political left, such as Halsey (1993) and Dennis and Erdos (1992), as well as for politicians (Hansard, 1993) and the media (BBC 1993), concerns about the differences between one-

and two-parent families have ranged well beyond the matter of material support. All have argued that the successful socialisation of children requires the active involvement of two parents. Dennis and Erdos (1992) sought to trace the rise of the 'obnoxious Englishman' to family breakdown. Their chief concern was the effect of lone motherhood on the behaviour patterns of young men; lone motherhood was, in their view, responsible for at best irresponsible and at worse criminal behaviour in the next male generation.

Dennis and Erdos's convictions about the link between lone motherhood and rising crime rates has not been tested for any large scale British sample. From the beginning of the 1980s, however, psychological research in Britain and America has provided convincing evidence of the detrimental effects of divorce on the educational achievement, employment and personal relationships of children and young adults (Hetherington et al. 1978; Wallerstein and Kelly 1980; Richards 1982, 1993), and while it is too early to come to any firm conclusions regarding the effects on the large numbers of children born to unmarried mothers since the mid-1980s, earlier studies showed their life chances to be lower at birth when compared with children from two-parent intact families (Burghes 1994).

However, as the Finer Committee recognised in the early 1970s, it is well nigh impossible in a liberal democratic society for Government to seek directly to control marital and reproductive behaviour. Nevertheless, Conservative Governments at the end of the 1980s set out on a course that if pushed to its logical conclusion would have attempted to do this. Early in the 1990s the Lord Chancellor announced his intention of introducing measures to cut the rate of divorce. However, in a 1995 White Paper (Cm. 2799) on mediation and the grounds for divorce, he proposed instead a collection of measures intended to make divorce less expensive and more amicable. According to The Independent (24/4/95), he had 'recognised an important truth – that the state has limited ability and little right to intervene in the personal relationships of private individuals'. However, the effects of the 1996 Family Law Bill, which aims to make divorce possible after a one year 'cooling off' period during which couples will be encouraged to seek mediation, are difficult to predict. Access to legal aid, which has been crucial to women both in enabling them to initiate divorce and in securing financial settlements, is being severely curtailed, meaning that those who would be reliant on it will effectively be forced to use the (cheaper) mediation service, which in the United States has been shown to work to the detriment of women and children (Mason 1994). Thus it may be that women will be deterred from seeking divorce.

The 1991 Child Support Act can also be interpreted as seeking fundamentally to change reproductive behaviour by making fathers responsible for all their biological children. However, the protests, chiefly from middle class men but also from their second wives, have been so strong that the legislation has been substantially diluted. In the words of the Secretary of State, Peter Lilley, the Child Support Act was intended to reverse 'the inadvertent nationalisation of fatherhood' (cited by Land 1994). All biological fathers, unmarried and divorced, were given a persistent obligation to maintain and the long-established practice by which the state assumed that the man would maintain his second family while it would support the first, was formally abandoned. The primary obligation of fathers is to the state rather than the child, the amount payable being a proportion of assessable income. The formula employed contained an element for the support of the mother as well as the child, which prompted opposition from feminists concerned about the perpetuation of female dependence on men. The formula is also considerably more draconian than that used historically to determine the amount payable by 'the liable relative' and one of the main criticisms of the legislation has been the tendency to reduce the man's second family to social assistance levels. This legislation has proved very difficult to implement, for the reason that in the 'flexible' labour market of the 1990s, far fewer men earn a 'family wage', and because major errors were made in implementation.

In a sense, the child support legislation has tried to enforce the old assumptions of traditional marriage, whereby wives and mothers care while husbands and fathers maintain. This interpretation is strengthened when the legislation is placed in its larger context. Faced with the profound change in marital and reproductive behaviour which means that it is no longer possible to attempt to enforce the traditional obligations of husbands and wives, Government has sought to enforce parental responsibility, an option that is logical in the face of widespread marriage breakdown and increasing cohabitation, but which is also in line with the determination of successive Conservative Governments to enforce individual rather than collective responsibility. Thus the Children Act of 1989, which addressed the problem of care for children, firmly supported the idea of care by both parents, and Eekelaar (1991) has traced the way in which responsibility in the sense of a preference for parental responsibility over state responsibility came to predominate over the simple meaning of responsibility by parents for children. Just as the 1996 Family Law Act seeks further to deregulate marriage by consigning the negotiations over property and children to lay mediators, so the official guidance accompanying the Children Act stated firmly that children do better in the family with both parents playing a full part and without resort to legal proceedings (Department of Health 1990).

Furthermore, the emphasis on parental responsibility in the legislation tended to assume traditional roles on the part of mothers and fathers. For the first time unmarried fathers were given the right to share parental responsibility by making an informal agreement and without resort to court proceedings. This recognises the importance now attributed to the presence of a father in the life of the child by the academic literature, but absent fathers have no automatic recognition in respect of care comparable to the absolute obligation to maintain laid upon them by the child support legislation. Indeed, the traditional assumptions regarding the male obligation to maintain being paramount remains. One aspect of the child support formula that was subjected to the most severe criticism was the lack of regard for travelling expenses incurred by fathers who maintained contact with the children of their first family (Garnham and Knights 1994).

Thus it may be argued that the 1990s have seen the emergence of a new parenthood contract designed to secure the responsibilities of parents and to limit those of the state in an environment where the norms and expectations associated with marriage can no longer be counted upon. However, when both gender roles in the family and in the workplace and the structure of personal relationships are changing rapidly, an attempt to solve the problems that are posed for children by reimposing elements of the traditional marriage contract look rather dubious. Such an approach does nothing to recognise the problems that women have in combining paid and unpaid work and does little to encourage men to share the unpaid work of caring. Indeed, Britain is one of the few northern European countries not to have taken seriously the problems that all parents face in combining family and work responsibilities. In France, it is an explicit policy goal to help parents to do this, while in Britain Government remains officially neutral on the subject, maintaining a strict division between what is perceived as the public and private spheres, with the result that mothers and fathers must work out their own salvation. Britain is near the bottom of the European child care league and has opposed European Commission proposals in respect of parental leave. Lone mothers pay a particularly heavy price in terms of the barriers that are thereby erected to their participation in the labour market.

There is also increasing evidence as to a lack of investment on the part of Government in children, in terms of the increasing levels of child poverty. Between 1979 and 1991, the number of children living in households with below 50 per cent of average income trebled to 3.9 million. The rise in child poverty means that the British Government will have difficulty in implementing Article 27 of the UN Convention on the Rights of the Child, which refers to the 'right of children to a standard of living adequate for children's physical, mental, spiritual, moral and social development' (Wilkinson 1994; Bradshaw 1990). Questions have also been raised about educational investment. Kiernan's (1996) data suggest that a strong predictor of young unmarried motherhood is poor educational attainment. One of the most striking findings of Phoenix's (1991) qualitative study of young mothers was that had they waited another year or two before having a child it is highly unlikely that their socio-economic circumstances would have changed. In other words, their opportunities were extremely limited. The contrast with the position of young German women, who are much more likely to be in some form of education or training, is striking (*see* Chapter 1). There are limits to what individual parental responsibility can achieve, particularly when there is only one resident parent. However, in the 1990s Government has continued to pursue its goal of reducing collective provision for lone mothers. In 1996, it abandoned the special benefits and premiums paid to lone parents drawing state benefits since the 1970s in recognition of their greater needs. Announcing the proposal in 1995, the Department of Social Security made reference to the huge rise in dependency of lone mothers on social assistance and the especially sharp rise in the number of never married lone mothers, while the Chancellor of the Exchequer's budget speech made an explicit commitment to redress the 'discrimination' in favour of lone parent as compared to two-parent households. This is a milder version of the American attempt to discourage lone motherhood by removing state support altogether. In addition, the 1996 Housing Bill has reversed the legislation of the late 1970s and has removed the right of homeless families to permanent housing.

Conclusion

The treatment of lone mothers in Britain can to a considerable extent be predicted from the nature of the welfare regime. Historically, policies towards lone mothers separated out widows, who could legitimately be treated as dependants of their dead husbands and therefore included under social insurance, something that continues to this day, and problematised those women with children and without an identifiable breadwinner. In the case of these women, the state had to decide on what terms to support them. As part of the post-war settlement and under the influence of theories that stressed the evils consequent on maternal deprivation, divorced and unmarried mothers were given the right to draw social assistance so long as they had children of school age. However, what is interesting is the relatively small numbers who did so until the 1970s. This was in part because the numbers of lone mothers who were divorced or unmarried were actually relatively small and because a much higher percentage went out to work, usually finding childcare within their family of origin. During the 1970s, as the numbers of lone mothers increased rapidly, so also the stigma surrounding lone motherhood diminished. Lone mothers increasingly lived independently and were prepared to claim social assistance benefits as of right. Government policies attempted to encourage lone mothers to work, but the special needs of lone mothers were also recognised within the social assistance scheme, and given the cost of childcare and the low wages commanded by women, it became less and less worthwhile for lone mothers to enter the labour market. In the late twentieth century the British pattern of high labour-market participation on the part of married mothers (albeit largely part-time) and the low participation rates of lone mothers is highly unusual. However, it is possible to explain it in terms of:

(1) The partial move away from a commitment to a male-breadwinner model towards a dual-earner model. While explicitly promoting equal opportunities at the workplace, Government has nevertheless drawn a firm boundary between the public and private spheres, such that it refuses to take any responsibility for reconciling the demands of family and work, particularly in respect of childcare. The ambivalence that is felt particularly on the political Right, but elsewhere on the political spectrum too, about women with small children going out to work means that any decision to do so has been defined as a private decision in which Government plays no part. This has had especially severe implications for lone mothers.

(2) The nature of the social security system, which relies heavily on means-tested social assistance in meeting all types of need and which, while less generous than many other countries, means that lone mothers are not as stigmatised as claimants as they are in systems where social insurance predominates. In addition, because the system is nationally determined, it is not possible for local officers to discriminate against them as it is in some continental European assistance schemes. Even though the social security system sought to reinforce traditional ideas about roles and responsibilities within families through regulations such as the cohabitation rule, the availability of the means of subsistence and of housing made it possible for lone mothers to eke out an autonomous existence on benefit.

The steeply rising cost of lone mother families to the state has led the British Government to attempt to recoup the costs from the only other possible source, the absent fathers, a strategy that has been further legitimated by increasing anxiety about the behaviour of young men and the effects on children of being raised by a lone parent. The focus on fathers rather than on husbands or cohabitees has partially recognised the increasing individualisation of adult men and women. However, from the beginning the Child Support Act had more to do with bringing down public expenditure than with helping lone mothers and their children. The legislation sought to increase the number of lone parents receiving regular maintenance by 200,000, a reasonably modest objective given that there were over a million lone parents at the beginning of the 1990s and only one quarter were receiving maintenance. However, it is possible that the proportion of lone parents receiving maintenance may well have gone down since the child support agency began operating. Arrears totalled £738 million by September 1995 and were increasing at the rate of £47 million a month. The old 'liable relative' scheme would likely have saved more for the Treasury and lone mothers and their children have not profited from the new legislation. In the meantime, however, Government continues to take steps to decrease the amount of support provided by the state in terms of cash benefits and the provision of housing. The prospect for lone-mother families in Britain looks bleak.

References

Barker, M. (ed) (1995) *Health and Personal Social Services Statistics for England, 1995,* T.5.51, 76.

BBC (1993) *Panorama.* 'Babies on Benefit'. 20 September.

Black, S. and Sykes, M. (1971) 'Promiscuity and oral contraception: the relationship examined.' *Social Science and Medicine 5,* 637–643.

Bone, M. (1986) 'Trends in single women's sexual behaviour in Scotland.' *Population Trends no. 43,* 7–14.

Bradshaw, J. (1990) *Child Poverty and Deprivation in the UK.* London: National Children's Bureau.

Bradshaw, J. *et al.* (1996) *The Employment of Lone Parents. A Comparison of Policy in 20 Countries.* London: Family Policy studies Centre and Joseph Rowntree Foundation.

Bradshaw, J. and Millar, J. (1991) *Lone-Parent Families in the UK.* Department of Social Security Research Report no. 6. London: HMSO.

Burghes, L. (1994) *Lone Parenthood and Family Disruption. The Outcomes for Children.* London: Family Policy Studies Centre, Occasional Paper no. 18.

Bury, J. (1984) *Teenage Pregnancy in Britain.* London: Birth Control Trust, 33.

Carstairs, G.M. (1962) *This Island Now.* London: Hogarth Press.

Cd. 6404 (1942) *The Report of the Committee on Social Security and Allied Social Services.* London: HMSO.

Cm. 2799 (1995) *Looking to the Future: Mediation and the Ground for Divorce: The Government's Proposals.* London: HMSO.

Cmd. 8030 (1950) *Report of the National Assistance Board for 1949.* London: HMSO.

Cmd. 9210 (1953) *Report of the National Assistance Board for 1952.* London: HMSO.

Cmnd. 1730 (1961) *Report of the National Assistance Board for 1960.* London: HMSO.

Cmnd. 5629 (1974) *Report of the Committee on One-Parent Families.* London: HMSO.

Comfort, A. (1963) *Sex in Society.* London: Gerald Duckworth.

Daly, M. (1996) 'The gender division of welfare: the British and German welfare states compared.' Unpublished Phd. thesis, Florence: European University Institute.

Davis, G. and Murch, M. (1988) *Grounds for Divorce.* Oxford: Clarendon.

Davis, G., Cretney, S., Bader, K. and Collins, J. (1992) 'The relationship between public and private financial support following divorce in England and Wales.' In L. Weitzman and M. Maclean (eds) *The Economic Consequences of Divorce.* Oxford: Clarendon.

Dennis, N. and Erdos, G. (1992) *Families without Fatherhood.* London: IEA.

Department of Health (1990) *The Children Act: Guidance and Regulations, Vol I.* London: HMSO.

Eekelaar, J. (1991) 'Parental responsibility: state of nature or nature of the state?' *Journal of Social Welfare and Family Law 37,* 1.

Eekelarr, J. and Maclean (1986) *Maintenance after Divorce.* Oxford: Clarendon.

Fletcher, R. (1966) *The Family and Marriage in Britain.* Harmondsworth: Penguin.

Garnham, A. and Knights, E. (1994) *Putting the Treasury First: The Truth about Child Support.* London: Child Poverty Action Group.

Gilder, G. (1987) 'The collapse of the American family.' *The Public Interest. no. 89* (Fall).

Gillis, J. (1986) *For Better, for Worse: British Marriages, 1600 to the Present.* Oxford: Oxford University Press.

Greenland, C. (1957) 'Unmarried parenthood: ecological aspects.' *Lancet 19* January, 148–151.

Greve, J. (1964) *Homelessness in London.* London: Bell.

Gustaffson, S. (1994) 'Childcare and types of welfare states.' In D. Sainsbury (ed) *Gendering Welfare States.* London: Sage.

Halsey, A.H. (1993) 'Changes in the family.' *Children and Society 7,* 2.

Hansard (1993). House of Commons Debates, 3 December, C. 1283.

Hantrais, L. and L'Etablier, M-T. (1996) *Families and Family Policies in Europe.* London: Longman.

Haskey, J. (1989) 'One-parent families and their children in Great Britain: numbers and characteristics.' *Population Trends no. 55,* Spring, 27–43.

Haskey, J. (1993) 'Trends in the numbers of one-parent families in Great Britain.' *Population Trends 71,* Spring.

Hetherington, E., Cox, M. and Cox, R. (1978) 'The aftermath of divorce.' In J. Stevens and M. Matthews (eds) *Mother–Child, Father–Child Relations.* Washington DC: National Association for the Education of Young Children.

Hills, J. (1995) *Income and Wealth. Vol II.* York: Joseph Rowntree Foundation.

Hunt, A. (1967) *A Survey of Women's Employment. Vol. I.* Report. Government Social Survey. London: HMSO.

Joshi, H. (1990) 'Obstacles and opportunities for lone parents as breadwinners in Great Britain.' In Lone Parent Families. *The Economic Challenge.* Paris: OECD.

Kiernan, K. (1996) 'Family change: parenthood, partnership and policy.' In D. Halpern, S. Wood, S. White and G. Cameron *et al.* (eds) *Options for Britain: A Strategic Policy Review.* Aldershot: Dartmouth Press.

Kiernan, K. and Estaugh, V. (1993) *Cohabitation. Extra-Marital Childbearing and Social Policy.* London: Family Policy Studies Centre. Occasional Paper 17.

King, D. (1987) *The New Right. Politics, Markets and Citizenship.* Basingstoke: Macmillan.

Land, H. (1994) 'Reversing "the inadvertent nationalization of fatherhood": the British child support act 1991 and its consequences for men, women and children.' *International Social Security Review 47,* 3–4.

Land, H. and Lewis, J. (1997) *What the Problem of Lone Motherhood has been About.* (Forthcoming).

Lewis, J., Kiernan, K. and Land, H. (forthcoming) *Lone Mothers in Twentieth Century Britain.* Oxford: Oxford University Press.

Macaskill, H. (1993) *From the Workhouse to the Workplace: 75 years of One-Parent Life, 1918–93.* London: National Council for One-Parent Families.

McLanahan, S. and Sandefeur, G. (1994) *Growing up with a Single Parent. What Hurts, What Helps.* Cambridge, Massachusetts: Harvard University Press.

Mason, M.A. (1994) *From Fathers' Property to Children's Rights: The History of Child Custody in the United States.* New York: Columbia University Press.

Marsden, D. (1969) *Mothers Alone. Poverty and the Fatherless Family.* London: Allen Lane.

Mead, L. (1986) *Beyond Entitlement.* New York: The Free Press.

Millar, J. (1989) *Poverty and the Lone Parent Family: The Challenge to Social Policy.* Aldershot: Avebury.

Millar, J. (1996) 'Family Obligations and Social Policy.' Inaugural lecture, University of Bath.

Morgan, P. (1995) *Farewell to the Family. Public Policy and Family Breakdown in Britain and the USA.* London: IEA.

Moore, K.A. and Burt, M.R. (1982) *Private Crisis, Public Cost: Policy Perspectives on Teenage Childbearing.* Washington: Urban Institute Press.

Murray, C. (1984) *Losing Ground. American Social Policy, 1950–1980.* New York: Basic Books.

National Audit Office (1991) *Department of Social Security Support for Lone-Parent Families.* Report by the Controller and Auditor General. House of Commons Paper 153. London: HMSO.

Nicholson, J. (1968) *Mother and Baby Homes.* London: National Council for the Unmarried Mother and her Child. London: NCUMC.

Novak, M. *et al.* (1987) *A Community of Self-Reliance: The New Consensus on Family and Welfare.* Marquette University, Milwaukee: American Enterprise Institute.

OPCS (1987) *Birth Statistics: Historical Series 1837–1983*, Table 12.5, Series FM1 no. 13. London: HMSO.

Parker, S. (1990) *Informal Marriage. Cohabitation and the Law, 1750–1989.* London: Macmillan.

Pedersen, S. (1993) *Family Dependence and the Origins of the Welfare State in Britain and France, 1914–1945.* Cambridge: Cambridge University Press.

Phoenix, A. (1991) *Young Mothers.* Cambridge: Polity.

Rainwater, L., Rein, M. and Schwartz, (1986) *Income Packaging in the Welfare State.* Oxford: Clarendon Press.

Registrar General (1971) *Statistical Review*, 1964, Part III, Commentary. London: HMSO.

Richards, M.P.M. (1982) 'Post-divorce arrangements for children: a psychological perspective.' *Journal of Social Welfare Law*, May, 133–51.

Richards, M.P.M. (1993) 'Children and parents and divorce.' In J. Eekelaar and P. Saricevic (eds) *Parenthood in Modern Society. Legal and Social Issues for the Twenty First Century.* Dordrech: Martinus Nijhoff.

Robinson, J.A.T. (1963) *Honest to God.* London: SCM Press.

SBC (1971) *Cohabitation.* Report by the SBC to the Secretary of State for Social Services. London: HMSO.

Selman, P. and Glendinning, C. (1996) 'Teenage pregnancy. Do social policies make a difference?' In J. Brannen and M. O'Brien (eds) *Children in Families. Research and Policy.* London: Falmer Press.

Skocpol, T. (1993) *Protecting Soldiers and Mothers.* Cambridge, Massachusetts: Harvard University Press.

Smart, C. (1984) *The Ties that Bind: Law, Marriage and the Reproduction of Patriarchal Relations.* London: Routledge and Kegan Paul.

Wallerstein, J. and Kelly, J. (1980) *Surviving the Breakup: How Children and Parents Cope with Divorce.* London: Grant McIntyre.

Wilkinson, R. (1994) *Unfair Shares. The Effects of Widening Income Differentiation on the Welfare of the Young.* London: Barnardo's Publications.

CHAPTER THREE

Lone Mothers: the Case of Ireland

Pauline Conroy

For close to 150 years, lone mothers in Ireland have been marginalised in social policy, treated punitively in legislation and socially isolated or exiled by public opinion. Only in the late 1980s and 1990s have lone mothers begun to experience a normalisation of their status in social policy, which assimilates their situation to that of other unequally treated women.

As in Britain, the nineteenth century Irish Poor Relief Act of 1838 established the first state provision for destitute unsupported mothers, under an Irish version of the Poor Law. It was assumed under this system, that unsupported and destitute mothers should support their children by labour and those who could not were taken into the Poor Houses with their children (Burke 1987). So great was the stigma attached to unmarried parenthood, that mothers of so-called illegitimate children were not always allowed to be appointed to jobs in the workhouse even when they were long-stay inmates (O'Hare *et al.* 1987). The workhouse population of women was only gradually diminished at the beginning of the twentieth century, with unsupported mothers being treated outside the workhouse according to whether they were considered deserving or non-deserving of blame for their situation. By the early part of the century, unmarried mothers who were pregnant for the first time began to be catered for in harshly run, large mother-and-baby institutions administered by religious orders, and designed to isolate them in anonymity from society at large. Those with second pregnancies or 'fallen women' were placed in even more severe closed religious institutions or asylums. Widows were left to their own devices and were expected to take employment to support their children in contrast to unmarried mothers who were expected to leave the country, or give their children away and stay at home. The development of mother and baby homes was one of the responses to a 1906 report on Poor Law Reform (O'Hare *et al.* 1987, p.5). The five largest homes established between 1919 and 1935 had accommodation for 580 unmarried mothers at any one time (Flanagan and Richardson 1992 p.51). The mother and baby homes began to close down between the 1960s and the 1980s and in some instances were replaced by smaller homes or housing accommodating up to 15 unmarried mothers.

The establishment of an independent Irish State in 1922 did not alter this regime of either socially excluding or incarcerating mothers and children without a male breadwinner. Married women were excluded from the state insurance system in 1929. A widow's pension was only introduced in 1935. The repressive and extraordinarily harsh treatment of unmarried mothers by religious and state authorities alike created a fear bordering on terror in many women which endures in some instances to this day. O'Connor in her contemporary Irish folklore interviews notes that 'abortion and infanticide are equally regarded with horror though infanticide is spoken of relatively more freely' (O'Connor 1985, p.87). Young girls went to extraordinary lengths to conceal a pregnancy and birth, tragically risking their own lives and that of the child (McCafferty 1985; McCafferty 1992). The high levels of emigration from Ireland of women and girls as young as 14 years until the early 1960s may in part be explained by the harsh conditions of living for women and girls and the impossibility of an unmarried pregnancy (Jackson 1984, p.1004).

By the early 1990s the Irish birth rate was beginning to approximate that of other European countries, but was still high by European standards at 14.6 births per 1000 population (Department of Health 1993). The relatively high birth rate was all the more noteworthy in that it was accompanied by a fall in the marriage rate. By 1993 an ever greater proportion of a shrinking number of births was occurring outside the institution of marriage (see Table 3.1 below).

Table 3.1 Marital and extra-marital births, Ireland 1978–1993

	1978	1983	1988	1993
Total number of live births	70,299	67,117	54,600	49,456
Total number of births outside marriage	3003	4552	6336	9664
Births outside marriage as % of total	4.3	6.8	11.6	19.5

Source: Central Statistics Office, Dublin.

Just under 20 per cent of all births in 1993 occurred outside of marriage. Of these 9664 births, about 25 per cent, were to teenagers under the age of 20 years; of which 57 births were to child-mothers aged under 15 years old. This minority of births has attracted extensive policy and media comment as symptomatic of a decline in morality and the family. Public policy describes teenage pregnancy as 'a matter for concern…(a) high proportion of these young mothers come from deprived urban areas. Factors associated with the rising number of such pregnancies are sexual activity without contraception, irresponsible use of alcohol and addiction to other drugs' (Department of Health 1995, p.55). The social profile of unmarried teenage mothers conveyed by the public authorities with benevolent intent, nevertheless carries resonance of American debates on the alleged rise of an underclass of welfare dependent women and children.

Discussing illegitimacy and IQ, American advocates of the underclass analysis remark that the 'less intelligent the woman is, the more likely that she does not think ahead from sex to procreation, does not remember to use birth control, does not carefully consider when and under what circumstances she should have a child' (Hernstein and Murray 1996, p.179). The casting of Irish lone mothers into the role of reproducers of an Irish style underclass has already been signalled by a former Minister of Education who has proposed that it may be 'economically rational' to encourage higher-income parents to have more children and low-income families to have fewer, since a larger share of the child population is accounted for by single parents and low-income families (Cullen 1996, p.6). This exchange of views illustrates the changes occurring in the traditional conception of the family in the context of anxieties about the differential birth rate.

Family and familialism

The family has a special place in Irish law. It is recognised in the Irish Constitution of 1937, which states:

> The State recognises the Family as the natural primary and fundamental unit group of Society and as a moral institution possessing inalienable and imprescriptible rights, antecedent and superior to all positive law. (Bunreacht Na hEireann 1937, Article 41.1.)

The Constitution derives certain conclusions from Article 41.1. These are laid out in Article 41.2. which states that 'in particular, the State recognises that by her life within the home, woman gives to the State a support without which the common good cannot be achieved', and also that 'the State shall, therefore, endeavour to ensure that mothers shall not be obliged by economic necessity to engage in labour to the neglect of their duties in the home'.

Against this legal backdrop, successive waves of women's organisations have attempted to wrest autonomous rights and entitlements to an emancipated status for women in Ireland (Conroy Jackson 1993; Meaney 1993; Tweedy 1992; Ward 1988). The right of married women to work, the right to equal pay, the right of married women to own property, the right to use contraception, have had to be fought for one by one. The struggle for the right to equal treatment in social security lasted from 1984 to 1997. A bitterly fought campaign for a limited form of pregnancy termination to be made available began in 1982 and continues to this day. It is only during the 1990s, with some issues beginning to see resolution, that the family itself has come under scrutiny (O'Connor 1995).

Despite the prominent position of the family in the written Constitution of Ireland up to 1997, there had never been a Minister or a Ministry responsible for the family. In October 1995 a first Commission on the Family was established under the auspices of the Minister for Social Welfare. Its membership includes a psychiatrist, a GP, civil servants, the Catholic Church and experts in family law. Surprisingly its membership did not include the only University centre for the study of the family. Its establishment was reactive rather than proactive. The 1995 Referendum to approve the introduction of the first divorce law in Ireland had seen wild claims as to the demise of the family projected from publicity billboards and television screens. According to the Minister for Social Welfare there is a clear need for new realistic policies and strategies to 'strengthen and support families' (Department of Social Welfare 1996). The Commission was asked to report its findings on the family by June 1997. In the meantime no explicit family policy surfaced. The Parliamentary Joint Committee on the Family, also established in 1995, had no better luck. After a year of deliberations and technical support, the Committee could not agree on a definition of the family. It recommended the establishment of a family affairs unit in the Department of Finance to co-ordinate policy and expenditure programmes.

The policy shifts during the 1970s and 1980s

Immune from the upheavals of World War II and devoid of heavy industry, the social and economic situation of women in Ireland hardly changed from the 1920s to the 1960s. It was not until the 1970s that changes in the status of women in general and lone mothers in particular, began to emerge (Conroy 1993). The large religious institutions which housed lone mothers continued to function until the 1970s, when demographic changes in the extent and composition of lone parenthood began (McCashin 1993). In 1971 the extra-marital birth rate represented only 2.9 per cent of all births, by 1993 this had reached 19.5 per cent of all births (Department of Health 1993). The rise in extra-marital births as a proportion of all births was especially sharp from 1987 onwards (McCashin 1993, p.117). In some instances the actual increase in numbers of extra-marital births was quite small (200 additional non-marital births).

Nevertheless, in a context of a falling overall birth rate, these increases had significance. The use of adoption as a solution to unmarried parenthood began also to decline. Adoptions as a proportion of non-marital births were over 70 per cent in 1971 and fell to just 8 per cent by 1991. Changes inside the family began to surface as well. The numbers of women in situations of marital breakdown rose from 5,000 in 1979 to almost 30,000 in 1991 – a five fold increase (McCashin 1993, p.32). Widowhood declined as life expectancy increased among younger married men. Changes from the 1970s thus modified the composition of lone parenthood and dispersed lone parents among a number of new categories, while it simultaneously increased their numbers (Yeates 1995).

Some of these changes are explored in studies generated by social work during the 1980s (*see* for example; Flanagan and Richardson 1992; O'Hare *et al.* 1987), which found that unmarried mothers in particular were reluctant to give up their children for adoption and were beginning to create new self-sufficient units composed of mother and child. The growth in visibility of women's organisations and the women's movement in Ireland would have had an influence on this, notwithstanding the low priority accorded in feminist publications and actions to the issue of motherhood (Conroy Jackson 1993).

Rapid changes in marital behaviour and in births outside marriage between the 1970s and 1990s were illustrative of modernising behaviour, despite a legislative and social infrastructure locked into nineteenth century attitudes and values. Between 1979 and 1987, the birth rate turned sharply downwards. It fell from 21 per 1000 population, at which rate (or higher) the birth rate had been maintained since 1949, to 16.5. Between 1983 and 1993 the proportion of all births to mothers with four or more children fell by 6 per cent, the average age at first birth rose to 29 years for women and there was also a rise in the proportion of births to mothers aged over 35 years. These are the demographic changes one would expect to observe in a society where the labour force participation and educational participation of women is rising from a low base level.

By 1993 the birth rate had fallen to only 13.9 per 1000 population. At a time when the birth rate was falling, the fact that a growing proportion of births were taking place outside marriage made lone mothers all the more visible. Changes in attitudes to, and the availability of, contraception played a part in the changing patterns of births and spacing of children. The sale and prescription of contraceptives was illegal until 1979. Abortion was not and is still not available. There was not and there still is no sex education in schools. In the first large scale contemporary study on women's health, Wiley and Merriman (1996, p.45) found that half the women interviewed did not find family planning services accessible and just under 80 per cent had difficulties with their efficacy. Indeed, the study found high proportions of sexually active women using no form of contraception. Somewhat surprisingly, the study found that between half and three quarters of women with second level education or higher did not know when a women is at her greatest risk of pregnancy. It would appear that the rapid fall in the birth rate during the 1970s may be partly attributed to the use of contraception by women, notwithstanding difficulties in obtaining it, a reduction in the numbers of children per mother and a postponement of marriage and first maternity.

It was during the early 1970s when births outside marriage were still a low proportion of all births and marital breakdown was not very evident, that lone mothers were singled out for special treatment inside the social security system. The introduction of an unmarried mothers social welfare allowance in 1973 followed lobbying by Catholic interests to deter Irish Catholic girls from using the UK 1967 Abortion Act. The introduction of a deserted wives benefit and allowance continued the categorical treatment of women by offering them payments based not so much on need as the causes which gave rise to the absence of a male in their family. Thus wives deserted by insured husbands were paid more than unmarried mothers. Widows were treated better than either of the above. All payments supposed that lone mothers would stay at home and mind their children full-time at a time when the labour force participation rates of all women were gradually rising. Just as earlier treatment of lone mothers had isolated them in closed institutions, so the new social welfare treatment of lone mothers in the 1970s treated them apart from other women and encouraged them to stay at home.

The new provisions re-enforced the model of the male-breadwinner regime inside Irish social welfare. Large proportions of women in employment were excluded from social insurance by virtue of working in agriculture, or in non-recognised employment such as child-care, by having interrupted insurance records through absence for child-care or by being in part-time and casual employment. Those who were inside the insurance system were discriminated against by lower payments of shorter duration compared to those of insured men. This discrimination was to be outlawed by a European Community Directive of 1979 on equal treatment in social security. Ireland implemented the Directive after the 1984 deadline, and only then with new discriminatory clauses. The situation led to several years of legal cases in the European Court of Justice, which finally vindicated the right of women to equal treatment with men under social security. As a result, back-dated compensation payments to formerly unemployed married women were still being paid in instalments in 1996. Payments are to be finally completed in 1997, some 18 years after married women's lawful entitlement to equal treatment was prescribed by the European Community. The system of separate consideration of lone mothers was thus grafted onto an already segregated and unequal system, fusing inequity with inequality in the treatment of lone mothers.

Lone mothers became a major subject of public debate during the 1980s with two proposals to alter the Irish Constitution which had been enacted in

1937. The first proposal was to entirely ban abortion by placing an amendment in the Constitution to prevent the legislature from introducing a change in the law. The second proposal was to amend the Constitution to permit divorce in Ireland. The first Amendment – known as the Pro-Life Amendment – was passed after a vitriolic campaign dividing the country. The second Amendment was not passed and the prohibition on divorce remained. In less than ten years, this decision was reversed.

The case of Ms X, a young school girl of 14 years made pregnant by an older man, caused an outcry in 1994. In December 1991, Ms X disclosed to her parents and to the police that she had been sexually abused by an older married man. It emerged that she was pregnant and both parents and daughter came to the conclusion that the best course of action was to go to England for an abortion. Her parents reported to the police that a crime had been committed against their daughter and asked for their help in preparing evidence to prosecute the perpetrator. In February 1992 the Attorney General issued proceedings against Ms X and her parents to restrain them from 'interfering with the right to life of the unborn' from 'leaving the jurisdiction of the Courts' and from 'procuring or arranging a termination of pregnancy or abortion' (McDonagh 1992, p. 8). Ms X a child victim of rape and her parents were effectively interned on the island of Ireland. Ms X subsequently had a miscarriage. In the course and aftermath of the X case, there were an enormous number of court cases, hearings, television debates, public meetings and protests in the Irish and European Parliament. Deep fears and uncertainties concerning motherhood permeated the whole society embodied in the single case of a child who did not want to be a mother.

It was the Ms X case too, which brought to public attention for the first time that there was a European dimension to the issues it raised. Some weeks earlier, unknown to Parliament and to the public, a 42 word Protocol had been added to the revised Maastricht Treaty of European Union, by the Irish Government. The Protocol provided that a section of Article 40 of the Irish Constitution, which prohibited abortion, would not be affected by any European Treaty. The Protocol had been agreed by all the Governments of the European Union. The fact of the existence of the Protocol which placed the reproductive rights of women outside the scope of European law and the secretive manner of its introduction, added additional fuel to the controversy.

The Ms X case played a significant part in changing social attitudes and in triggering legal change. Three new amendments to the Constitution were proposed to allow for a limited form of abortion and for abortion information to be available in Ireland. These amendments were eventually passed by referendum. The legislature, however, has never enacted a law to allow abortion under any circumstance, including rape or incest, in any Irish clinic or hospital, so Irish women and girls continue to go to England for abortion. In 1995 an amendment to the Constitution was voted to allow for divorce.

Lone mothers and the labour market

The numbers of lone mothers in Ireland are not large in absolute figures. In 1995 there were approximately 97,000 lone mothers (*see* Table 3.2).This is a slight underestimation since it is based on the Labour Force Survey; a household survey which will tend to under-estimate the number of young teenage mothers living with their parents. In the absence of divorce, lone mothers fall into a limited number of analytical categories: unmarried (single), those with a court separation or divorce obtained overseas, those who are married but separated and those who are widowed. The increase during the 1990s has been among the category of those who are separated. There is no data available on the proportions of households living in consensual unions, so it is not possible to say how many of those who are categorised as single or separated, are, in fact living as a couple with a partner.

Table 3.2 Lone parents with children, Ireland 1993–1995 (1000s)

	Men (thousand)	Women	Total	Women as % of Total
1993	18.3	89.0	107.3	82.9
1994	18.5	92.8	111.3	83.3
1995	18.1	97.1	115.2	84.2

Source: Central Statistics Office, *Labour Force Survey, 1993, 1994 and 1995*, Stationary Office, Dublin, tables 43

Ireland has a low rate of employed mothers compared to other European countries. In 1993 34 per cent of women with a child under 15 years were employed, of these 68 per cent were employed full-time. This rate contrasts with 58 per cent employment rate in the UK of which only 33 per cent worked part-time (Meijvogel and Petrie 1996, p.41). The labour-force participation rate (employed and unemployed) of lone mothers with a child under 14 was also 34 per cent in Ireland in 1995 (*see* Table 3.3). This rate is lower than for women as a whole (39.5%) but higher than for all lone mothers with children (24.6%) – a category which includes women of all ages and older widows with older children.

Table 3.3 Labour force participation rates of women, aged 15 years and over in Ireland by marital status 1993–5 (%)

	1993	1994	1995
Single	49.9	50.0	49.7
Married	36.2	37.8	38.9
Separated/divorced	45.9	48.7	48.6
Married and separated	36.7	38.4	39.5
Widowed	8.5	7.7	7.8
Total	38.2	39.1	39.5
Lone parent with child(ren)	24.6	24.4	24.6
of which: Lone parent with one or more children aged 0–14	32.8	34.1	34.3

Source: Central Statistics Office, *Labour Force Survey 1993, 1994 and 1995*, Stationary Office, Dublin, Tables 33B and 43.

During the 1990s the labour force participation rates of lone mothers with young children rose in tandem with the labour force participation rates of women in general. This may suggest that, independent of public opinion and the values embedded in state policies, the labour market behaviour of younger lone mothers conforms more to that of 'women' as a category than that of 'mother'.

Lone parents are the subject of special treatment in the Irish tax system. In the calculation of allowances, lone parents with a dependent child(ren) are treated as single persons and allowed a single persons allowance (subject to certain conditions). In addition, they are also granted a second 'lone parent' allowance equal to a single persons allowance. In effect, this double allowance provides them with the same allowances as a married couple. The outcome of this special treatment is that a lone mother is not subject to taxation on her earnings from employment as fast as a single person without children and is thus provided with an incentive to enter employment. This fiscal policy is a form of positive discrimination towards lone parents.

Fiscal policy is not entirely neutral in outcome, once lone mothers have entered the tax system and begin to earn higher wages. Within the tax regime, a lone mother in the lower rate tax bands is on par with a married couple. However, fiscal calculations comparing the treatment of lone-parent households with two-adult households reveals that lone parents are at a disadvantage compared to two-person households when their earnings rise, since they enter higher tax bands comparatively faster. This disadvantage was discussed by a parliamentary committee on the family (Houses of the Oireachtas 1996) and the committee decided not to propose any change, thus maintaining a fiscal bias towards married couples in the tax system.

Policy changes in the 1990s

The 1990s heralded a series of important policy changes in the public treatment of lone parents in Ireland. These changes are of particular significance, in that they announced a limited departure from a tradition of over one hundred years of replicating British social welfare policy in Ireland. Of equal importance is the fact that the Irish changes moved in a different direction from those being introduced in the UK during the same period.

The high level of readership of British newspapers, the availability of all British T.V. channels in Ireland and the extensive professional and commercial interchange between the countries, rendered any major change in the UK visible in Ireland. This was the case in respect of the 1991 Child Support Act. This Act was based on a UK Government White Paper entitled 'Children Come First' issued in October 1990 and had the benefit of all-party support in the Houses of Parliament in London. The policy changes it was to introduce were of considerable interest to Ireland where social welfare legislation was based on similar principles to that of Britain.

The UK House of Commons Social Security Committee described the changes brought about by the Child Support Act as:

> ...the most far reaching social reforms to be made for forty years. The assumption that in broken marriages or partnerships taxpayers should assume the financial responsibility for the first family is, at long last, challenged. The prime responsibility is placed where we believe it has always rested until recently, i.e. with natural parents. (House of Commons 1993)

Under the Act, a Child Support Agency was set up, which moved the entire field of child maintenance from the individual and the courts to a centralised administrative agency whose aim was to assess parents as to their liability to support their biological children from previous relationships or marriages and to enforce maintenance payments.

Ireland was facing a rise in the numbers of lone parents, mainly mothers, claiming a variety of state social welfare benefits to support themselves and their children; creating an unsatisfactory system of maintenance for children (Daly 1989). The enormous policy change in the UK towards children, families, lone parents, the distribution of liability and the role of the state provided a ready-made model which Ireland might follow. One of the factors giving rise to the need for a policy change in the UK was the perception that the system for eliciting financial contributions from fathers had failed. The perception that the legal system was failing to deliver maintenance to dependent children was also keenly felt in Ireland. An Irish study of 1990 (Ward 1990) revealed the unsatisfactory nature of the operation of the Family Law (Maintenance of Spouses and Children) Act 1976. In over 80 per cent of a sample of cases reviewed, the wife was awarded less from the Court than she would have received in state benefits. The study also found that maintenance was not paid in 87 per cent of the orders processed through the District Court. In 28 per cent of these, there was no record of any payment having been made at all and almost half were in arrears of six months and therefore of no practical import to a lone mother and children. The system of individual wives pursuing individual husbands, with or without the aid of lawyers, through the legal system was simply not working for the overwhelming majority of women.

The situation was particularly difficult for separated wives/mothers who wanted to claim state benefits for themselves and their children. Until 1990, despite the negligible benefit to themselves, separated or deserted wives who made an application for state benefits had to make 'reasonable efforts' to trace and obtain maintenance from their spouses (Cousins 1995, p.90). The 'liable relative' system in Ireland was at that time similar to that of the system of the Department of Social Security in the UK. Under this system, any monies obtained by the wife (or husband) from the former partner were deducted from her (or his) state benefits. About one in three claims for unsupported mothers were refused on the grounds that the wife had failed to make reasonable efforts to track down her husband and enforce maintenance by taking him to court. This was despite the fact that these proceedings had to be issued, often repeatedly and without legal representation, by the wife personally in the Courts with little to no prospect of any financial benefit.

A more systematic policy of pursuit of maintenance payments for children of lone parents was approved by the Irish Government in 1990 and instigated in 1991. The Department of Social Welfare decided to pursue only the partners of married or separated women for maintenance, and not to bother with the putative fathers of children of unmarried mothers in receipt of social welfare payments. The policy was far less interventionist than that introduced in the UK.

In 1990 the 'liable relative' requirement was changed thus softening the impact of the policy. From then on a claimant had merely 'to make and continue to make appropriate efforts' to obtain maintenance. In practice, social welfare payments are made unless the Department of Social Welfare considers that maintenance is at such a level that no social welfare payment is required as a consequence. In other instances, the Department itself pursues the husband or spouse under the 'liable relative' provisions of the 1989 and 1990 Social Welfare Acts.

The operations of the legal system and the 'liable relative' clauses of the Social Security Acts were the two planks of child support altered in the UK. In the overly optimistic words of the Chief Executive of the UK agency:

> ...the Agency is comprehensively replacing the previous arrangements for child maintenance that were administered by the courts and by the

DSS liable relative sections...our current estimates are that a maintenance assessment will be made in about 750,000 cases...we have been set a target in our first year of saving £530 million in Social Security benefits. (House of Commons 1993, p.5)

The relatively modest changes made in Ireland have not generated a large centralised agency for the pursuit of errant fathers. The UK model was not adopted. Indeed, no great priority has been given to pursuing fathers by the Irish Department of Social Welfare. Only four civil servants were allocated to the unit charged with tracing and enforcing maintenance from 'liable relatives' throughout Ireland during 1996. The unit is located in a provincial town outside the capital Dublin. It produces no separate annual report and its work is not reported in the Annual statistical report of the Department of Social Welfare. It is not well known either to the general public or other public servants. According to an *Irish Times* article on the subject '...as in many other welfare issues, the State is endeavouring to learn from mistakes made across the Irish sea' (McNally 1996, p.13).

The results of the 'liable relative' unit of the Department of Social Welfare are summarised in Table 3.4 below.

**Table 3.4 Outcome of liable relative cases pursued by
Department of Social Welfare 1991 to June 1996**

Number of cases pursued:	17,956
of which persons concerned:	
at work	4792
in receipt of social welfare	8538
no trace	4626
of which orders made against:	
(persons at work)	640
of which:	
refusal/difficulty to pay	299
change of circumstance	35
now paying	306

Source: Communication from the Planning Unit. Department of Social Welfare, Dublin, July 1996.

An analysis of Table 3.4 shows that just over 26 per cent of the 17,956 fathers pursued by the Department of Social Welfare, were deemed to be liable to make a payment for a child. The remainder were either in receipt of social welfare payments themselves and were thus presumed to be unable to pay and/or could not be traced.

Of the 17,956 pursued over a five year period, a payment was 'recovered' from a father in response to an order issued by the Department of Social Welfare in just 1.7 per cent of all cases pursued. Thus, the number of fathers of children in families headed by a lone mother in receipt of social welfare payment who are effected by the policy is small: just 306. As a consequence, the net financial benefit of the policy to the State is extremely limited.

Categorising women, mothers and wives

The category-by-category treatment of women within the Irish social welfare system continued throughout the 1990s despite the existence of a coalition government which included a left-wing Minister of Social Welfare. Minister Prionsias de Rossa of the Democratic Left party had joined the Cabinet in the 1990s. He came from a modest North Dublin background, had a long record of political activism and belonged to a party pledged to reform on issues of concern to the working class among which figured social welfare.

In anticipation of the 1995 Referendum on divorce, the Minister proposed in 1995 to alter social welfare legislation to take account of divorce. This might have been an opportunity to review the legislation and abolish all the various male-defined categories under which women were or were not entitled to benefits and allowances as dependent wife, widow, deserted wife, and prisoner's wife, in addition to unmarried mothers.

This was not to be. In an explanatory Memorandum to the Social Welfare (No. 2) Bill 1995 the Minister proposed to introduce a new range of women-based categories into the system. In a complicated proposal, the Minister proposed merely to ensure that no spouse was disadvantaged in social welfare entitlement as a result of their status changing from married, separated or deserted to divorced. This was a laudable objective. At the time of the debate on the Bill, divorce did not exist. However, the Bill, which became the Social Welfare (No. 2) Act 1995, created a form of 'social welfare polygamy' whereby in Social Welfare law, a man could confer benefits on two spouses simultaneously. In other words, a wife who, up to then, was receiving deserted wives' benefit, would continue to receive deserted wives' payments after a divorce, while her former husband, if he became unemployed could claim his (second) spouse as a dependant and obtain benefit on her behalf. In other words the Act allows family income supplement to be claimed by divorced husbands on behalf of wives with whom they are not living. This extraordinary Act involved defining divorced person to mean 'spouse', spouse to mean in addition 'cohabitant', and divorced partner of a prisoner to mean 'wife'.

The dilemma faced by the Parliament was that the categorical treatment of women within a male defined social security system conferring primarily derived or discretionary entitlements on women, is not amenable to reform.

Change can only occur by fusing two or more categories or by the addition of more categories. The Minister made the latter choice and doubled the number of categories, from seven to fourteen, into which a lone mother might have to slot herself in order to prove her entitlement to state support. The Minister then announced a streamlining of entitlements for later in 1995 with a new Social Welfare Bill (Social Welfare 1996).

The Dáil (lower house of Parliament) debate on the 1995 Bill had elements of farce as the Democratic Left Minister supported by his Labour Party and Christian Democratic allies defended the extraordinary categorisation of lone parents as spouses, former spouses, divorced-spouses and might-have-been spouses. No women's organisations were present in the Dáil for the debate, nor were the poverty or other lobby groups. Claiming that the Bill was merely intended to redress social welfare anomalies that might arise in the event of the divorce referendum passing, the Minister refused all amendments in the Dáil at Committee Stage and again later in the Seanad (upper house of Parliament).

In the course of the debate, in a letter to the *Irish Times* of June 27th 1995, Nicola Yeates, a social policy researcher at University College Dublin criticised the Bill for extending the web of dependency for women and failing to introduce individualised rights to social security for women, and made the accusation of 'social welfare polygamy'. In an unusual step, the Minister replied to her personally in a letter to the *Irish Times*. In the course of a lengthy reply defending the Bill, the Minister stated:

> Like Ms Yeates, I would like to see the process of 'individualisation' accelerated; but in practice it will take time and major restructuring of the social welfare code. In the meantime it is essential to protect those women who have not had the opportunity to build up contributory pensions and other social welfare entitlements in their own right. (De Rossa 1995)

Despite the Minister's defence of his proposals, opposition and independent women senators attempted to force amendments into the Bill in the Seanad (upper house) to confer more individual rights on women. They sought more opportunities for women to claim income support payments in their own name and in their own right rather than as the dependant of a male. These proposals were rejected. An amendment to ensure that welfare payments were paid to whichever spouse was in charge of children went to a vote. This had been recommended by a Government appointed Commission on the Status of Women. The amendment was defeated but the Government parties survived this defeat by only one vote.

In 1996 the treatment of lone mothers was the subject of further changes. The Social Welfare Act 1996 abolished Deserted Wives' Benefit for all new claimants and combined other lone parents allowances and payments into a newly entitled 'One-Parent Family Payment' to be introduced in 1997 (Social Welfare 1996). The One-Parent Family Payment unifies into a single category (for new claimants) those welfare payments previously paid to different categories of lone mothers according to the status of their spouse (absent, in prison or other categories). This rationalisation will bring the payments to lone mothers in Ireland in line with the system that prevailed in the UK twenty years ago, but which has since been radically altered under the new system of income and child support.

The abolition of Deserted Wives' Benefit (except for those already in receipt of it) constituted a financial saving for the Government. This payment was insurance-based and as such, deserted wives and children were paid about 20 per cent more than unmarried lone parents. In addition, women in receipt of this benefit could receive some income from earnings and maintenance payments without losing their entitlement to this benefit. This change brought about an effective downward harmonisation of the conditions of all lone mothers to a lower level of payment.

Labour market integration of lone mothers

The notion of 'welfare dependency' can be found in research on lone mothers in Ireland. McCashin (1996, p.79) argues that there is 'a high level of dependence among lone mother families on State transfer payments and low level of labour market participation'. This may not be so strongly the case as is argued. McCashin's studies have had a particular focus on lone parents in receipt of social welfare or living in relatively deprived areas. The focus of Millar's (1992) study was on poverty among lone parents, while Ward's (1990) examined maintenance payments pursued through the Courts. Ward did not and could not have included privately funded maintenance agreements which are not registered with the Courts. In fact, the labour force participation rates of some categories of lone mothers are not particularly low (see Table 3.3). The labour force participation rates of mothers with children are low compared to women with no children. The correct comparator for lone mothers is the participation rate of married mothers with the same number of children, but this comparison is rarely made (Conroy, 1993). When it is, it shows that the labour force participation rates of lone mothers compares well with those of married mothers.

The economic activity rates of lone mothers includes that of very young teenage mothers whose peers are at school. Lone teenage mothers have prematurely exited the school education system and frequently share a low level of labour force participation with other girls of reduced educational attainment. To compare the activity rate of these young mothers with those of separated women in a different age cohort is not appropriate. The conflation of categories enlarges the apparent number of lone non-economically active mothers. In other words, the lone-parent/ poverty nexus may be stretched in Ireland beyond the data available to confirm it.

Since 1990 the explicit aim of public policy has been to encourage those lone mothers who are dependent on state social welfare payments to gradually move into paid employment. A number of separate steps have been taken in this direction, via earnings supplements and labour market access. Lone parents in receipt of state payments have been allowed to package together different kinds of income and benefit. Irish lone mothers can combine earnings from paid employment, a lone parents payment and a wage subsidy (Family Income Supplement or FIS) to achieve a 'basic income'. The notion of a 'basic income' has gained currency among a minority of policy makers in the public and non-profit-making sector, who calculate that in the absence of full employment, the state should co-ordinate measures to allow individuals both to work and be in receipt of some state support. It is conceptually distinct from a 'minimum income' attached to various fixed threshold levels.

The combining together of wages, welfare and subsidies has a logic. According to the Department of Social Welfare 'The rationale behind this is to encourage lone parents to pursue a course into employment and thus away from dependency' (Houses of the Oireachtas 1996). The implication in this state-ment is that lone mothers' entitlement to state support generates a form of dependency on social welfare which is not only unacceptable behaviour, but ought to be changed by monetary incentives. The same employment-oriented argument is not used for stay-at-home wives with children, or for wives of unemployed men or other unemployed women with children. Indeed, there is no evidence that Irish lone mothers on state benefits remain on these benefits for long uninterrupted periods, or longer than claimants of other benefits. Thus this particular form of beneficial treatment of lone mothers places them, theoretically, in a more advantageous position than, for example, the wives of unemployed men.

However, the advantage is only theoretical since the take-up rate of Family Income Supplement is very low and there are hidden traps. In 1995, about 18 per cent of FIS claimants were lone parents: 2004 mothers and 76 fathers (Second Progress Report 1996, p. 23). The combining of state payments, earnings and employment subsidies may well generate a basic gross income higher than that from social welfare alone, so long as the person is in a low-paid job. Once the earnings from paid employment increase, either by better pay or working more hours, FIS may be lost and the increases may also unexpectedly propel a lone mother forwards into the tax system, reducing net take-home pay, and giving rise to a poverty trap which the combined-income system was designed to prevent.

Access to employment

The view that lone mothers should not be on State benefit and should enter employment was advanced by the Second Commission on the Status of Women in 1993. The Commission held the view that:

> ...younger lone parents should be encouraged and facilitated to return or to take up employment in their own long-term interests and those of their children. This involves such issues as eligibility for placement on education and work training courses and the provision of créche facilities and earnings disregards to remove disincentives to taking up employment. (Second Progress Report 1996, p.23)

Community employment schemes offer year-long employment opportunities to persons who are unemployed or at risk of becoming unemployed. This is the principal labour market integration programme for the long-term unemployed and is supported by the European Social Fund and European Regional Fund. Lone mothers are considered and treated as long-term unemployed for the purposes of entry to the programme. Indeed, lone mothers in receipt of lone parents' allowances from the Department of Social Welfare are a target population group intended to benefit from such job or integration opportunities. Lone parents with a dependent child and in receipt of an allowance for a year are eligible for this scheme. Eleven thousand participants were involved in these schemes during 1995. Of these, some 9 per cent were lone parents, almost exclusively mothers, in receipt of an allowance. Under the previous equivalent 1994 scheme, only 4 per cent of participants were lone mothers. The special targeting appears to have had the effect of doubling the rate of participation of lone mothers in this important labour market programme (Fás 1996, p.8). The eligibility for these schemes functions in such a way that lone mothers may continue to receive their social welfare allowance while obtaining, in addition, a labour market allowance. This effectively doubles their income immediately, while enabling them to retain important secondary social welfare benefits and the security of their original weekly welfare entitlement. In this regard, the scheme is a subsidy to lone mothers to enter the labour market via a labour market integration programme. A change in the scheme from April 1996 allowed participants to remain in the programme for up to three years.

Among lone mothers, those specifically targeted by the programme are those in receipt of lone parent based welfare benefits. A closer examination of the group most likely to avail of this opportunity, shows that it is composed of two categories of lone mothers: never married mothers and mothers separated from their partners. This group of about 38,000 women (1994) in receipt of welfare payments have some 60,000 children between them, who require child-care or after school care while their mothers attend training and other programmes. In the absence of a national child-care or nursery service, this child-care service has to be paid for privately from the income of mothers.

Lone-parent organisations

A measure of the singular status of lone mothers, is the existence of one parent organisations representing them directly or representing their interests. Such organisations have existed in Ireland since the early 1970s. The first such organisation was called Cherish. This self-help organisation took its name from a word appearing in an Irish National Declaration of half a century earlier. It thus identified itself clearly as an organisation of outsiders placing themselves within Irish social and political history. It was the first public refutation of the stigma of illegitimacy. Other organisations have since appeared such as Gingerbread, a self-help organisation for separated parents and the Parents Alone Resource Centre which operates actively in North Dublin and is a member of the National Women's Council of Ireland. Equally active is the federation of Women's Aid Refuges which provide support to women preparing to separate and live alone following flight from violence in intimate relationships.

The founders and governing bodies of Cherish, Women's Aid and Parents Alone have maintained close connections to developments in feminist thinking on the family. They have been active in lobbying the government, the legislature and public services to change their attitudes and services specifically directed to mothers living alone with their children.

Fathers as carers, providers, or nurturers have not figured largely on the agendas of lone mother organisations. The question as to whether the model father was ever a family provider has been rarely been asked in public policy or scholarship. An implicit maternalism is sustained in law by a Guardianship of Infants Act which automatically confers legal guardianship of a non-marital child on the mother. Joint guardianship with the father can be established through legal process. A review of actual judicial decisions in this area reveals that the Courts remain sceptical and 'unwilling to recognise that any significant weight should be given to paternal bonding' (Jackson 1993).

Conclusion

A policy change to encourage and remove barriers to lone mothers' access to the labour market has begun to be implemented in Ireland. This has been based in part on assumptions of welfare dependency among lone mothers which remain to be demonstrated. As is argued by Lewis (see Introduction) in a perverse sense this represents a full turning of the policy circle towards lone mothers back to the mid-nineteenth century, when they were expected to fend for themselves and their children on the labour market. The isolation of lone mothers from other mothers in respect of social policy, leaves relatively untouched the general subordination of women as secondary earners and beneficiaries within the Irish welfare regime.

References

Bunreacht Na hEireann (1937). Dublin: The Stationary Office.

Burke, H. (1987) *The People and the Poor Law in Nineteenth Century Ireland.* West Sussex: The Women's Education Bureau.

Conroy Jackson, P. (1993) 'Managing the mothers – the case of Ireland.' In J. Lewis (ed) *Women and Social Policies in Europe.* Aldershot: Edward Elgar Publishing.

Cousins, M. (1995) *The Irish Social Welfare System – Law and Social Policy.* Dublin: The Round Hall Press.

Cullen, P. (1996) 'Former FF Minister suggests family limits.' *The Irish Times.* Dublin: The Irish Times Newspapers Ltd.

Daly, M. (1989) *Women and Poverty.* Dublin: Attic Press and Combat Poverty Agency.

De Rossa, P. (1995) 'Social welfare entitlements' letter to the *Irish Times,* 3.07.95, Dublin: Irish Times Newspapers Ltd.

Department of Health (1993) *Health Statistics 1993.* Dublin: Stationary Office.

Department of Health (1995) *Developing a Policy for Women's Health.* Dublin: The Stationary Office.

Department of Social Welfare (1995) Message from Minister Prionsias De Rossa, on 8.03.96. Dublin: Information Service.

Department of Social Welfare Leaflet 08.03.96.

Department of Social Welfare (1995) *Statistical Information on Social Welfare Services.* Table C13. Dublin: Stationary Office.

Fás (1996) *Community-Employment Review 1994–5.* Dublin, Fás May.

Flanagan N. and Richardson, V. (1992) *Unmarried Mothers: A Social Profile.* Dublin: Department of Social Policy and Social Work, University College.

Hernstein, R.J. and Murray, C. (1996) *The Bell Curve – Intelligence and Class Structure in American Life.* New York: Free Press Paperbacks.

House of Commons Social Security Committee (1993) *The Operations of the Child Support Act, First Report, Session 1993–94.* London: HMSO.

Houses of the Oireachtas (1996) *First Report of the Joint Committee on the Family: The Impact of State Tax and Social Welfare Schemes on the Family.* Dublin: Stationary Office.

Jackson, N. (1993) 'Family law: fertility and parenthood.' In A. Connelly (ed) *Gender and the Law in Ireland.* Dublin: Oak Tree Press.

Jackson, P. (1984) 'Women in 19th century Irish emigration.' *International Migration Review, vol.18.* Winter. New York: Center for Migration Studies, NY.

McCafferty, N. (1985) *A Woman to Blame – the Kerry Babies Case.* Dublin: Attic Press.

McCafferty, N. (1992) 'The death of Ann Lovett.' In A. Smyth (ed) *The Abortion Papers – Ireland.* Dublin: Attic Press.

McCashin, A. (1993) *Lone Parents in the Republic of Ireland, Enumeration, Description and Implications for Social Security.* Paper No 29. Dublin: Economic and Social Research Institute.

McCashin, A. (1996) *Lone Parents in Ireland – A Local Study.* Dublin: Oaktree Press.

McDonagh, S. (ed) (1992) *The Attorney General v. X and Others*. Dublin: Incorporated Council of Law Reporting for Ireland.

McNally, F. (1996) 'Rise and rise of the welfare mother.' *Irish Times*. Dublin: Irish Times Newspapers, 6.03.96. p.13.

Meaney, G. (1993) 'Sex and nation: women in Irish culture and politics.' In A. Smyth (ed) *Irish Women's Studies Reader*. Dublin: Attic Press.

Meijvogel, R. and Petrie, P. (1996) *School-age Child-care in the European Union*. European Commission Network on child-care and other measures to reconcile employment and family responsibilities, Brussels.

Millar, J., Leeper, S. and Davies, C. (1992) *Lone Parents, Poverty and Public Policy in Ireland*. Dublin: Combat Poverty Agency.

O'Connor, A. (1985) 'Listening to tradition.' In L. Steiner Scott (ed) *Personally Speaking – Women's Thoughts on Women's Issues*. Dublin: Attic Press.

O'Connor, P. (1995) 'Understanding continuities and changes in Irish marriage: putting women centre stage.' *Irish Journal of Sociology* 5,135–163, Dublin.

O'Hare, A., Dromey, M., O'Connor, A., Clarke, M. and Kirwan, G. (1987) *Mothers Alone – A Study of Women who Gave Birth Outside Marriage*. Dublin: Federation of services for unmarried parents and their children.

Second Progress Report of the Monitoring Committee on the Implementation of the Recommendations of the Second Commission on the Status of Women (1996) Dublin: Stationary Office.

Social Welfare Bill, 27.02.1996 and Explanatory Memorandum. Dublin: Stationary Office.

Tweedy, H. (1992) *A Link in the Chain, the Story of the Irish Housewives Association 1942–1992*. Dublin: Attic Press.

Ward, M. (1988) *Unmanageable Revolutionaries, Women and Irish Nationalism*. Dingle: Brandon Books.

Ward, P. (1990) *The Financial Consequences of Marital Breakdown*. Dublin: Combat Poverty Agency.

Wiley, M. and Merriman, B. (1996) *Women and Health Care in Ireland – Knowledge, Attitudes and Behaviour*. Dublin: Oak Tree Press.

Yeates, N. (1995) *Unequal Status, Unequal Treatment, the Gender Restructuring of Welfare: Ireland*. Working Paper Gender and European Welfare Regimes. Dublin: WERRC.

CHAPTER FOUR

Lone Mothers in the Netherlands

*Jet Bussemaker, Annemieke van Drenth, Trudie Knijn
and Janneke Plantenga*

Introduction

The history of social policy towards lone mothers in the Netherlands is a history
of shared responsibilities between the state, the private and voluntary sectors
and families. These responsibilities were determined by the principle of subsidiarity, meaning that the family as the lowest social unit has the primary duty
to provide. Local government gave financial assistance only when no other
resources were available from either the family or the voluntary sector. Parents
and parents-in-law were legally obliged to care for (married) children; even
grandparents had this obligation to their grandchildren, and vice versa (Loo
1981, p.206). If the family had no means to support the lone mother, charitable
organisations were asked for financial assistance. These voluntary initiatives
originated in various religious and charitable organisations, of which the
so-called Protestant 'poor boards' and the Roman Catholic Associations of St.
Vincent were the most significant. Organisations of this kind played a role in
providing income for lone mothers until after World War II, although over time
an increasingly greater responsibility was gradually assumed by municipal poor
relief (Valk 1986, p.104). In 1949, 41.9 per cent of Catholic and 44.5 per cent
of Protestant female family heads received support from their respective
church-linked organisations. Ten years later, in 1959, these figures had fallen
to 30.5 and 35.5 per cent respectively (Valk 1986, p.103).

The strictly segregated church-linked organisations have been an important
aspect of the Dutch welfare state in general. The history of policies towards
lone mothers is an illustration of particularism in the context of pillarisation.
Pillarisation refers on the political level to a highly segmented but stable society
in which confessional parties were dominant but were never big enough to rule
alone. A strong effort to reach consensus was the result. On the socio-cultural

level, pillarisation refers to denominational segregation in social organisations such as schools, broadcasting, newspapers, sporting clubs unions etc., often encouraged and subsidised by the state. Charity and social work were also organised in a 'pillarised' way. As a consequence, aid to lone mothers had the character of a specific sort of 'particularism'; the church-linked charitable organisations took care of the lone mothers belonging to their own faith or 'pillar' (for the pillarised history of the Dutch welfare state *see* Kersbergen 1995).

A major change in financial support for lone mothers took place in the 1950s and 1960s. The introduction of the General Widows and Orphans Act in 1959 and the General Assistance Act in 1965 meant that the decentralised and strongly personalised system of poor relief was transformed into a collective arrangement, and that a discourse of favour and goodwill made way for a discourse of rights and duties. In fact these Acts represent two tracks of the three-track Dutch Welfare regime (Nelson 1990). The first track is composed of rather generous insurance schemes funded by employers and employees which have traditionally been of special importance for breadwinners. Lone mothers rarely benefitted, because they seldom met the criteria. The second track is composed of national social insurance which is funded by premiums paid by all inhabitants. The benefits are flat rate and are not means-tested. This track provides flat-rate state pensions. The General Widows and Orphans Act was a clear example of this sort of benefit. The Act granted an income at a social minimum level to all widows who are 40 years old and above or who have children under 18 years. The General Assistance Act belongs to the third track of social assistance, funded by taxation. It provided means-tested benefits for those who were not covered by any insurance system. After its introduction divorced and never-married mothers were increasingly covered by this scheme. The two types of benefits for lone mothers effectively stratifies them. The distinction between a particular non-means-tested insurance for widows and a general means-tested benefit for other categories of lone mothers (divorced and never-married) emphasised in the Netherlands, as well as in many other countries, a moral border between 'deserving' and 'undeserving' lone mothers (Gordon 1994, p.293).

Both sources of financial support for lone mothers are part of the extreme breadwinner–caretaker regime that has been the Dutch welfare state. The post-war Dutch welfare state was founded on the assumption of the nuclear family in which the husband was supposed to earn an income and the wife was supposed to be a full-time mother. First, the Dutch government discouraged married women from entering or remaining in the labour market. Until the end of the sixties there were no laws to protect them from being fired when they married, became pregnant or gave birth. Married women who were employed were also not entitled to pensions, and the tax system imposed disincentives on secondary earners. Second, the identification of men with maintenance implied that the breadwinner earned a family wage and that all kinds of financial support for families were given to him. He received child-allowances and his wife and children were included in all kind of insurances without having to pay additional contributions (Sainsbury 1994). Finally, the generosity of the welfare system implied that benefits were either linked to the man's previous wage, or to the legal minimum wage level. As a result of this linkage, every man was enabled to maintain a family, without it being necessary for wives to earn an additional income (Bussemaker and Kersbergen 1994; Knijn 1994b; Sainsbury 1994). In consequence married women had hardly any financial autonomy.

The breadwinner–caretaker regime, however, is based on the assumption of a two-parent family. Since even breadwinners can die, or disappear, the dilemma of how to envision mothers without breadwinners forced the Dutch government, like the British, to make a choice: whether to view them simply as mothers or as breadwinners without a spouse. With respect to widows, this dilemma was clearly solved in favour of motherhood. Until recently they were sure to get an income at the legal minimum level for the rest of their life. With regard to other categories of lone mothers the dilemma had not been solved until the mid 1990s. Since the introduction of the General Social Assistance Act, Parliament has discussed this issue from time to time. Until recently the tendency was to favour the idea that lone mothers should be able to form an autonomous household without being employed. In order to protect these mothers' ability to care, benefits were paid at a level linked to the minimum wage and the mothers were exempted from any obligation to work until the children reached the age of 18 years. As a result almost all lone mothers – like all married mothers – in the Netherlands were full-time mothers until the beginning of the 1980s.

In the 1990s, however, this rather generous regime of social assistance was increasingly questioned. In fact their right to get an income linked to the social minimum level without having an obligation to work has now been almost completely dismantled as part of a total restructuring of the Dutch welfare state. The nurturing/breadwinning division of labour, which was once the mainstay of social policy toward the family, is now considered restrictive, passé and too expensive. This has had major consequences for lone mothers in particular because it has redefined the way in which they are treated, which in turn has implications for their identity. They can no longer consider themselves exclusively as mothers; the state now makes increasing demands on their capabilities as breadwinners.

More specifically this transition from lone mother as carer to lone mother as breadwinner can be attributed to at least three major developments. First, the composition of this group has changed dramatically. In particular there has been an increase in divorced and never-married mothers. In addition there has been a decline in rigid marital and parental moralities. Both tendencies have led to a decline in social solidarity towards lone motherhood which is increasingly seen as a personal problem, rather than a social responsibility (Bussemaker 1993; Knijn 1994b). Second, since the 1980s there has been a growing lobby for a society in which every individual, regardless of his or her circumstances, should attain economic independence through labour-market participation. In this debate both cultural and economic arguments are used. Paid employment according to this argument is an important element in participatory citizenship. At a time when other integrative ties are withering participation in the labour market is especially important for social cohesion. The economic argument refers to the negative consequences of a low male and female participation rate on the Dutch competitive position since it generates a high tax environment and employers as well as employees have to pay high premiums in order to maintain the level of insurance benefits (WRR 1990). The fact that (lone) mothers have been included in this strategy to stimulate participation in the labour market is linked to a third development – a changing ideology of motherhood. The long-held attitude in Dutch society that children prosper only if they are given a mother's undivided attention has come under fire from feminists since the 1970s. Their criticism is aimed primarily at female dependency on a male partner but also at the taboo on child care being provided outside the family. In the 1990s this thinking has been taken up by politicians. The assumption now is that children will do just as well in the care of third parties.

The next section looks at the characteristics of lone motherhood in the Netherlands. We then look at the recent shift in social policy that seeks to make lone mothers breadwinners and also take up the issue of care for mother and child.

Lone motherhood since 1945

Prior to World War II most lone mothers were widows. The number of divorces was limited and compared to other countries the percentage of never-married mothers was relatively small. The most common response to extra-marital pregnancy was a marriage. This picture remained virtually unchanged in the first post-war decades (cf. Godefroy 1960). For the Netherlands the 1950s, often headlined as a time of 'restoration', 'stability' and 'conformity', proved in retrospect to have been a period of significant cultural change. This resulted in significant changes in behaviour at the end of the 1960s, when the idea that marriage was not necessarily 'forever' began to be expressed and the first cautious forays into alternative family structures began to emerge. Since then the number of lone-parent families has increased strongly.

Some 6500 couples a year were divorced in the Netherlands during the 1950s and 1960s, but by 1985 this figure had risen to approximately 34,000 a year (Tas 1989). If these data are related to the total number of marriages then calculations show that the chance of marriage ending in divorce has risen from 17 per cent in the first half of the 1970s to 28 per cent in the second half of the 1980s (Tas 1992). This change in behaviour is commonly held to reflect the declining influence of organised religion, community and family on the stability of a marriage. The economic function of marriage has become less important and the demands made on the emotional aspects of the relationship have grown, while the option of leaving an unsatisfactory relationship has become available to more people (Kooy 1978; Damsma 1993).

Changes in marital and family morality are also apparent from the increasing number of extra-marital births. Whereas only 2.5 per cent of the total number of live births took place out of marriage in 1971, this percentage had risen to 12 per cent in 1991. Although precise data are lacking it seems that around two-thirds of these children are born to unmarried, cohabiting partners. The rest are born to mothers who have made a more or less conscious choice for lone parenthood (Delft and Niphuijs-Nell 1988, p.27). These babies are generally wanted children and this is supported by evidence of an increase in the number of extra-marital births in higher age groups. The number of never-married teenage mothers in the Netherlands is very small and has continued at this stable low level since the 1950s: two to three births per 1000 to 15–19-year old never-married women (Delft and Niphuijs-Nell 1988, p.45). There are several reasons for this small number. One is the custom that was widespread until the 1960s of marrying a pregnant bride even when she was very young. The second more current reason is that contraceptive practices have become widely accepted for girls; general practitioners prescribe contraceptive pills for girls without telling their parents and condoms can be bought in every supermarket. Girls also have easy access to abortion clinics and one in two teenage pregnancies ends in abortion (Bogt 1992; Niphuijs-Nell 1992, pp.141–2).

Finally, the increasing number of lone-parent families should be linked to the changing composition of the Dutch population as a result of migration flows. Immigration from Surinam and the Dutch Antilles is of particular significance here. Lone motherhood is the dominant family structure among women from the Dutch Antilles (62%) and it is almost dominant among women from Surinam (47%) (Hooghiemstra and Niphuis Nell 1995, p.109). In this so-called Caribbean family structure the mother is central and the father occupies a fairly peripheral position. He is frequently absent, often for lengthy periods and even permanently. The family is not, or not wholly, maintained by the man/father (Keller 1985). The origins of this system can probably be traced back to slavery but Caribbean machismo and the high unemployment of black men have also played their part. Women appear to have adjusted to this situation in the sense that they expect little financial support from the man, perceive adultery more or less as a fact of life, and stress their own autonomy and independence (Dijke *et al.* 1990, p.171ff; Hooghiemstra and Niphuijs-Nell 1995, p.109ff).

The consequences of all these changes for the number of lone-parent families are summarised in Table 4.1. A lone-parent family is defined here as a household in which one adult lives permanently with, and is responsible for the care of, one or more young children. In more concrete terms this means that there is no permanent partner present and that there is at least one child under 18. From this table it appears that the number of lone-parent families almost doubled in the period 1971 to 1985. A slight decline occurred after 1985 mainly as a result of a fall in the divorce rate. In 1993 the Netherlands had 180,200 lone-parent families, or 10 per cent of all families with children under 18. Equally this table shows that the vast majority of lone-parent families consist of a mother with one or more children; only a small percentage has a male head of the family.

Table 4.1 Lone-parent families, 1971–1993

	Absolute numbers	With female head (%)	Lone-parent families as % of all families with children under 18
1971	107,500	85.0	n.a.
1981	153,600	88.8	8
1985	203,500	88.9	10
1989	191,500	87.5	11
1993	180,200	89.1	10

Source: Niphuijs-Nell 1997; Olde Daalhuis 1978, p.71.

Major changes in the types of lone parents are illustrated in Table 4.2. While around half of all lone-parent families in 1971 were still created by the death of a partner, this percentage had fallen to 7.7 per cent of the total of lone mother families and 25 per cent of lone father families in 1993. In contrast the importance of divorce as source cause rose strongly – over 60 per cent of (male and female) lone-parent families are formed as a result of divorce. Never-married lone-parenthood is also clearly gaining ground: in 1993 about one-quarter of female lone-parent families were never-married. After 1985 there appears to be a rising trend in this respect for men too. These are probably never-married fathers who have separated from co-habitants and care for their children alone or possibly in association with their former partner.

Table 4.2 Lone-parent families by marital status and gender of parent, 1971–1993 (%)

	1971	1981	1985	1989	1993
WOMEN					
widowed	46.1	27.2	16.1	9.7	7.7
divorced	32.8	54.2	58.3	60.6	63.1
married	10.9	8.4	8.5	6.9	4.5
never-married	10.2	10.3	17.1	22.8	24.7
Total	100.0	100.0	100.00	100.0	100.0
Absolute Numbers	91,400	136,400	180,900	167,400	160,600
MEN					
widowed	52.8	42.4	25.7	27.9	25.0
divorced	22.4	43.0	64.2	62.9	61.7
married	20.5	10.0	8.8	7.1	6.6
never-married	4.3	4.7	1.3	2.1	6.6
Total	100.0	100.0	100.0	100.0	100.0
Absolute Numbers	16,100	17,200	22,500	24,000	19,600

Source: figures based on Olde Daalhuis 1978, p.109 and Klooster-van Wingerden *et al.* 1979; Niphuijs-Nell 1997.

Labour-market participation

One of the characteristic elements in lone parenthood is that in principle 'nurturer' and 'breadwinner' have to be combined in one person. In a society based on a separation of labour and care this becomes a problem that demands a solution. The practical application of assumptions informing the Dutch welfare state meant that government provided assistance to mothers who had lost their breadwinner. Through various income-replacement measures, lone mothers were defined primarily as mothers and the responsibility for maintenance was taken from them.

Given this situation, it is hardly surprising that lone mothers' labour-market participation has been traditionally low, although an increase can be observed, especially in the 1980s. Table 4.3 provides details on the period 1985 to 1993. The table shows that lone-mothers' labour participation in 1985 was 24 per cent; 4 per cent lower than the participation of mothers in two-parent families. Participation levels of widows and never-married mothers were the lowest; of these groups 14 and 17 per cent respectively were active in the labour market. Divorced women participated slightly more than the average for lone mothers and their participation rates almost equalled those for mothers in couples. By 1993 participation rates for all mothers had risen. Of lone mothers in 1993,

37 per cent were active in the labour market but the percentage for mothers in two-parent families had risen to 45 per cent. Thus the gap between lone and married mothers was actually higher in 1993 than in 1985. In order to discover the extent to which labour-market participation is influenced by the age of children at home Table 4.3 also gives data on mothers with children under 12. Not surprisingly the presence of young children has a negative effect on labour market participation among lone mothers.

Table 4.3 Labour-market participation levels[a] of mothers by type of household, 1985–1993 (%)

	Child under 18		Child under 12	
	1985	1993	1985	1993
Mothers in two-parent families	28	45	25	44
Lone mothers	24	37	18	31
Widows	14	27	7	24
Divorced mothers	29	40	21	34
Never-married mothers	16	29	15	28

[a] Has income from employment or own company.

Source: Niphuijs-Nell 1997.

Finally, Table 4.4 provides information on average working hours. This table shows that lone mothers put in relatively long working weeks: 36 per cent work more than 35 hours per week, against only 13 per cent of mothers in two-parent families. Conversely, 44 per cent of the mothers in two-parent families work less than 20 hours against only 25 per cent of lone mothers. This is easily explained by the fact that if they have no income from paid work, lone mothers have to make use of the General Social Assistance Act (*see* the following section). Since a social assistance benefit is liable to income testing, and beneficiaries are only allowed to add a small amount of wage-income to their benefit, it does not pay to work only a few hours a week. Thus, lone mothers are confronted with a choice, they can opt for a benefit paid at a social minimum level, or income from paid work, but choosing the latter will in most cases only be economically worthwhile if they work at least 32 hours (cf. Delft and Niphuijs-Nell 1988, p.68).

Table 4.4 Working hours of mothers by week and in hours, by type of household, 1993

	Average working hours per week	Working hours per week				
	hours	< 10 hours	10–19 hours	20–34 hours	ծ35 hours	Total
Mothers in two-parent families	21	15	29	43	13	100
Lone mothers	28	8	17	40	36	100
Widows	#	#	#	#	#	
Divorced mothers	27	8	17	39	36	100
Never-married mothers	29	9	10	40	41	100

\# number in sample was below 25.

Source: Niphuijs-Nell 1997.

The figures in Table 4.3 and 4.4 confirm that, comparatively speaking, the labour participation rates of Dutch mothers are rather low. At this moment 50 per cent of married mothers and 60 per cent of lone mothers with children under 18 are still full-time housewives, and of those who are employed a majority work part-time. These figures illustrate the fact that most mothers see employment as a matter of social participation rather than as a route to financial independence. Whereas for men paid work is an important if not primary basis for identity, women are identified first and foremost as spouses, housewives and mothers (Knijn 1994a; Plantenga 1996). Nevertheless the employment of Dutch mothers is growing, especially among the middle class and more highly educated.

Lone mothers and sources of income

The General Widows and Orphans Act

In comparison to most other industrialised countries, which introduced legislation for providing incomes for widows before World War II, the Dutch government was rather late in making this kind of provision. Most probably this can be explained by the fact that the Netherlands was not involved in World War I, with the result that the number of widows was comparatively low. Moreover, the principles of particularism and subsidiarity which characterised the Dutch welfare state from the end of the nineteenth century kept the responsibility away from the national government. However, changing attitudes regarding the allocation of social responsibility, together with the low income levels of lone mothers, led to an increasing demand for collective measures which resulted in the introduction of the General Widows and Orphans Act (*Algemene Weduwen- en Wezenwet*: AWW) in 1959.

In some respects, the AWW was the successor to two other acts which had provided benefits for widows and orphans: the Industrial Injuries Act (*Ongevallenwet* 1901) and the Invalidity Act (*Invaliditeitswet* 1919). The benefits paid out under these pieces of legislation were, however, considered inadequate and the number of those insured too limited. As the Explanatory Statement to the AWW put it: 'It can be stated that the inadequate provision for widows and orphans after the demise of a breadwinner has become a general social phenomenon' (TK 1958–1959a, p.21). In view of these circumstances, it was seen as government's duty to intervene 'not only to relieve existing need, but also to prevent future need' (TK 1958–1959a, p.21). Thus, there was an implied recognition of a man's obligation as breadwinner to maintain his family and of government's responsibility to do so if the man died.

The potential needs of widowers, who in all probability would also be unable to manage to combine work and care, were not even mentioned. This is probably because the AWW was seen as an insurance against financial destitution, something that was not considered relevant for widowers, so the possible nature of their needs was not taken into account. In practice widowers did have recourse to the home help service. However, the eligibility criteria for a home help stated categorically that the service was intended to provide temporary help for families where the mother was unable to care for her husband and children because of illness or other problems. If the wife and mother died then the eldest daughter or other female relatives were expected to take on care responsibilities or paid (household) help had to be sought (cf. Schouten and Boelhouwer 1976, p.183; Bruggen-Grevelink 1985). More pressure was thus indirectly brought to bear on widowers than on widows to find a new partner.

Besides a gender distinction, the AWW also differentiated between widows. A widow's pension was awarded to a woman of 40 years or more, or to a woman caring for one or more unmarried children under 18. A temporary widow's benefit was made available to women under 40 and to those not caring for unmarried children under 18. The categorisation was thus formally linked to 'age' and 'children'. In practice these criteria are complementary: the vast majority of mothers with children over 18 will be over 40 years old. Young widows with no family obligations were expected to provide for themselves after a period of grace:

> Rather than moping around, which is what a permanent widow's pension would allow, she would be far better off, also from a mental welfare point of view, going out and finding employment. Under these circumstances, the population cannot be expected to make sacrifices for women who

may have had the misfortune to lose a husband, but who are still capable of work and thus do not require a widow's pension. (TK 1958–1959a, p.24)

Divorced women whose former husband died were also excluded from entitlement to a widow's pension, even if the man had paid maintenance and thus fulfilled the role of breadwinner. According to government, the amount of maintenance paid was overly subject to numerous coincidental circumstances and as such could not form the basis for entitlement to an AWW benefit (TK 1958–1959b, p.3).

The General Social Assistance Act

There has never been a piece of legislation in the Netherlands under which other categories of lone mothers, such as the divorced or never-married, could claim benefits. The General Social Assistance Act (*Algemene BijstandsWet*: ABW) which came into effect in 1965, gave entitlement to a benefit, but the Act's primary function was to provide a safety net for all those men and women who no longer had any recourse to other kinds of social welfare benefits. The safety-net aspect is most clearly expressed in the fact that the ABW comprises a collection of various regulations and eligibility criteria, each of which is tailored to various groups. The so-called ABW-sec was especially relevant to lone mothers, because it was specially aimed at people with limited ties to the labour market. People receiving benefit under the ABW-sec regime were covered by a categorical exemption from any obligation to seek work; in other words, they did not have to be available for employment. Table 4.5 shows that lone mothers have been the largest group of ABW-sec beneficiaries; comprising 60 per cent of claimants. By placing lone mothers under the ABW-sec regime, and thus exempting them from the job-seeking, the government defined them primarily as full-time carers for their children.

The position occupied by divorced and lone mothers within the ABW has always been subject to debate: are they a specific group with specific needs, or is their individual situation just as varied as that of other social security clients? Initially, when the Act was implemented in 1965, never-married and divorced mothers were considered to be 'marginal groups comprising individual cases' for whom the local authority should determine the level of benefit required on a case-by-case basis. This often led to confusion, should, for example, a 17-year-old lone mother living with her parents be considered as an independent social security client or as a daughter? The rapidly growing numbers of lone mothers, partly as a consequence of changes in divorce legislation in 1971, made this individual, decentralised approach increasingly difficult to sustain. Lone mothers thus quickly became a recurring problem in political debates about the level of benefit, the relationship of ABW to other benefits

Table 4.5 People under 65 receiving ABW-sec benefits, by household, 1978–1991

	1978		1980		1985		1991	
	1000s	%	1000s	%	1000s	%	1000s	%
Married couples	10.3	10	10.1	9	19.0	11	11.5	6
One-parent families								
– women	60.0	58	70.9	61	111.6	62	103.7	59
– men	0.7	1	1.2	1	1.6	1	2.1	1
– women's share		99		98		99		98
Singles								
– women	24.8	24	25.5	22	37.2	21	46.7	26
– men	7.2	7	8.0	7	8.9	5	10.5	6
– women's share		78		76		81		82
Others	0.4	0	0.1	0	0.5	0	2.7	2
Total	103.4	100	116.0	100	178.8	100	177.2	100

Source: Hooghiemstra and Niphuijs-Nell 1993, p.157.

and the relationship between centrally determined criteria and local authority discretion (Bussemaker 1985; Weuring 1996).

The difficulties in finding an agreed position on lone mothers also frustrated attempts to create a categorial benefit for lone, especially divorced, mothers. Such a benefit had been created for, among others, artists, the self-employed and invalids. However, most political parties were afraid that this type of measure would lead to the acceptance of divorce as 'a normal social risk' (Holtmaat 1992, p.157–158; Weuring 1996). Moreover, it was felt that divorced mothers exhibited too little homogeneity to warrant categorial treatment. The reasoning was on the one side that there were too many similarities in the position of 'incomplete families' to create a separate benefit for divorced women and on the other side that the group of divorced women itself was too mixed to permit a common treatment, some having an income of their own from earnings or maintenance and others not. The debate died a natural death with the introduction of a new income stipulation which linked the ABW to the minimum wage level in 1974.

Another important point of discussion, the improvement of the lone mother's income through encouraging the labour market participation, also failed to result in concrete policy change. After the ABW was linked to the minimum wage level in 1974 lone-parent families were allowed to keep about a third of their earnings in addition to the benefit, up to a maximum of 25 per cent of the minimum wage (in contrast to 15% for couples) (Weuring 1996, p.35). However, when in 1982 the social democrats proposed to allow single mothers to keep a greater portion of earnings alongside their state benefits in order to promote their labour market participation, the majority of the Second Chamber argued that this would result in inequity between different kinds of breadwinners, that is between those with and those without a spouse, on social security benefit. It was also argued that lone mothers were first and foremost mothers with a care task. Their special position as both mother and breadwinner was not recognised.

In the first half of the 1980s the position of lone mothers became strongly politicised. Feminist groups spoke of the 'feminisation of poverty' and set up a number of action campaigns in conjunction with committees formed by women on welfare. These committees, the first of which was established in 1979, were especially active on behalf of divorced women with children and would rapidly develop from support to action groups. The action campaigns, which were concentrated in the winter of 1982/83, proved controversial and led to all manner of public and political debate on improving the position of women on welfare (Bussemaker 1985). While little real change was achieved, there was a clear shift in attitudes. On the one hand, a greater understanding emerged as to the difficult position in which these 'caring mothers' found themselves. On the other, the link with feminist action groups also led to a perception of these mothers as 'demanding feminists'. Although lone mothers on benefits are not formally treated as a separate group, they were seen as such by public opinion. The term 'welfare mother' soon became common parlance. The official terminology for one-parent families also changed. In Parliament the loaded term 'incomplete families', which suggested that lone parents were to some extent deviant families, was replaced by one-parent or lone-parent families, which while politically neutral identified lone parents as just another kind of family. This shift in meaning firmly underlined the increasing tolerance of the diversification of families.

The treatment of lone mothers under the social security system has been somewhat ambivalent. The Netherlands has no categorial benefits for lone mothers. Welfare benefits for lone mothers were justified by the fact that they and their children represented families in distress rather than in terms of the mother's role as carer or her former role as housewife. However, social assistance permitted the development of a category of benefit recipients with no obligation to work. The identification of lone mothers as 'welfare mothers' was particularly important for the way they were viewed by the general public. Feminists and lone mothers themselves drew attention to the position of lone mother families on benefit in order also to draw attention to their poverty. However, this made lone mothers visible as a main category of welfare dependents.

Restructuring social provision

From the beginning of the 1980s the nature of the Dutch welfare state has been subject to a measure of restructuring. The need for austerity in terms of public expenditure together with a new emphasis on the citizen's own responsibility and obligations began to influence the political climate. There was a growing belief that increased labour market participation by all – including women – would reduce the costs of the social security system. This together with changing perceptions of marriage and family morality gave new impetus to debates on the political legitimacy of arguing the case for social solidarity to deal with the results of 'private' decisions, such as the ending of a marriage and the termination of a man's financial responsibility for his wife and children. Thus never-married and divorced mothers became the focus of debates on labour-market participation, gender relations and the structure of the Dutch welfare state. As a result the demand for a thorough revision of social security legislation began to gain ground.

The first move towards revision came in 1989 with significant proposals for the simplification of provisions and decentralisation of administration. Simplification was primarily a response to a public discussion on the abuse of the system, in which it was assumed that extensive fraudulent reporting of household composition was taking place. Given the fact that social assistance benefit is subject to means testing, it was highly unattractive for 'welfare mothers' to cohabit 'officially' with a (potentially earning) partner. The difficulties in finding proof of *de facto* cohabitation gave rise to all manner of arguments in which the right to privacy and to an independent life came into conflict with a sense of morality and the responsibility that should be assumed by the state out of a sense of social solidarity. The second proposal – decentralisation to local authority level – was aimed at closing administrative loopholes. However, the most central element in the new social assistance legislation has been the emphasis which it places on improving what is called the 'activating effect'. Rather than a safety net, social assistance should be more of a 'trampoline' to paid work. One consequence in this shift in thinking is that the obligation to work, or at least to apply for work, has been extended to a much larger group of people.

These proposals had major consequences for lone mothers because care for children as such is no longer considered a reason for exemption from work. There has been discussion only on the question of whether an exception should be made for mothers with very young children and if so where the age boundary should be drawn. A 'New General Social Assistance Act' finally came into force on 1 January 1996. One of its provisions is that

> …policy must be aimed at preventing a situation whereby a period of care for young children would represent a structural impediment to

achieving economic independence, especially for women. This is why the new ABW begins from a position which stresses the importance of the claimant maintaining his or her ties with the labour market and making preparations for future participation during periods when caring tasks are being carried out.

In plain language this means that the obligation to work also applies to women with children. A general exception is made, however, for a parent who has to care for one or more children under five; this implies that at least one (of the) parent(s) of children under five is exempted from the obligation to work. By simply extending the obligation to work to a large category of mothers without simultaneously introducing a right to public child care an opportunity was missed to develop specific legislation for those who also have an obligation to care, in particular lone mothers.

The 1959 General Widows and Orphans Act has also been subject to revision. As early as the mid-1980s, it was recognised that this Act no longer reflected the social reality in that the line between breadwinners and carers was no longer as absolute as the legislation assumed. It also transpired (in December 1988) that the Act contravened the non-discrimination principle laid down in the International Convenant on Civil and Political Rights (ICCPR). Thus widowers have also been given access to AWW benefits. These new claims have proved expensive for the Treasury, especially as there is often no real financial need for the benefit. Initial attempts to revise the AWW had foundered in the First Chamber but government finally got legislation through in 1995 and the AWW was replaced by the General Next of Kin Act (*Algemene NabestaandenWet*: ANW) on 1 July 1996.

One significant difference between the AWW and the ANW is that the latter has dropped all explicit references to gender. Entitlement to benefit is formulated in gender neutral terms and is given to next of kin with children under 18 or to childless next of kin if they were born before 1950. The assumption here is that widows and widowers with children under 18 have a care obligation and thus have more difficulty in combining work and care than people without children and parents who share care tasks with their partner. This group should not, therefore, be obliged to perform paid work. However, given that this type of care obligation ceases to exist when the children are older the entitlement to benefit expires. An exception is made for people born before 1950. Older widows who do not usually have jobs and either no, or an outdated, training are thus exempted. A second significant difference is that the ANW is means-tested. The introduction of this income test has resulted in a considerable saving on public expenditure.

The new approach towards lone mothers characteristic of both new pieces of legislation, forms a clear break with the idea that lone mothers of young children should, and could, focus their undivided attention on caring for their offspring regardless of how they became lone mothers. The new legislation stresses the lone mother's responsibility for self maintenance and entitlement to benefit is increasingly linked to availability for work. These measures thus show government underpinning a development which was already signalled in the previous section; the increasing labour-market participation of lone mothers.

Sources of income

Table 4.6 provides a general overview of sources of income for different types of families in 1993.

Table 4.6 Personal sources of income (%)[a] and disposable household income[b] (x Dutch florins[c] 1000 per annum) in 1993

	wages	self-employed earnings	ABW	RWW	WW	WAO/AAW	AWW/pension	Other	Disposable household-income
Lone parents	37	4	42	8	5	6	9	2	27.3
Lone mothers	34	3	47	8	4	5	7	2	25.9
Widows	19	7	1	1	1	5	88	2	35.9
Divorced mothers	39	3	47	8	5	6	0	2	25.4
Never-married mothers	27	2	60	11	3	4	0	2	23.9
Lone fathers	56	12	6	8	6	11	21	3	38.7
Divorced fathers	63	12	8	9	6	13	3	5	36.0
Mothers in two-parent families	41	5	0	1	2	2	0	2	52.7
Fathers in two-parent families	79	13	1	2	3	6	1	2	52.7

a: More than one source is possible: e.g. a lone mother can also receive (supplementary) benefit when her earnings (for instance from a part-time job) are below the level of benefits.

b: This refers to the disposable household income of man and/or woman (jointly), in other words any income earned by children is not included.

c: UK £1 – 2.6 Dutch florins.

Explanation of abbreviations:

ABW = Algemene Bijstandswet (General Social Assistance Act)

RWW= Rijksgroepregeling Werkloze Werknemers (State Group Regulation for Unemployed Employees, including school leavers)

WW/WWV= Werklozenwet (Unemployment Act)

WAO/AAW= Wet Algemene Arbeidsongeschiktheid (Disability Act)

AWW= Algemene Weduwen- en Wezenwet (General Widows and Orphans Pension Act)

Source: Niphuijs-Nell 1997.

The data in Table 4.6 illustrate the particular importance of ABW benefit; 47 per cent of lone mothers receive it. For lone fathers the percentage is only 6. The vast majority of widows (88%) appear to be dependent on the AWW. The ABW accounts for 47 per cent of income for the divorced, and 60 per cent of income for never-married lone mothers. Maintenance from fathers is not included in the table, but this does not mean that divorced Dutch women do not get any. About 40 per cent of the divorced mothers received money for their children, while about 27 per cent of these mothers get alimony payments for themselves. Only 14 per cent of divorced mothers receive both forms of maintenance from fathers (Niphuijs-Nell 1997).

In terms of actual disposable income (including income from earnings and benefits, but not alimony) it appears that the income level of never-married and divorced mothers is especially low, a direct result of the fact that these groups are strongly dependent on welfare benefits. In principle these benefits are linked to the minimum wage level and calculated at 90 per cent of the benefits for couples. Recently the level of benefits has declined as a result of the increase in wage dispersion and the general policy to increase the differential between benefits and wages. Moreover, if the disposable income is standardised by taking into account the composition of the family it appears that the standardised income of lone-parent families increasingly lags behind that of two-parent families. While the disposable income per person in lone-parent families was 25 per cent less than in two-parent families in 1985, it was 35 per cent less in 1993. This was not only due to the relative decline of benefits but also to the increase in the number of secondary earners (i.e. working mothers) in two-parent families (Niphuijs-Nell 1997). Not surprisingly a large majority of divorced and never-married mothers are dissatisfied with their financial position. According to the research that Van Gelder carried out in 1984, 29 per cent of lone-parent families say their income is inadequate, against 5 per cent of two-parent families (Gelder 1987). The financial position of lone-parent families where benefits are the only source of income is even more difficult. Of these 44 per cent say their income is inadequate. Current research shows lone-parent families belong to the poorest households in the Netherlands (Muffels et al. 1995).

Lone mothers and care

A second thread in state intervention in respect to lone mothers is concerned not so much about the level and source of income, but with the mother/child relationship. So long as the social assistance legislation and the widow's pension schemes achieved their objective of giving lone mothers the opportunity to care, measures to facilitate the combination of work and care were seen as unnecessary and in fact undesirable. As a result the Netherlands has very little by way of state provision for the care of children in the form of child care or parental leave. Even where it exists lone mothers have sometimes been prohibited from using it. For instance when in 1930 maternity leave was introduced as part of the Health Act lone mothers were exempted from it. Members of Parliament argued that such a provision might provide an incentive to immoral behaviour. It was only under the German occupation during World War II that lone mothers got access to maternity leave (Plantenga 1993, p.109). Child-care provision has only appeared in state budgets since 1975 and an explicit relation between child-care and labour-market considerations was first recognised at the national level at the end of the 1980s. On 1 January 1990 the Stimulatory Measure for Child-Care 1990–1993 was introduced which aimed to expand public and private child-care and to achieve a better spread of facilities throughout the Netherlands. The measure was extended until 1996 and has indeed resulted in a major growth in both state subsidised and employer provided child care. However, even in 1995 the public funded services only covered about 8 per cent of all children under 3 years (European Commission Network on Childcare 1996, p.148). Parental leave schemes are also a rather new phenomenon in the Netherlands. It was only in 1991 that a measure of parental leave was legislated. At present civil servants enjoy the most favourable arrangement. Not only can the leave be spread over a longer period but it is also paid at a rate of 75 per cent of the normal salary. In the private sector parental leave is subject to negotiation between the social partners and is usually unpaid.

Care provisions for never-married mothers exist mainly in the form of homes and advisory offices for (teenage) never-married mothers. Those provisions belong to the domain of 'social surveillance' and have a long history in which concern about morality has played a crucial role (Drenth 1991, 1994). Individual women and girls were looked after in order to guide them towards a normal female life; meaning being a decent housewife and mother. In the second half of the nineteenth century, the greatest anxiety was expressed about 'fallen women' and the battle against immorality. The 'homes' that were founded then, especially by representatives of the Protestant Dutch Revival movement, sheltered numerous never-married mothers and their children. Women received relief and got assistance in finding work (Graaf 1923). The Catholics quickly followed suit and convents took on the care of never-married mothers (Wiemann 1988, p.340). There were also initiatives from the early feminist movement, including a home in Amsterdam opened in 1905. In 1929, the existing relief organisations concerned with care of never-married mothers in the Netherlands joined together in the National Federation of Institutions for the Never-Married Mother and her Child (FIOM), whose main task was to provide services and to guide these mothers and their children during the first years after giving birth. As a result 24 homes were set up which could provide shelter for 385 of the 700 mothers who asked for it. Those who could not be placed were obliged to turn for support to the child's father and their relatives (Hueting and Neij 1990, p.39).

In the first instance, the FIOM saw its task as protecting the mother/child relationship. It was important for the child that 'the only bond it has in this world, the bond with its mother, is not severed' (Jong 1984, p.121). The mother was expected to keep her child and a certain moral obligation to care for it was imposed on her. It was a form of penance: '…let the mother atone for the wrong she did through her negligence' (Jong 1984). Nevertheless this attitude would eventually change in the 1950s. Influenced by the professionalisation and application of (especially psychological and psychiatric) scientific insights, the problem of unmarried motherhood was redefined. 'Saving' these women through repentance and reform was no longer the focus but rather helping them, showing them understanding and instilling in them the notion that the situation of a never-married mother was 'maladjusted'. According to this diagnosis, never-married mothers suffered from developmental problems which required support (Trimbos 1955; Heijmans and Trimbos 1964).

This new approach raised the question of whether, in view of their 'psychological maladjustments', they were capable of taking good care of their children and of satisfying the 'modern' demands of raising children. The lack of a father was also problematised and the importance of achieving a 'normal' family situation emphasised. As a result of these changes the previously almost unassailable concept of the bond between mother and child was called into question and the placement of the child in a foster family through adoption was increasingly advocated. A number of homes assumed that the mother would give up her child and separated mother and baby immediately after birth (Hueting and Neij 1990). At the end of the 1960s, almost one-quarter of all never-married mothers gave up their babies. In total this affected about 700 children, 90 per cent of the total number of children adopted in the Netherlands (Wel 1992, pp.433–438).

Attitudes changed yet again in the 1970s. Pioneering criticism questioned whether lone mothers were actually a problem in themselves, or whether they were turned into a problem (Hueting and Neij 1990, p.153–154; Wel 1992, p.439). At that point in time the ABW had given lone mothers a right to their own income and the pill and abortion had brought about a decline in the number of unwanted pregnancies. Moreover, the growth in the numbers of divorced women, mothers who also had to tackle raising their children alone, meant that lone-parent families were more common. It should be noted here that this did not result in the disappearance of social work assistance to lone-mother families but rather that the traditional homes for never-married mothers were replaced by so-called 'support and guidance centres for lone parents and children in crisis or emergency situations' (Hueting and Neij 1990, p.160).

In the 1980s the term 'never-married mother' became the new name for a new category of lone mothers; women who had made a deliberate, conscious choice 'not to marry and to have a baby'. These women created their own new support and self-help networks. An advertisement placed by a woman in a national daily newspaper in 1977 illustrates the mood of the times: 'I am looking for a number of women who – like me – have made a conscious choice to become pregnant, or are considering this. Aim: exchanging experience, mutual support, cooperation in solving practical matters' (quoted in Holtrust 1995, p.51). In contrast to their predecessors these so-called BOM-mothers (*Bewust Ongehuwde Moeder* – literally 'consciously never-married mother') got a great deal of press attention. They were a new phenomenon. They were also, however, a phenomenon which in terms of their characteristics and their problems appeared to be little different from other categories of lone mothers. At the end of the 1980s Wiemann could therefore conclude: 'their social standing has risen and never-married mothers were not any longer perceived as a group in need of professional social treatment: pregnancy out-of-marriage and never-married motherhood is in itself no longer grounds for assistance from an agency or home' (Wiemann 1988, p.359).

The fact that these women would take on the care of their child(ren) became accepted. The BOM-mothers also drew attention to the role of the father and fatherhood, because they developed all manner of new forms of 'fatherhood', varying from the straight-forward biological semen donor whose identity would be made known to the child on request to the social father-at-a-distance (Holtrust and Hondt, 1987). Moreover, increased attention on fatherhood was fostered by the fact that a small but increasing number of fathers were assuming sole care for children after divorce. As a result they too became part of the group targeted by organisations involved in providing support for lone parents.

Conclusion: breadwinning, nurturing and the Welfare State

The changed position of lone mothers in the Netherlands should be placed against the backdrop of changes in the Dutch welfare state. In the 1950s and 1960s the welfare state was anchored to a strongly asymmetrical and complementary gender regime. The prevalent breadwinner ideology generated comprehensive measures which provided men (and their families) with financial security. The strong motherhood ideology justified a complementary structure in which mothers could make claim to relatively generous social benefits if they had no breadwinner (Bussemaker and Kersbergen 1994; Knijn 1994b).

The complementary breadwinner/motherhood ideologies led to very limited labour market participation by mothers. On the one hand this implied a major level of socio-economic dependence. On the other it also furnished mothers with the assurance that they could always care for their children at home. Both the Widows and Orphans Act and the General Social Security Act created, unintentionally, an environment in which lone mothers could combine care for their children with socio-economic independence. In other words both social benefits offered lone mothers the opportunity to form and maintain an autonomous household (Orloff 1993). The ABW also contributed indirectly to the increased independence of married women, they now had an 'exit option'. If the marriage did not meet their expectations they were assured of a social safety net created by the welfare state (Hobson 1994). The state appeared to have become a relatively trustworthy alternative breadwinner (Stolk and Wouters 1983). Nonetheless, there was another side to this relatively generous regulatory environment; the right to care for one's children also implied an obligation to do so. The strong complementary breadwinner–carer regime offered mothers few other options. The post-war Dutch welfare state comprised almost no arrangements which would enable a combination of care and work. Childcare and parental leave were not part of the deal and structures based on the breadwinner model made married women's paid work financially unattractive.

It was only in the 1990s that drastic changes occurred in policy towards lone mothers. As we have already seen these were linked to the increased differentiation in the kinds of lone mothers, the increase in the importance attached to labour-market participation and related changes in the importance attached to the ideology of motherhood and the restructuring of the welfare state. Individualisation and the fragmentation of life styles gave rise to the perception that lone motherhood was a self-selected life style which no longer required social protection. Exceptions were made only for lone mothers with children under five. Thus lone mothers are now considered to be breadwinners like any other adult, raising her children in one of many possible family arrangements. Although the emphasis on labour market participation, which has been chosen as a point of departure for the restructuring of the Dutch welfare state in the 1990s, implies that the gender regime has changed its character, it does not mean that men and women are also autonomous individuals. The motherhood ideology that was so omnipresent in the post-war welfare state is disappearing and no longer gives rise to social benefits for a special category of mothers. Now they too have an obligation to be active in the labour market. However, this ignores their double role as breadwinner and carer.

A rather complicating aspect in this process is the move towards decentralisation which has been part of social security reform. Although aimed at lightening administration it in fact gives rise to lots of problems at the administrative level. Since the national framework of a general obligation to work is not accompanied by a national framework for care (lone) mothers cannot claim access to public child care or part-time work. Therefore the municipalities that are now responsible for implementing the legislation lack the means to get lone mothers into the labour market. For the moment they make different choices in dealing with these issues. They either; (1) strictly apply the legislation (punishing those who do not make efforts to find a job); (2) marginalise lone mothers as a category of benefit recipients who cannot be readily employed; or (3) use their discretion creatively in order to support lone mothers according to their needs.

The result of the changes in the gender regime of the Dutch welfare state allow no single interpretation. For those lone mothers who are (to all intents and purposes) able to meet male norms very little will change, if they work outside the home they still lack an entitlement to care for their children. For those mothers who have built their identity primarily on full-time motherhood the changes are radical, they often lack both the mindset and the capacity to make their way in the male-oriented world of work. In addition the inequality in treatment between inhabitants of different municipalities which may be expected will result in a high degree of uncertainty about rights and duties.

In the end we can conclude that lone mothers were never an easy fit in the strict Dutch post-war gender regime. Never-married and divorced mothers were especially difficult to place in the complementary regulatory environment based on the breadwinner/motherhood ideologies. In spite of all the changes which have taken place over time relating to their position and to policies concerning them there has been little change in one major respect – the Dutch welfare state continues to be badly tailored to the needs and situation of lone mothers.

References

Bogt, T. ter (1992) *Jongeren op de drempel van de jaren negentig.* Den Haag: VUGA/SCP.

Bruggen-Grevelink, M. van der (1985) *De duizendpoot in de gezinsverzorging.* Utrecht: SWP.

Bussemaker, J. (ed.) (1985) *'Zielig zijn we niet'. Het politieke verzet van bijstandsvrouwen.* Amsterdam: Van Gennep.

Bussemaker, J. (1993) *Betwiste zelfstandigheid. Individualisering, sekse en verzorgingsstaat.* Amsterdam: SUA.

Bussemaker, J. and Kersbergen, K. van (1994) 'Gender and the welfare state: some theoretical reflections.' In D. Sainsbury (ed) *Gendering Welfare States.* London: Sage.

Damsma, D. (1993) *Het Hollandse huisgezin (1560-heden).* Utrecht/Antwerpen: Kosmos – Z and K Uitgevers.

Delft, M. van and Niphuijs-Nell, M. (1988) *Eenoudergezinnen: ontstaan, leefsituatie en voorzieningengebruik.* Sociale en Culturele Studies 9. Rijswijk: Sociaal en Cultureel Planbureau.

Dijke, A. van., Hulst, H. van and Terpstra, L. (1990) *Mama Soltera. De positie van 'alleenstaande' Curaçaose en Arubaanse moeders in Nederland.* Den Haag: Warray.

Drenth, A. van (1991) *De zorg om het Philipsmeisje. Fabrieksmeisjes in de elektrotechnische industrie in Eindhoven (1990–1960).* Zutphen: Walburg Pers.

Drenth, A. van (1994) 'Zorg-en-de-macht. Over sociale constructie van gender-identiteit.' *Psychologie en Maatschappij 67*, 19, 2, 141–155.

European Commission Network on Child-care (1996) *A Review of Services for Young Children in the European Union, 1990–1995*. Brussels: European Commission Directorate General V (Employment, Industrial Relations and Social Affairs) Equal Opportunities Unit.

Gelder, K. van (1987) *Alleen Zorgen: Een onderzoek naar het functioneren van eenoudergezinnen*. Den Haag: NImawo.

Godefroy, J. (1960) *Buitenechtelijke geboorten in Nederland. Een sociaal-statistische beschrijving*. Tilburg: Instituut voor Arbeidsvraagstukken.

Gordon, L. (1994) *Pitied but not Entitled. Single Mothers and the History of Welfare*. Cambridge/Massachusetts: Harvard University Press.

Graaf, A. de (1923) *De ontwikkeling van den strijd tegen de onzedelijkheid: De strijd tegen de prostitutie*. Utrecht: Ruys.

Heijmans, H.F. and Trimbos, C.J.B.J. (1964) *De niet-gehuwde moeder en haar kind*. Hilversum: Brand.

Hobson, B. (1994) 'Solo mothers, social policy regimes and the logics of gender.' In D. Sainsbury (ed) *Gendering Welfare States*. London: Sage.

Holtmaat, R. (1992) *Met zorg een recht? Een analyse van het politiek-juridisch vertoog over bijstandsrecht*. Zwolle: Tjeenk Willink.

Holtrust, N. (1995) 'De geschiedenis van de afstandsmoeder. Dikke bult, eigen schuld.' In *Publiek geheim. Deprivatisering van het vrouwenleven*. Amsterdam: Clara Wichmann Instituut/Nemesis.

Holtrust, N. and Hondt, I. de. (1987) *Bewust ongehuwd moeder*. Baarn: Ambo.

Hooghiemstra, B.T.J. and Niphuijs-Nell, M. (1995) *Sociale atlas van de vrouw. Deel 2: Arbeid, inkomen en faciliteiten om werken en de zorg voor kinderen te combineren*. Rijswijk: Sociaal en Cultureel Planbureau.

Hooghiemstra, B.T.J. and Niphuijs-Nell, M. (1995) *Sociale atlas van de vrouw. Deel 3: allochtone vrouwen*. Rijswijk: Sociaal en Cultureel Planbureau.

Hueting, E. and Neij, R. (1990) *Ongehuwde moederzorg in Nederland*. Zutphen: Walburg Pers.

Jong, N. de (1984) 'Van zondig tot ongezond. De Christelijke Vereniging Zedenopbouw over moederschap en seksualiteit.' In S. Sevenhuijsen e.a., *Socialisties-Feministiese Teksten 8*. Amsterdam: Sara.

Keller, S. (1985) 'Caraïbische gezinstypen en hun toekomst in Nederland.' In R.A. de Moor (ed) *Huwelijk en gezin: wat is hun toekomst in West-Europa?* Baarn: Ambo.

Kersbergen, K. van (1995) *Social Capitalism. A Study of Christian Democracy and the Welfare State*. London: Routledge.

Kooy, G.A. (1978) *Seksualiteit, huwelijk en gezin in Nederland*. Deventer: Van Loghum Slaterus.

Klooster-van Wingerden, C.M. van't, *et al.* (1979) 'Huishoudenssamenstelling en samenlevingsvormen.' In *Monografien volkstelling 1971, nr 11.*'s. Gravenhage: Staatsuitgeverij.

Knijn, T. (1994a) 'Social dilemmas in images of motherhood in the Netherlands.' In *The European Journal of Women's Studies 1*, 2, 183–207.

Knijn, T. (1994b) 'Fish without bikes: Revision of the Dutch Welfare state and its consequences for the (in)dependence of single mothers.' In *Social Politics, International Studies in Gender, State & Society 1*, 1, 83–105.

Loo, F. van (1981) *'Den arme gegeven'. Een beschrijving van armoede, armenzorg en sociale zekerheid in Nederland, 1784–1965.* Meppel/Amsterdam: Boom.

Muffels, R., Dirven, H.-J. and Fouarge, D. (1995) *Armoede, Bestaansonzekerheid en Relatieve Deprivatie: Rapport 1995 (Tisser-study).* Tilburg: Tilburg University Press.

Nelson, B. (1990) 'The origins of the two-channel welfare state: workmen's compensation and mother's aid,' In L. Gordon (ed) *Women, the State and Welfare.* Madison: university of wisconsin Press. 123–157.

Niphuijs-Nell, M. (1992) *De emancipatie van meisjes en jonge vrouwen.* Rijswijk: SCP.

Niphuijs-Nell, M. (1997/forthcoming) 'Eenoudergezinnen, stiefgezinnen en uitwonende ouders.' In *Sociale Atlas van de vrouw 4.* Rijswijk: Sociaal en Cultureel Planbureau.

Olde Daalhuis, A. (1978) 'Gescheidenen en verweduwden.' In *Monografien volkstelling 1971, nr 3.*'s-Gravenhage: Staatuitgeverij.

Orloff, A. (1993) 'Gender and the social rights of citizenship: The comparative analysis of gender relations and welfare states.' In *American Sociological Review 58*, 3, 303–328.

Plantenga, J. (1993) *Een afwijkend patroon. Honderd jaar vrouwenarbeid in Nederland en (West-)Duitsland.* Amsterdam: SUA.

Plantenga, J. (1996) 'For women only? The rise of part-time work in the Netherlands.' In *Social Politics, International Studies in Gender, State and Society 3*, 1, 57–71.

Sainsbury, D. (1994) 'Women's and men's social rights: Gendering dimensions of welfare states.' In D. Sainsbury (ed) *Gendering Welfare States.* London: Sage.

Schouten, C.W. and Boelhouwer, R.H. (1976) 'Economie en maatschappelijke dienstverlening.' In R.M. Lampré (ed.) *De economie van de welzijnszorg.* Alphen aan de Rijn: Samson.

Stolk, B. van and Wouters, C. (1983) *Vrouwen in tweestrijd.* Deventer: Van Loghum Slaterus.

Tas, R.F.J. (1989) 'Echtscheidingen in Nederland, 1950–1987.' In *Maandstatistiek voor de Bevolking*, nr. 3, 17–29.

Tas, R.F.J. (1992) 'Huwelijksontbindingstafel naar duur van het huwelijk, 1986–1990.' In *Maandstatistiek voor de Bevolking*, nr. 6, 31–37.

Trimbos, C. (1955) *Zorgenkinderen.* Utrecht: Het Spectrum.

TK (Tweede Kamer) 1958–1959a. Algemene weduwen- en wezenverzekering, Memorie van toelichting, 5390, nr 3.

TK (Tweede Kamer) 1958–1959b. Algemene weduwen- en wezenverzekering, Nota naar aanleiding van het verslag, 5390, nr 9.

Valk, L. van der (1986) *Van pauperzorg tot bestaanszekerheid. Armenzorg in Nederland 1912–1965.* Amsterdam: IISG.

Wel, F. van (1992) 'De ongehuwde moeder in de media van de jaren zestig.' In *Jeugd en Samenleving*, nr. 7/8, 430–444.

Wiemann, B. (1988) 'Opkomst en neergang van de ongehuwde-moederzorg in Nederland (1880–1985).' *Amsterdam Sociologisch Tijdschrift 15*, 2, 337–368.

Weuring, R. (1996) *Alleenstaand moederschap: Een zelfstandig bestaansrecht?* Doctoraalscriptie Vakgroep ASW, Universiteit van Utrecht.

WRR (Wetenschappelijke Raad voor het Regeringsbeleid) (1990) *Een werkend perspectief. Arbeidsparticipatie in de jaren '90.'s.* Gravenhage: SDU uitgeverij.

CHAPTER FIVE

The Parent–Worker Model: Lone Mothers in Sweden[1]

Barbara Hobson and Mieko Takahashi

Lone mothers have become a visible and disputed category in policy discourse in many Western democracies. They are the subject of expert commissions, they have been discussed as a social problem or social threat in the media, and they are now confronted with new laws and policies that affect their economic and social well being. This rising tide of moral panic around single-parent house-holds, most notably in Britain and the United States, reflects concern about marital dissolution and increasing numbers of never-married mothers (Lewis and Ostner 1995; Lister 1993; Mclanahan, Sorensen and Watson 1989). Not to be forgotten in the politicised discourse on lone motherhood, however, is the competition for provisions and services in an era of welfare state retrench-ment, what Nancy Fraser (1989) has aptly called the welfare wars.

The lone mothers category has been conspicuously absent in Swedish discourse and policymaking since the 1970s. If one were to characterise the central principle guiding Swedish social policy toward lone mothers, the keywords would be *integration* and *inclusion* within the policy framework developed for working parents. This principle has hidden or made invisible the economic and social pressures placed upon lone parents as breadwinners and carers in families. However it has meant that lone mothers have not been stigmatised or singled out as a deviant group.

In this chapter we want to suggest that Sweden is a paradigm case of the weak male breadwinner society through a set of policies that promoted a two

1 We are indebted to Joakim Palme for his valuable help with the LIS data and Åsa Enström for her contribution as legal researcher. Ingegerd Municio gave us helpful comments. We are also very grateful Jane Lewis for her insightful reading of the manuscript at different stages and to the helpful suggestions from the other contributors in this project.

earner family, what Hobson (1995) has referred to as a parent–worker model. What does this imply for lone mothers? To what extent has the dismantling of the male-breadwinner wage undermined the category of lone mothers in policy content as well as neutralised the differences between lone and partnered mothers? What are the costs of the parent–worker model for the lone mother? Finally, we want to consider whether the current fiscal crises and subsequent welfare state retrenchment may reverse the last two decades of inclusion and integration of lone mothers, as they appear more and more as a deviant category in a policy formula that seeks to transfer greater economic responsibility to individual family members.

Before turning to the assumptions underlying the early formulation of policy for lone mothers, we want to summarise the basic contours of the parent–worker model that Sweden exemplifies. The male-breadwinner ideology, which has characterised most European welfare states, is weakest in the Scandinavian countries. The parent–worker model assumes all mothers will be active labour force participants and that care services are available and affordable for working parents. It also provides compensations for care (benefits for parental leave and payment to care for sick children) that are based upon one's employment status and calculated as a proportion of one's salary. These policies have enabled Swedish women to form autonomous households without the risk of poverty and stigmatisation. In comparison to countries with moderate and strong male-breadwinner ideologies, the parent–worker model has resulted in low rates of economic dependency in marriage (*see* Figure 5.1) and low rates of poverty for single mothers. Earnings are the main source of the lone mothers income package (*see* Figure 5.2).

However, there are costs and benefits in the construction of the lone mother as parent–worker (Hobson 1995). In order to evaluate what are the positive or negative features of the model for lone mothers both in the period of welfare state expansion and current period of contraction, it is useful to consider exactly how lone mothers have been fitted into a specific policy logic.

This chapter has three parts: the first looks at early formation of policy toward lone mothers. The second considers the continuities and discontinuities in the parent–worker model. In the third, we compare lone and partnered mothers across a range of variables and present some of the recent debates of the consequences of welfare state retrenchment for lone mothers in a weak male breadwinner policy framework.

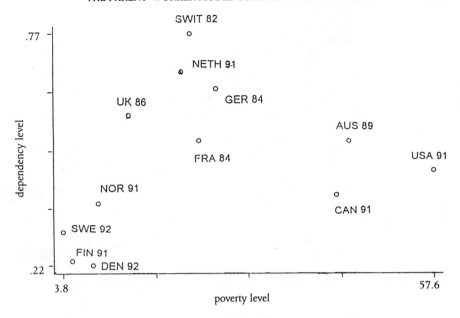

Source: LIS data (The above numbers are years.)

Figure 5.1 Economic dependency of married women and poverty rate of lone mothers, different years

Country, year	Dependency level	Poverty level
Sweden, 1992	.30	3.8
Norway, 1991	.37	8.9
Finland, 1991	.23	5.1
Denmark, 1992	.22	8.1
Netherlands, 1991	.68	20.9
France, 1984	.52	23.5
Germany, 1984	.64	26.0
UK, 1986	.58	13.3
Switzerland, 1982	.77	22.2
USA, 1991	.45	57.6
Australia, 1989	.52	45.2
Canada, 1991	.39	43.4

Note: We would like to thank the research staff at the LIS.

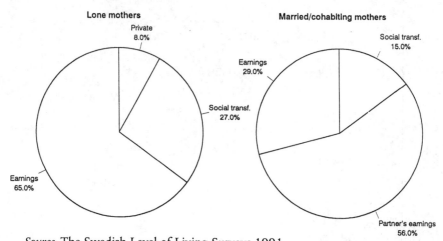

Source: The Swedish Level of Living Surveys 1991

Figure 5.2 Household income packages: lone and married/cohabiting mothers, 1991

Policy development

Swedish lone mothers have always been breadwinners for their families, and since the first decades of the twentieth century the state has taken responsibility for protecting their children. But the interpretation of their needs and their fit into the broader policy logic changed dramatically in the parent–worker model developed in the 1970s. The response to lone mothers is a history of struggles and conflicts involving the interpretations of family, as reflected in debates framed around gender and class inequalities and breadwinning and caring. Most importantly, it is story about *parents* and children, that is about the construction of motherhood and fatherhood and the welfare state's interventionist stance in defining the best interests of children (Ohrlander 1986).

A radical break with the past occurred with the 1917 Swedish law (*Svenska för fattnings samlig*: SSFS 1917, p.376), which established new principles concerning the rights of children born outside wedlock to know both their mother and father. This new policy ended a long-standing tradition that permitted even the mother to remain anonymous, which dated back to 1778 when the Swedish King sought to prevent child murder by allowing unmarried mothers the right to have their names omitted from the parish registers (Malmström 1969). Clearly, however, it was the father's anonymity that the law sought to end and the rationale was twofold:

(1) to ensure the child's right to know his or her mother and father[2]

---

2   Before this change in the law a 1910 investigation by Statistical Central Bureau of Sweden showed that only 5 per cent of the fathers were brought before the court – the procedure used for formal registration of paternity for children born outside of wedlock (Elgán 1990, p.483).

(2) that registered fathers would then bear the cost of supporting their out-of-wedlock children and thus improve the situation of the lone mother and her child (Social Handbook 1925).

The debates and investigations that preceded and followed the passage of this legislation underscored the high risk of poverty and crime among children born outside of wedlock; fathers who did not take responsibility for their children, more than lone mothers, were viewed as blameworthy. The remedy was therefore to develop policies to legally bind fathers to provide economic support for their children born out-of-wedlock. This involved a court proceeding to determine paternity and to assess the amount of child support.

Establishing paternity was only the first step in the highly interventionist stance of the Swedish local and national authorities. The legal principle guiding paternity law was negative probability, a man had to prove that he was not the biological father: this often meant obtaining evidence that the mother had intercourse with other men during the period of conception (Agell 1986; Saldeén 1993). The 1917 law provided fairly strong measures for enforcing paternity obligations. Once assigned by the court as the biological father, a man could have support deducted directly from his pay.[3] Debt collectors could confiscate his property to pay his share of child support. Fathers of children born outside of marriage were not permitted to leave the country. The most draconian measure was commitment to the workhouse; the threat of virtual imprisonment hung over biological fathers of illegitimate children who lacked employment or a steady income, referred to in policy discourse as a 'failed breadwinner'. A central component of the 1917 law concerning children born outside of wedlock was the assignment of a social welfare officer appointed by the local municipality, to oversee the financial support and care of children born outside marriage. The role of the social welfare officer included establishing paternity and enforcing child supports payments from the father.

In practice, the law did not work as intended. The process was cumbersome: first tracking down the father who failed to provide economic support, then bringing him to court and finally obtaining a judgement in court against him. As the welfare officer was unpaid (in the majority of cases it was a woman) there were not enough volunteers to pursue delinquent fathers (Elgán 1990). By the end of the 1930s a Swedish Commission found that while the majority of children born out-of-wedlock knew their fathers, their economic situation was not improving[4] (SOU 1936: 47, p.40).

---

3   One contemporary source claimed that this was used often by the Children's Board (*barnvårdsnamnd*) (Social Handbook 1925), but it is important to keep in mind that a very small percentage of fathers were actually taken to court.

4   Among children born outside wedlock in the 1930s, only 9 per cent in cities and 13 per cent in the countryside did not have a known father (SOU 1936: 47, p.30).

During the 1930s the Social Democratic party became the dominant political party in Sweden and new policies were put in place to protect the rights of children, some of which directly or indirectly addressed the economic situation of lone mothers. In 1937 advanced income payment (*bidrogsförskott* – hereafter referred to as income maintenance payments) for lone mothers was introduced in Sweden (SFS 1937: 383 and SOU: 1936: 47). Lone mothers, who were divorced, separated, or never-married were assured payment from the state for child support and the state then sought to collect what it could from the absent father. Unlike the widow's pension, which was an entitlement for a wife's service to her worker husband, this benefit was means-tested. It was not, however, a care allowance which was the rationale for the American child welfare system (Aid to Dependent Children) which assumed mothers on welfare would not be wage-earners.

As a result of her low wages and poverty the lone mother could not assume the breadwinner role without the support of the biological father and the financial backing of the state. Therefore the absent father's economic contribution was calculated as part of the family wage, that is as support for children rather than support for mothers who cared for children at home. In this context of the family wage and male breadwinning, the state acted as mediator or middle man, as the collector and distributor of this benefit, by forwarding payment when fathers were delinquent. Though mothers were still economically dependent on a husband's contribution they nevertheless did not have to negotiate directly with him. However, lone mothers who were unable to name the father or who refused to name him were denied income maintenance payment; those who were poor had to rely on social assistance. This stipulation in the law, which required lone mothers to name the father in order to be eligible for advanced payment did not change until the 1970s.[5]

In this early stage of welfare state formation one can discern the ambivalent attitude of policymakers toward the respective responsibilities of the mother, the father, and the state. On the one hand, the lone mother was assumed to be the mainstay of support for her children, with the dual roles of breadwinner and carer. On the other hand, the lone mother was characterised as someone who could not take care of herself and was in need of guardianship and strict supervision. Up until they were 16 all children born out-of-wedlock, whether the parents were cohabiting or living alone, had a social welfare officer assigned to them. Implicit in this construction of guardianship was social control and surveillance (Ohrlander 1986; Winkler 1996). The social welfare officer exhorted mothers under her charge to breast feed and every month she reported on how they managed their household economy and used state benefits (Elgán

---

5   Readers may wish to compare the history and the current debates on child support in Britain, see Chapter Two.

1990).[6] Alva Myrdal in her book on family and nation written at the end of the 1930s, remarked on the oversight and supervision exerted by the child welfare officer, stating that parents often married to get rid of them (Myrdal 1948).

Thus in the social policy of the emerging Swedish welfare state, lone mothers were placed within the category of the irresponsible poor rather than within a gender specific discourse of immoral women. Much of the debate in this period revolved around removing the stigma attached to illegitimate children (*oakta barn*) and there were even debates on whether children born outside marriage should have inheritance rights (Elgán 1990).[7] In the redistributive family policies of the 1930s lone mothers were given the same general benefits as married mothers. As mothers they were entitled to free pre- and post-natal care, as poor mothers they were given a means-tested benefit aimed in fact at working mothers to encourage them to have more babies (Ohlander 1991). Finally, as citizen workers unmarried and divorced mothers were protected under the married women's 'right to work' law (Hobson 1994) which forbade employers from firing a woman who married or became pregnant. Equally lone mothers could take advantage of the right to mother's leave for three months, which was paid in the public sector and unpaid with the right to return to their jobs in the private sector (SOU 1938: 2).

Over the following decades two trends in Swedish social policy helped to remove both the stigma attached to lone motherhood and the distinctions between children born inside and outside of marriage: the dismantling of the male-breadwinner wage through the radical restructuring of tax laws and the recasting of custody and marriage laws; and the move toward universalising benefits for children and working parents.

Continuities and discontinuities

Dismantling the male-breadwinner wage

The dismantling of the male-breadwinner wage was the major reform of the 1970s, a watershed decade in Swedish social policy, in which a range of policies were introduced that sought to remove or at least reduce gender differences in both labour-market participation and care responsibilities. Perhaps more than any other reform the introduction of individual taxation shook the foundations of the male breadwinner wage. Whereas the tax laws had always favoured a working man with a dependent wife, the new law actually penalised single

---

6 The social welfare officer became less involved with paternity cases and tracking down delinquent fathers after the introduction of the income maintenance policy. As the state took over the job of collecting child support from absent fathers, the social welfare officer became more absorbed in overseeing home conditions.

7 The question of inheritance rights was resolved in the 1970s revised parental codes that removed distinctions between children of married and unmarried parents (*see* discussion below).

earner families. Every crown a married women earned was extra income in the two earner family (Gustafsson 1990; Gustafsson and Bruyn-Hundt 1992) Extensive daycare, parental leave benefits and the right to work part-time during the early years of childrearing were part of the incentives to induce women to enter the labour market (Sundström and Stafford 1991).

It is important to keep in mind that all these reforms followed a decade of debate around what should be the role of social policy in promoting family forms – whether there should be family-centred policies versus individual-centred policies and whether the goal should be to redistribute resources to reduce inequalities among families or within families, that is whether claims for low-income families should take precedence over claims for gender equality (Winkler 1996).

These contests were bound up with debates around the 'freedom to choose' that involved compensations for care either in the form of services or mother's care allowance. The Conservative Party, now called the Moderate Party, sought a tax deduction. On the other hand the farmers party called the Centre Party, argued for a care allowance to be paid to the mother for staying at home with her children, similar to the proposal for mother's endowment in Britain in the pre-war period (see Chapter 2). Women in both the Liberal Party and the Social Democratic Party realised that it was not possible to have both extensive municipal daycare and care allowances.[8] Strategically Social Democratic women sought to undermine support in their party for the allowance by employing a discourse of class solidarity. They argued that a care allowance was 'unsolidaris-tic' with working mothers and lone mothers who did not have the freedom of choice; it was a freedom only for a class of women who were married and whose husbands earned enough to support a family (Winkler 1996).

The question of the right to choose was addressed in the published report of the Commission on Family and Marriage which reported in 1972. A long and exhaustive document analysing policy and its consequences for changing patterns in Swedish families, the report acknowledged that while certain kinds of measures would stimulate married women to enter labour market work others would have a 'break' effect. This opened up the debate on social policy initiatives and gender equality (SOU: 1972: 41).

Many of the changes in policy toward lone mothers were the result of this pathbreaking government Commission on Family and Marriage which altered the discursive terrain on the family and made policy recommendations that

---

8   One can find parallels between the arguments made by Social Democratic women against the care allowance (care voucher) that was enacted by the right wing coalition in the 1990s and these earlier debates of the 1950s and 1960s. The 1990 law allowed women to take a small subsidy instead of a municipal daycare place, or even reduce their use of daycare hours and take a partial subsidy. Social Democratic women in the 1990s were unanimous in their opposition to the care voucher system (whereas in the 1960s some Social Democratic women favoured a care allowance). Their vigorous campaign led to its demise when the Social Democrats returned to power in 1994.

resulted in a revamping of the laws pertaining to marriage and cohabitation. The main conclusion of the Commission was that policy should be neutral in relation to family forms, and furthermore, how parents organise their relationship should not affect their rights and duties to their children. Joint custody was put forward as the norm for divorced parents and the revised law gave non-married parents the same rights to joint custody. The guiding principle in this policy was that it was to the child's advantage to have good contact with both parents even if the child lived with only one parent. In contrast to earlier policy on the father's obligations, joint custody was taken to imply both cash and care responsibilities. Not only did the legal distinctions between children born within and without marriage disappear,[9] but the distinctions between married and unmarried parents were blurred in law and withered away in practice.[10]

The 1972 Commission recommendations were a response to broader societal shifts in ideologies and practices: changing patterns of marriage and cohabitation, the rise in women's labour force participation, and the growing numbers of women who were now wage-earners, all of which helped to produce greater equality among men and women in families. Embedded within the policies that emerged from the new family policy was a view of father's responsibility for care. The joint-custody norm now implied that this was expected of divorced fathers. At the same time the assumption that women would be in the labour force and be economically independent shadowed the construction of the father's financial obligations.

Wide variations existed in the amount of maintenance fathers had to pay throughout the post war period since it was calculated on the basis of ability to pay and the child's needs. However, it became more and more common to permit the biological father to reserve income for his new family. Beginning in the 1970s fathers were able to get approval for reducing support for many reasons. One notable court case allowed a father to discontinue his support because he took leave from his job to further his education, which the court construed as a valid claim since it could be interpreted as a response to labour market conditions (see NJA 1978, p.362.)

Alongside unmarried fathers' rights in custody cases was a growing recognition of lone mothers' rights to form autonomous households. One of the Family and Marriage Commission's recommendations was to abolish the requirement for mothers to name the father as a condition of eligibility for the child support guarantee (SOU 1972: 34, 318). Hence the social rights of

---

9   In the 1977 revised codes, children born out-of-wedlock were given the same rights and the same legal standing as children of married parents (Saldeén 1993).

10 Although the parental code of 1949 had brought together the obligations of both parents to support children whether married or unmarried, these distinctions appeared no longer relevant with the changing family patterns and the expanded role of the state support for lone mothers.

mothers were expanded and the assumption that lone mother families were 'incomplete families' was no longer embedded in the law.

Finally, the policy of assigning never-married mothers a social welfare officer was abandoned in the 1970s. This was the last remnant of the 1917 law that defined lone mothers as a category in need of guardianship by the state. The arguments against it were expressions of a new feminist and gender consciousness. Several motions by women in Parliament openly challenged guardianship for lone mothers as discriminatory to women who chose not to marry (see Winkler 1996). They claimed that to be assigned a welfare officer because of one's marital status labelled lone mothers as category of weak and incompetent mothers. Furthermore, they maintained that over half the lone mothers were not young women and that many married mothers were in need of supervision. Those who defended the principle of guardianship argued that unmarried mothers not in need of supervision should support those vulnerable teenage mothers who needed guardianship (Winkler 1996). At the heart the matter was whether the state should promote certain family forms. Equally important, this debate made visible the issues of gender equality and linked them to a mother's right to form a household.

Within the discourse and policy that emerged in the 1970s one could see a changing perception of lone mothers as no longer a distinct group of mothers but rather as marking a stage in the life course. In fact, the more universal benefits and services became, the more invisible lone mothers became in family policy.

Universalising benefits

In the post World War II era the Swedish welfare state developed its unique model defined by its institutional or universalist construction of social citizenship rights (Korpi 1989; Esping-Andersen 1990). Within family policy the shift toward universalist entitlement came early with the introduction of the child allowance policy in 1947. The universal benefit implicitly challenged the rationale for means-testing benefits for income maintenance payments to lone mothers. More and more policymakers recognised that children of lone mothers should enjoy the greater prosperity of Swedish society and the higher wages that workers, mainly men, were now getting (Winkler 1996). Payments to lone mothers increased in the 1950s but the core of the policy remained, that fathers should support children and women were tied to fathers economically. However, in 1964 the child support payment became a child support guarantee (meaning that the state benefit was raised above the income maintenance payment fixed in law). The state benefit not only raised payments but indexed them to inflation (SFS 1964: 143). Thus the benefit took the form of a social citizenship right that assured children of lone mothers a better living standard.

Another crucial component in the universalist mode of providing benefits and services came in the form of subsidised public daycare for children. The massive investment in municipal daycare that sought to create a high quality single standard of care for children broke down the distinctions between public care of poor women's children (many of them lone mothers) and private care of the children in the majority of families. Subsidised daycare centres were few and far between in the period before the expansion in the 1970s and those that existed were for poor working mothers, many of them lone mothers (Nyberg 1996). Poor working women were those who used the public daycare system;[11] middle class children attended private nurseries for pedagogical reasons and because their mothers were in paid work. Once again Social Democratic women were key actors in the discursive battles around childcare. First, they maintained that means-testing and prioritising daycare for lone mothers tended to create a stratified system of daycare. Second, they argued that investment in daycare would eliminate the distinctions between married and unmarried women.

The living standards of lone mothers rose in the post-war period with increased benefit levels for the worst off beginning with the housing allowance in the 1950s. Though means-tested, this had a high threshold that took into account the number of children and a range of the expenses that both lone and coupled parents faced in their daily lives. Throughout the 1960s and 70s, the wage solidarity policy, in which unions negotiated the highest pay rises for low wage-earners, benefited female workers in general (le Grand 1994) and improved the living standard of lone mothers, who were often low waged workers and the main breadwinners for their families. Parental leave benefits, public subsidised daycare, and paid sick days for parents to care for children were benefits for all working parents and supported women who wanted to combine labour market work with childrearing responsibilities.

Workers, mothers, and carers

From one perspective one can see that the policy logic regarding lone mothers remained constant during this period of innovation around parenting and paid work. It was always assumed that lone mothers would be employed full-time. As Celia Winkler (1996) points out, the Swedish Parliamentary debates about the dilemmas arising from women's roles as mothers and carers considered only married mothers. Such a position was evident in the 1955 Commission on families and work: 'When an unmarried or divorced woman begins her existence as a lone mother, society assumes that she obtains funds for her support and her children's support through paid work' [author's translation] (SOU: 1955: 29, 283). Similarly

---

11 Anita Nyberg (1996, p.98) found that throughout the 1940s and as late as 1955, approximately 40 per cent of Swedish children in public daycare were those of lone mothers, which included widows and divorced women as well as never-married women.

the 1963 Social Policy Committee appointed by Parliament to investigate single mothers, cited two causes of their economic distress: (1) low wages of the mother; (2) lack of a second income to the family economy. No one in the Commission addressed the double burden of lone mothers as primary breadwinners and carers (Winkler 1996).

The refusal to target benefits for lone mothers as a special category could be seen as a strategy to prevent stigmatisation. This was the position of Social Democratic women. From another perspective, however, it was also a reflection of a policy framework that did not make distinctions between different types of workers. Thus when the Liberal Party put up a motion to provide sick pay for single working mothers it was rejected by the Social Democratic party because it did not apply to all parents and could be subject to abuse (Winkler 1996). Lone mothers could enjoy this benefit only after it became a universal benefit for all working parents in 1972.

By the end of the 1970s the social services and parental leave benefits that formed the core of the parent–worker model were in place. The process of inclusion and integration of lone mothers involved a radical restructuring of policies and changing ideologies and practices. First and foremost, the policy supports for the male breadwinner wage were dismantled and the male-breadwinner ideology was abandoned.[12] The dominant idiom in the 1970s was *jamlikhet* (equality between different groups) which expressed the goal of equal participation of men and women in work and family life. However, the discourse on sex roles and the policies that ensued from it reveal its reformist rather than its radical approach to restructuring of the private sphere through individual taxation and family reforms (daycare and parental leave (Sainsbury 1993). In effect the false universalism embedded in the ideology of equality between the sexes underscored the disjuncture between the rhetoric of equality and the practice. This was revealed in the studies of low rates of fathers taking parental leave (Näsman 1995) and the persistence of high levels of married women's economic dependency (Hobson 1990).

However, what did occur throughout the 1970s and 1980s was a lessening of differences between married and lone mothers. This is evident as one examines both the trends in lone parenting and the similarities and differences between lone and married/cohabitant mothers.

Comparisons of lone and married mothers[13]

Trends

Despite the fact that over the last two decades the proportion of Swedish single parent households has almost doubled (*see* Table 5.1), lone mothers have not

---

12 This is in comparison to the strong breadwinner ideology that was sustained throughout this period of feminist activism in Holland (Knijn 1994) and Britain (*see* Lewis in this volume and Land 1994).

13 Data for this section are derived from the Swedish Level of Living Surveys conducted by the Swedish Institute for Social Research in 1968, 1981 and 1991 (for more detail about the survey and data, *see* Erikson and Åberg 1987; Fritzell and Lundberg 1994). We have selected persons under age 66 who had at least one child under 17 years old living in their household during the time of the survey.

been targeted as a problem group in policy debates. As is the case in most welfare states, there have been changes in the marital status of lone mothers; the vast majority are divorced or never-married mothers rather than widows (*see* Table 5.1). Another shift in the composition of lone-parent households is that the proportion of lone mothers who have at least one child under seven years has increased over the last two decades (*see* Table 5.2) Nevertheless, a discourse on the decline of the traditional family has little resonance in Sweden in contrast to the situation in Britain and the United States. This is a reflection of the tolerance for different patterns of partnering in Scandinavian countries, as discussed above, in which cohabitant couples are given the same recognition in the social system as married couples.[14]

Table 5.1 Proportion of lone-parent families: 1968, 1981 and 1991 (%)

	1968	1981	1991
Two parents	91.3	87.2	85.0
Solo mothers	7.3	11.1	13.0
Solo fathers	1.4	1.7	2.0
Total	1003	973	857

Source: The Swedish Level of Living Surveys 1968, 1981 and 1991

Table 5.2 Marital status of lone mothers: 1968, 1981 and 1991 (%)

Year	Age	Single*	Divorced	Widow	Total	Age (%)
1968	19–29	70.0	25.0	5.0	20	27.4
	30–44	12.9	37.4	9.7	31	42.5
	45–65	13.6	50.0	36.4	22	30.1
	ALL	28.8	54.8	16.4	73	100.0
1981	19–29	91.3	8.7	-	23	21.7
	30–44	29.4	64.7	5.9	68	64.1
	45–65	6.7	73.3	20.0	15	14.1
	ALL	39.6	53.8	6.6	108	100.0
1991	19–29	93.7	6.3	-	16	14.8
	30–44	56.3	42.3	1.4	71	65.7
	45–65	19.1	57.1	23.8	21	19.4
	ALL	54.6	39.8	5.6	108	100.0

*Single means persons who have never been legally married.
Source: The Swedish Level of Living Surveys 1968, 1981 and 1991.

---

14 In contrast to the United States, where a significant proportion of lone mothers are 'single' and have not cohabited with the father of their child (particularly Afro-American women), Swedish lone mothers tend to have cohabited with at least one partner (86.4 per cent of those who are lone mothers claimed this).

Surveys in the early 1990s reveal that lone and partnered (married\cohabitant) mothers had become strikingly similar to one another across a range of variables: average age, education, labour force activity, and socio-economic class. Perhaps the dimension that is key to interpreting the experiences of married and lone mothers is that both spend a significant part of their time in paid work. Over 84 per cent of mothers in Sweden are labour force participants and the numbers of women in full-time employment has increased in the last ten years. Lone mothers were less like married mothers before the dramatic surge in women's labour force participation in Sweden. Whereas in 1968 only 15 per cent of lone mothers were housewives compared to 55 per cent of married mothers, by 1991 as many married mothers as lone mothers were participating in the labour market.

The social and economic costs for lone mothers

Clearly there are costs involved in lone parenting that are made invisible by treating them as single income earners who happen to be parents. Lone mothers have fewer resources than married/cohabitant mothers, in terms of time, money, and social networks. Looking at the economic resources of working mothers, we can see that lone mothers are relatively much poorer on average than married mothers. If we compare adjusted income by family size, lone mothers have about 23 per cent less income than married mothers, have more than twice the poverty rate of married mothers and they are eleven times as likely to be receiving some form of social allowance. If we consider the income packages of lone mothers we find that income maintenance payments represent only eight per cent of lone mothers income package, whereas social transfers comprise 27 per cent (see Figure 5.2).

Suppose we consider time resources. Lone mothers have tended to opt for full-time work. Whereas only about a third of married mothers had full-time employment in 1981, more than half the lone mothers were in full-time jobs. A still larger proportion of lone mothers were in full time employment by 1991 (66.3% compared to 50.8%). Lone mothers are thus relatively time poor (considering both paid and unpaid work hours). Compared to married women, lone mothers spend on average an hour and a quarter more in employment than married mothers: their average work week, which includes both paid and unpaid work, is over 54 hours per week, 3.3 hours more than the 51 hour working week of married mothers (see Figure 5.3). This suggests that lone mothers have less time for leisure and less time to spend with their children.

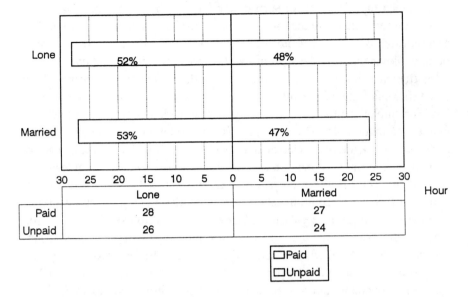

Source: The Swedish Level of Living Surveys 1991
Figure 5.3 Paid and unpaid work hours: lone and married/cohabiting mothers, 1991

Lone mothers in the current period of restructuring

Lone mothers In Sweden, as well in Denmark (see Chapter 6 in this volume), have been treated as single income earner families by policymakers. Thus the main source of their social citizenship rights has been their status as working parents and as parents in poor families in need of social assistance or housing allowances. Gender differences disappear in this conceptualisation, which does not take into account the gendered wage gap or the extent to which most women with children have previously been economically dependent on their husband's earnings.[15]

In fact the Swedish case underscores the dilemma in the construction of the parent–worker model because it assumes that women and men are similarly situated in the labour market. As Figure 5.2 illustrates, the differences in economic well-being between a lone mother and a married mother's household is due to a husband's wage (which on average accounts for 56% of the family income).

15 In Sweden in the 1990s women's economic dependency dropped precipitously over the decade. We used a standard measure of economic dependency in families (Hobson 1990), which represented the gap between the wife's and the husband's proportion of family income, based on pre-tax earnings. Thus we found that Swedish married/cohabitant women had a 24.2 per cent dependency rate. Among married/cohabitant women with children under 17, it was 31 per cent.

In the current fiscal crisis the threats to lone mothers in the parent–worker model are twofold: (1) reductions in social transfers and benefits that make up a significant portion of lone mothers' income; and (2) more ominous, the threat of unemployment itself. The parent–worker model is built around two assumptions that may no longer be relevant given the current restructuring of the Swedish welfare state that will reshape the organisation of paid work: (1) high levels of employment; and (2) a sharing of care work among parents (men and women) so that employers do not penalise workers who have to combine paid and unpaid work (i.e. those who do not have a partner who does all the carework).

Citizenship rights of parents, such as child sick days and parental leave, are policies that remain intact and are essential for married parents and for lone parents if they are to combine labour market work and family responsibilities. In a period of high unemployment, however, those who exercise these rights may be disadvantaged as competition for jobs increases. The most recent statistics (AKU 1995) suggest some disturbing trends: lone mothers show a steep rise in unemployment from 4 per cent in 1985 to 12 per cent in 1995. Married/cohabitant mothers have not reached these unemployment levels during the same period.

Conclusion

What has been distinctive about the Swedish response to lone mothers over the last two decades is their *inclusion* within the policy framework developed for working parents. This principle has made invisible the economic and social pressures on lone parents as breadwinners and carers in families. It has also camouflaged various forms of benefits that lone mothers receive – housing allowance, daycare subsidies and social assistance – that are in effect compensations for their care work. As parents who have the main responsibility for childrearing they are disadvantaged in the labour market. As single earners, they lack the economic resources to maintain a household. What feminist scholars have called 'women friendly' policies (Hernes 1987; Siim 1994) have been policies that have enabled lone mothers to be heads of households without the risk of poverty. However, the services and benefits for low-income families, in which lone mothers are over-represented, are no longer assured.

Things are changing so rapidly that for the first time in decades concern for lone mothers as a problem category has begun to emerge in public debate (Bjornberg 1996). While lone mothers are not seen as a threat, they appear as a group who do not fit into the current strategies to make Swedish industry more competitive by reducing social spending.

On the one side, one finds articles in the newspapers about the poverty and unemployment lone mothers are now experiencing. At the very same time, a recent Commission, which published its findings in the debate pages of the leading newspaper, argued against continuing a policy of granting social assistance for lone mothers. They maintained that this kind of assistance should be short term and was not meant for this category of full-time workers. Their conclusion was that full-time workers should have wages high enough to support themselves without having to rely on social assistance, but they did not offer any policy initiatives to achieve this.

The right to form one's own household without fear of poverty is being undermined in Sweden by the restructuring and retrenchment of the welfare state in the 1990s. This policy shift away from less universal benefits and services toward more privatised solutions for the care of children and the elderly foreshadows a widening poverty gap between women who are in two earner families and women who are lone parents (Hobson and Takahashi 1996). As care services become more expensive, only those women with highly paid and secure employment will be able to take part in the parent–worker model. This prospect suggests an increased stratification among Swedish women and even among lone mothers. In confronting a worsening situation for lone mothers Swedish women in Parliament (now 44%) and femocrats in the Swedish social welfare bureaucracy face a dilemma about whether to support targeted and categorical benefits for lone mothers. These would improve the economic situation of lone mothers, but equally would undermine the basic premises of the parent–worker model: that lone mothers should not be differentiated from all mothers and that a social service state should create policy incentives to encourage both fathers and mothers to be equal participants in paid work and family life.

References

Acker, J. (1992) 'Två diskurser om reformer och kvinnor i den framtida välfärdsstaten.' In A. Baude, U. Bjornberg and E. Dahlstrom (eds) *Kvinnors och Mäns Liv och Arbete.* Stockholm: SNA Förlag.

Agell, A. (1986) *Underhåll till Barn och Make.* Uppsala: Instus Förlag.

AKU (Labour Force Survey) (1985, 1995) Stockholm: Statistiska Centralbyrån (Data from 1995 is unpublished).

Björnberg, U. (1996) 'Ensamstående, mördrarm Sverige.' In *Kvinnorna och Välfärstaten.* FRN Report 96, 8, 82–94.

Elgán, E. (1990) 'En far till var kvinnas barn: Politik och debatt angående män, kvinnor och oäkta barn in Sverige och Frankrike vid seklets början.' *Historisk Tidskrift 4,* 481–505.

Erikson, R. and Åberg, R. (1987) *Welfare in Transition. A Survey of Living Conditions in Sweden 1968–1981.* Oxford: Clarendon Press.

Esping-Andersen, G. (1990) *The Three Worlds of Welfare Capitalism.* New Jersey: Princeton University Press.

Fraser, N. (1989) *Unruly Practices: Power, Discourse and Gender in Contemporary Social Theory.* Minneapolis: University of Minnesota Press.

Fritzell, J. and Lundberg, O. (1994) *Vardagens Villkor. Levnadsförhållanden i Sverige under tre decennier.* Stockholm: Bromberg.

Gustafsson, S. (1990) 'The labour force participation and earnings of lone parents: a review of Swedish policies and institutions with some comparisons to West Germany.' In *OECD Outlook, Lone-Parent Families,* Social Policy Studies. Paris: OECD.

Gustafsson, S. and Bruyn-Hundt, M. (1992) 'Incentives for women to work: a comparison between the Netherlands, Sweden, and West Germany.' *Journal of Economic Studies 18,* 30–65.

Hernes, H. (1987) *Welfare State and Women Power: Essays in State Feminism.* Oslo: Norwegian University Press.

Hobson, B. (1990) 'No exit, no voice: women's economic dependency and the welfare state.' *Acta Sociologica 33,* 235–249.

Hobson, B. (1994) 'Solo mothers, policy regimes, and the logics of gender.' In D. Sainsbury (ed) *Gendering Welfare States.* London: Sage Publications.

Hobson B. (1995) 'Remaking the boundaries of women's citizenship and the dilemma of dependency.' In T. Gordon and Kaupinen-Toropainen (ed) *Unsolved Dillemmas: Women, Work, and the Family in the United States, Europe and the Soviet Union.* London: Avebury.

Hobson, B. and Takahashi, M. (1996) 'Genusperspektiv på det sociala medborgarskapet. En studie av ensamstående mödrar.' In J. Palme and I. Wennemo (eds) *General Välfärd: Hot och Möjligheter.* Välfärdsprojektets skriftserie nr 3. Socialdepartementet.

Knijn, T. (1994) 'Fish without bikes: revision of the Dutch welfare states and its consequences for the (in)dependence of single mothers.' *Social Politics: International Studies in Gender, State, and Society 1,* 1, 83–105.

Korpi, W. (1989) *Power, Politics and State Autonomy in the Development of Social Citizenship, Social Rights During Sickness in Eighteen OECD Countries Since 1939.* Swedish Institute for Social Research. Report No. 245.

Land, H. (1994) 'The demise of the male breadwinner in practice but not in theory: a challenge for social security systems.' In S. Baldwin and J. Falkingham (eds) *Social Security and Social Change: New Challenges to the Beveridge Model.* London: Harvester Wheatsheaf.

le Grand, C. (1994) 'Löneskillnaderna i Sverige: Förändring och nuvarande struktur.' In J. Fritzell and O. Lundberg (eds) *Vardagens Villkor. Levnadsförhållanden i Sverige Under Tre Decennier.* Stockholm: Brombergs förlag.

Lewis, J. and Ostner, I. (1995) 'Gender and the evolution of social policies.' In S. Leibfried and P. Pierson (eds) *European Social Policy: Between Fragmentation and Integration.* Washington DC: Brookings Institution.

Lister, R. (1993) 'Tracing the contours of women's citizenship.' *Policy and Politics 21,* 1, 3–16.

Lister, R. (1994) 'The child support act: shifting family financial obligations in the United Kingdom.' *Social Politics: International Studies of Gender, State, and Society 1,* Fall, 211–222.

Malmström, Å. (1969) *Föräldrarätt.* P A Norstedts & Söners Förlag.

Mclanahan, S., Sorensen, A. and Watson, R. (1989) 'Sex differences in poverty, 1950–1980.' *Signs 15*, 1, 102–122.

Myrdal, A. (1948) *Nation and Family.* London: Kegan Paul, Trench, Trubner & Co.

Näsman, E. (1995) 'Time, work and family life.' In B. Arve-Parés (ed) *Reconciling Work and Family Life – A Challenge for Europe?* Swedish National Committee on the International Year of Family and the Commission of the European Communities.

NJA (Nytt Jurist Arkiv): 1978.

Nyberg, A. (1996) 'Från fostermor till förskollärare.' In A. Berggren (ed) *Kvinnorna och Välfärden.* Stockholm: Forskningsrådsnämnden. 96–105.

Ohlander, A.S. (1991) 'The invisible child? The struggle for a social democratic family.' In G. Bock and P. Tnane (eds) *Maternity and Gender Policies.* London.

Ohrlander, K. (1986) *I barnens och nationens intresse: Socialliberal reformpolitik 1903–1930.*

Orloff, A.S. (1993) 'Gender and the social rights of citizenship: the comparative analysis of gender relations in the welfare states.' *American Sociological Review 58*, June, 303–328.

Palme, J. (1992) 'Nations of welfare: Comparing income inequalities among the pre-retirement elderly.' Paper presented at the Department of Sociology, Stockholm University, November 24.

Sainsbury, D. (1993) 'Dual welfare and sex segregation of access to social benefits: income maintenance policies in the UK, the US, the Netherlands and Sweden.' *Journal of Social Policy 22*, 1, pp.69–98.

Saldeén, Å. (1993) *Barn & Föräldrar.* Uppsala: Instus Förlag.

SFS (Svenska färfattnings samlig) 1917:376 *Om barn utom äktenskap.*

SFS 1933:229 *Om blodundersökning i mål om barn utom äktenskap.*

SFS 1937:383 *Om förskottering av underhållsbidrag till barn.*

SFS 1964:143 *Lag om bidragsförskott.*

Siim, B. (1994) 'Engendering democracy: social citizenship and political participation for women in Scandinavian.' *Social Politics: International Studies of Gender, State and Society 1*, 1, 286–305.

Social Handbook: Översikt av Offenligt och Enskilt Smahällsarget i Sverige (1925) G.H. Von Koch (ed) Stockholm: Las Hökerbergs Bokförlag.

SOU 1936:47 *Förskottering av underhållsbidrag till barn utom äktenskap.*

SOU 1938:2 *Betänkande angående gift kvinnas förvärvsarbete.*

SOU 1955: 29 *Samhället och Barnfamiljerna: Betänkande av 1954 års familjeutredning.*

SOU 1972:34 *Familjestöd.*

SOU 1972:41 *Familj och Äktenskap.*

SOU 1977:37 *Underhåll till Barn och Frånskilda.*

SOU 1990:8 *Samhällsstöd till Underhållsberättigade Barn.*

Sundström, M. and Stafford, F. (1991) *Female Labour Force Participation, Fertility and Public Policy.* Stockholm Research Reports in Demography 63: Stockholm University.

Winkler, C.C. (1996) *The Canary in the Coal Mine: Single Mothers and the Welfare State, the Swedish Experience.* Ph.D. Dissertation. Department of Sociology, University of Oregon.

CHAPTER SIX

Dilemmas of Citizenship in Denmark: Lone Mothers Between Work and Care

Birte Siim

Introduction

During the last 30 years there have been dramatic changes in women's position as mothers, workers and citizens. During the same period the Danish welfare state has undergone profound changes in the policies, organisation and values of work and caring. From a feminist perspective, one of the most far reaching changes has been the move from a male-breadwinner to a dual-breadwinner norm, that is the public and cultural expectation that both women and men will be wage workers. From the beginning of the 1970s the dual-breadwinner norm has been the guiding principle in public policies and has gradually become an accepted part of the political culture and of people's daily lives.

The dual-breadwinner norm is manifested in the dramatic increase in the labour-force participation of women during the last 30 years, with the result that women's activity rates are today approaching those of men: 79 per cent of all mothers with children under 10 have wage work compared to 95 per cent of all fathers in the same group, the highest proportion of working mothers in all the EU countries (Stenvig, Andersen and Lauersen 1994, p.37). In the European context, it is surprising that mothers with small children today have higher activity rates than women in general. As a consequence mothers – as well as fathers – face new problems of balancing wage work and care for children. At the same time there has been an increase in the number of lone mothers in Denmark called *eneforsørgere*, or single breadwinners. The Danish term is gender neutral and focuses on the roles of single parents as wage workers.

The Danish welfare state is, like the Nordic welfare states, built on a universalist welfare system where the public sector has from the mid-1970s played a crucial role in providing and financing social services. Danish, and

Nordic, family policies have been described as *child-oriented*, because they are concerned with the well-being of children. Historically, policies toward lone mothers were part and parcel of welfare policies directed toward children in poor and low-income families. Social policies have certainly had an *implicit* family dimension but there has been no tradition of *explicit* family policies directed exclusively towards married couples.[1]

In Denmark during the last 20 years there has been a high degree of *universalism* in access to transfers and services, which are tied to citizenship, rather than labour-market performance or the needs of the family. This universalism has been combined with a high degree of *individualisation* of social rights and duties of citizens in the sense that the individual has as a rule replaced the family and the household as the legal unit in public policy (Koch-Nielsen 1995). In the Danish welfare system the principles of universalism and individualisation have been accompanied by an expansion of social citizenship and the state has taken on new obligations towards the individual citizens in the form of social service provisions, especially child care services and caring for the elderly, sick, handicapped and disabled (Siim 1993).

There is a public debate about the implications of the changes in the relationship between working life and family life, and the Equal Status Council has initiated a project to generate a debate on future equality in this area.[2] Feminist studies have pointed out that there is a dilemma associated with the dual-breadwinner norm for women in Denmark: on the positive side women have gained the right, and obligation, to work and consequently mothers are, in general, expected to be wage workers and they in turn expect to have access to publicly provided, high quality day care. On the negative side, caring work for children is still unequally divided and sex segregation in the labour market is a barrier to gender equality. Segregation means that women work predominantly in the public sector and men in the private sector, and women on average work fewer hours and earn lower wages than men.

In Denmark, lone mothers and their children were from the 1930s targeted as a vulnerable social group in need of economic support and their income has historically come from the labour market, the state and from the absent father. After World War II, the Danish welfare state gradually moved toward universal social policies and the provision of child care in particular has become a key

---

1   Borchorst differentiates between direct and indirect familism. Direct familism exists when married men and women have different rights and when legislation focuses on men as the head of households. Indirect familism exists when the housewife–male-breadwinner family type is supported by legislation, so that married women are made financially dependent on their husbands (Borchorst 1995, p.169)

2   The relationship between working life and family life is also an area of special priority in the Danish Government's Action Plan on Gender Equality. The anthology '*The Equality Dilemma. Reconciling Working Life and Family Life Viewed in an Equality Perspective – the Danish Example*', 1994 (Carlson and Larson) is one of the important contributions to this debate published by the Equal Status Council.

element in family policy. After the oil crisis in 1973 unemployment increased in Denmark and during the 1980s was above the OECD average. The social and economic problems of two-earner families became a public political issue and a new political consensus between Right and Left was reached about an 'income package' that included both an increase in direct cash benefits and social service provisions. Since 1987 child/family benefits have included a family allowance per child, independent of income and labour market attachment, and on top of that lone parents receive an extra benefit (Knudsen 1990).

The change from a male-breadwinner to a dual-breadwinner model has equalised the situation of all mothers and the cultural image of lone mothers has changed from that of a weak and dependent group to a strong and autonomous group. During the last 20 years there has been a gradual increase in the proportion of lone mothers to 18 per cent of families with children in 1995. Lone mothers have not been singled out as an ideological problem or as a political issue, but there has been public concern about the growing number who are either unemployed or marginal to the labour market. Danish research has illustrated that the general problems of combining wage work and care for children are experienced more acutely by lone mothers. Wage work is crucial for the incomes of all mothers, but unemployment is a special problem for lone mothers who are dependent on one wage. The investigations indicate that lone mothers do not form a homogeneous group. Since the 1980s there has been a growing differentiation between a well-educated, employed group, who often lack the time to care, and a low-skilled, unemployed group who lack material resources (Thalow and Gamst 1987; Larsen and Sørensen 1994). The tendency toward polarisation among lone mothers can be interpreted as an expression of more general polarisation among well-educated and unskilled women caused by unemployment.

The Danish case illuminates both the importance and limitations of universalist public policies *vis-à-vis* mass unemployment. There has been a general growth of public expenditures for the elderly, children and families during the 1980s, in spite of mass unemployment and a Conservative–Centre government with the explicit objective of cutting the size of the public sector (Plovsing 1994). There has also been a growth in public expenditures on behalf of all families, both in terms of cash benefits and in terms of provision of social services (Hansen 1990). On the one hand, public policies have not been able to prevent mass unemployment, including an above average unemployment rate for lone mothers. On the other hand, there are no signs of a general tendency toward social marginalisation among the unemployed, lone mothers included (Goul Andersen 1996).

Feminist scholars have suggested that the problems single mothers face balancing work and caring obligations are common to all mothers (Lewis 1993). The Danish case is a good illustration of this thesis. Here the situation of lone mothers can be interpreted as a concentrated expression of the general dilemmas of universal citizenship connected with the dual-breadwinner norm. This chapter suggests that in Denmark the dual-breadwinner model is not only based on the *explicit* norm of the two-earner family institutionalised in legislation, but is in fact based on a political *consensus* about state responsibilities for caring for the elderly, sick and disabled, and caring for children.[3] Indeed the dual breadwinner norm rests on an *implicit* and invisible premise about the need for parents to share caring work that contrasts with gendered practices.

The first section of this chapter discusses the new dilemmas for women in the Danish welfare state centred on wage work and caring work from a feminist perspective. The second section looks at the development of family forms and asks what are the implications of dual-breadwinner norm for couple-based families and lone-mother families? What does it mean for lone mothers that they are, like all mothers, expected to engage in wage work? The third section asks what the policy logic has been behind the caring dimension in social policies, looking both at developments in social services and at cash benefits for children and families. It also looks at what their relative importance has been for two-parent families, and for lone parents. The fourth section asks what the main tendencies of policies and debates have been in the 1980s and 1990s and what challenges does unemployment pose to the Danish model of work and care for women and men? The fifth section discusses the interplay between public policies and the strategies and values of single mothers. How do single mothers perceive the dilemma between work and care? The conclusion sums up the development of the policy logic of the Danish case in relation to work and care and discusses the strengths and weaknesses of the Danish welfare state from the perspective of women in general, and of lone parents in particular.

Women's autonomy and the dual-breadwinner model

The institutional structure, policies and values of the welfare state may explain why lone mothers have not been either an ideological issue or a political problem during the last 25 years. The gendered notion of the welfare state can help to explain why certain institutions, policies and values contribute to or impede women's autonomy as mothers, workers and citizens.

---

3   The Danish welfare state during the last 20 years has been based on a remarkable political consensus between Right and Left about what has been called the 'caring dimension' of the welfare state. Feminist scholars have defined different models of caring in relation to the welfare state. The notion of a caring dimension of the welfare state that includes the right of individuals to receive and give care has been introduced in a recent paper by Trudie Knijn and Monique Kremer (1995). The different obligations of individuals, families and the state to caring is a useful aspect of comparative studies of the interplay between work and care in different welfare states. The 'caring dimension' is a useful concept, because it captures an important aspect of welfare, but there is a need to develop the feminist notion of caring to incorporate a differentiation between the public and private dimensions of care and the way the two interact in different welfare states.

From an institutional perspective the Nordic countries have been characterised as welfare states in which social policies are based on the principle of
universal benefits to all citizens financed primarily by taxes. The Danish welfare
system is universal in the sense that services and transfers are tied to citizenship
and it includes a comprehensive system of cash benefits and an extensive public
system for the delivery of services in the area of health, education and welfare.
In terms of the state–market relationship the principle of universality in social
policy based on citizenship is differentiated from principles of insurance and
means-tested benefits based on previous occupation, income or contributions
(Andersen 1993, p.110).

Feminist scholars have generally evaluated the Scandinavian welfare states
positively. Helga Hernes' claim that the Scandinavian welfare states have the
potential to develop into 'women-friendly' states, based on her analysis of the
growing public commitment to social service provision described as 'reproduction going public', has been influential among feminists (Hernes 1987). From
this perspective it has been suggested that social welfare policies have empowered women in their daily lives as workers, mothers and citizens (Hernes 1987,
Siim 1988, Skjeie 1992). A small group has been critical of the 'state regulation
of daily life' arguing it has produced new forms of gender segregation and
hierarchy in the labour market (*see* Hirdman 1989).

Feminists outside Scandinavia have generally commented favourably on
women's high level of labour-force participation, the extended public responsibilities for caring for children and on women's ability to form autonomous
households (Orloff 1993, Lewis & Ostner 1994). Some have, however, been
critical of the employment-oriented model that tends to subsume caring work
under wage work. It has been argued that the Scandinavian 'model' is not
'friendly' toward caring work because it tends to force all mothers, including
lone mothers, to enter employment. The alternative is presented as a caring
model based on public support that enables lone mothers to give priority to
caring for children in the family for a shorter or longer period, as in the Dutch
case (Ostner 1994, Knijn 1994).

Scandinavian scholars have pointed out that there have in fact been important differences in the development of the 'Nordic model' from a gender
perspective as well as from a family or caring perspective (Borchorst and Siim
1987, Leira 1992). In Sweden and Denmark there has, from the 1960s, been
a parallel expansion of women's wage work and publicly provided day care.
This contrasts with Norway, where the entry of women into the labour market
on a large scale happened later and was not accompanied by an expansion in
publicly provided day care until the 1980s[4] (Leira 1992). Unlike Denmark,

---

4   Hege Skjeie has shown that there has been an uneven advance in the position of Norwegian women.
     In terms of political representation, Norway has been ahead of both Denmark and Sweden, but in
     terms of wage work and child care Sweden and Denmark have been ahead of Norway (Skjeie 1992).

first Sweden, and recently Norway, have pursued explicit public care policies aimed at changing the sexual division of work in the family. However, during the 1980s there was a tendency towards convergence in Scandinavian family policies (Knudsen 1990).

Feminist historians have argued that the male-breadwinner norm has never been strong in Denmark in public policies, in practice or in the cultural ideology. There was, for example, never a ban against married women's wage work in the 1930s and no ban against women working at night (Rosenbeck 1989). For the past 100 years Denmark has been dominated by a strong agrarian economy; industry did not become the dominant sector until around 1960. The majority of women of the working and peasant classes have always had to work to support their family, including married women. After the World War II, the ideology and practice of a male-breadwinner–housewife family form gradually spread from the bourgeoisie to the working classes but its impact was confined to the 1950s and the early 1960s.

The dual-breadwinner norm was never adopted as a conscious public policy but became institutionalised step by step in legislation from the beginning of the 1970s. One of the driving forces behind this has been the expansion of women's wage work, especially the growing labour force activity rates of mothers with young children. There has been a parallel change in the rights and obligations of citizens vis-à-vis the state as spouses, parents and children which has been expressed in social policies, tax changes, family law and political culture. The dual-breadwinner model today rests on the twin assumptions that individual women and men have the obligation to take care of themselves through wage work, and that the state will provide financial support for citizens who cannot do so themselves (as well as providing high quality services for children, the elderly, the sick and the disabled).

Lone mothers are, like all mothers, expected to be able to provide for themselves and their children through a combination of wage work, family benefits and social services. It can be argued that the dual-breadwinner model is in principle favourable to lone mothers, because they do not constitute a special category but are provided for via universal policies toward families with children. Thus, while it is presumed that lone mothers, like all mothers, must provide for themselves by earning, the state has taken on new 'caring' obligations in the form of child care and financial support for all mothers who are unemployed, sick or disabled. Lone mothers also receive a substantial child/family benefit to supplement their own earnings, a payment that since 1987 has been part of a universal family allowance. To sum up, lone mothers' dependency on wage work in Denmark is combined with a high level of benefits and services.

Nevertheless there is in practice an underlying dilemma for women connected with the dual breadwinner norm that is manifested both in the sex segregated labour market as well as in the unequal gendered division of caring work in the family. Like men, women have become dependent on the dynamics of the labour market. Segregation is a barrier to gender equality because women in general work fewer hours and earn less than men. Research has shown that low wages and unemployment are serious economic problems for lone mothers who are dependent on one wage, especially for unskilled mothers who have the lowest average wages and the highest risk of becoming unemployed. Furthermore, the sole responsibility for caring for children presents serious time problems for women, both in relation to the labour market and in their daily lives (Larsen and Sørensen 1994).

Lone-parent families and couple-based families

The dramatic changes in women's situation as mothers, workers and citizens during the last 30 years have had an impact on the situation of lone mothers. Since the 1970s lone motherhood has been regarded as a life-style choice and has been neither an ideological nor a political issue. Instead there has been a positive, and even heroic, image attached to lone motherhood and the women who struggle to combine wage work and caring for children. The proportion of children living with lone parents has grown: from 11 per cent of 0–17 year olds in 1980, to 16 per cent in 1995 (Statistical ten year review 1995, p.15).

General changes in family structure mean that families have become smaller and that the relative number of families with children has decreased. This is also a consequence of the decrease in the fertility rate between 1965–1975 in Denmark, in common with other EU countries. The birth rate began to increase slightly from 1983 for women aged between 25–34. However, the number of children being born in Denmark is still not big enough to reproduce the population (Stenvig, Andersen and Lauersen 1994, p.34). There is a general tendency in all EU countries for the number of first marriages to fall and the number of divorces to rise, which in Denmark has been accompanied by a dramatic increase in the number of cohabiting couples. In 1960 only 7.8 per cent of all children were born outside marriage; in 1994 the proportion had risen to 46.8 per cent. Twenty seven per cent of all families with small children were not married (Statistical ten year review 1995, p.15).

Another important change is the dramatic increase in women's labour-force participation, especially among married women. The gap in labour-force activity rates between men and women has been gradually closing during the last 40 years so that today there is only a small difference between the activity rates of women and men, a difference that decreases with age (Stenvig, Andersen and Lauersen 1994, p.36).

Percent

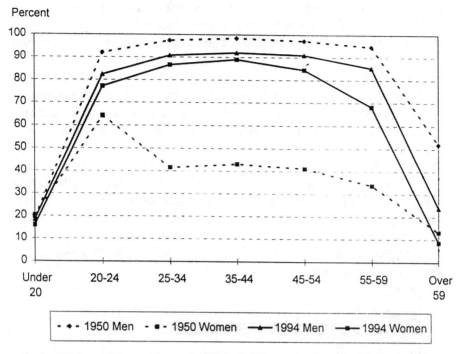

Source: 50-årsoversigten, Danmarks Statistik (50-year review, Danish Statistical Bureau)
Figure 6.1: Employed men and women by age, 1950 and 1994

The employment rate for women with children under 10 is 79 per cent, which is the same as that for women without children (Stenvig, Andersen and Lauersen 1994, p.37, Table 3.4). The implication is that marital status and the presence of small children no longer significantly affects labour-force activity. The role of housewife with small children has almost disappeared, and at present about half of all mothers with small children (under ten years) work full time.

As a result of the changes in family structure and the political ambition to create equality between different family types, a new definition of family was introduced in family statistics in Denmark in 1991 that made it easier to gain information about couples living together as man and wife.[5] Family statistics today count various types of families within the categories lone-parent families and couple-based families. Couple-based families (with and without children) include: (1) married couples; (2) registered partnerships (homosexuals); (3) cohabiting couples who have

---

5   The objective of this new family definition was to give a more realistic picture of couples living together as man and wife. One result was change age limit for children living at home who counted as members of the parents' family from 26 to 18 years. Another change was to create a new category for men and women with children from a previous relationship now living with new partners (Stenvig, Andersen and Lauersen 1994, p.33)

or have had children together or by other people. There has been a gradual decline in the number of families with children. In 1995 families with children accounted for only 23 per cent and families without children for 77 per cent of all families (Stenvig, Anderson and Lauersen 1994, p.33).

The sociological picture shows that during the 1970s and 1980s there has been a small increase in the number of lone parents, due to the rising number of divorces (Christoffersen 1996). In 1970 lone mothers accounted for just over 10 per cent of families with children (Qvortrup 1994, p.123). Table 6.1 and Figure 6.2 show first that the proportion of lone-parent families has gradually increased due to the fall in the number of two-parent families with children. Second, only 13 per cent of all the single parent families in Denmark are lone fathers and they account for only 2.3 per cent of all families with children. This percentage has been stable during the last decade. In 1996 the total number of single parents with children was 119,450, which is 18 per cent of all families with children, and there were 104,841 lone mothers with children and 14,609 single men with children.

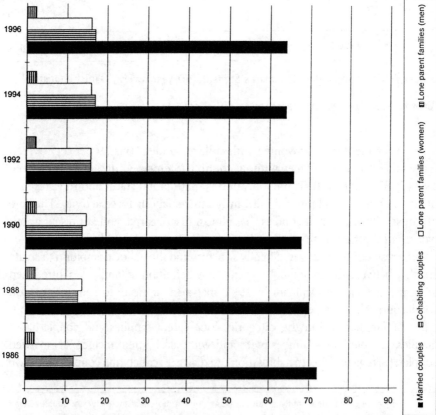

Source: 10-års oversigt, Danmarks Statistik 1995 (10 year review, Danish Statistical Bureau) 1996

Figure 6.2: Families with children, 1986–1996 (%)

Table 6.1 Families with children, number and proportion (%) for selected family types, 1986–1996

	1986		1988		1990		1992		1994		1996	
Married couples	489,036	72.0%	470,933	70.0%	449,144	68.0%	430,216	66.0%	413,745	64.0%	411,957	64.0%
Cohabiting couples*	81,289	12.0%	88,578	13.0%	94,605	14.0%	103,061	16.0%	109,533	17.0%	113,037	17.0%
Lone parent families	110,450	16.0%	112,663	17.0%	117,402	18.0%	118,072	18.0%	119,570	19.0%	119,450	19.0%
3a: women	94,718	14.0%	96,591	14.0%	101,184	15.0%	102,327	16.0%	104,363	16.0%	104,841	16.0%
3b: men	15,732	2.3%	16,072	2.4%	16,218	2.5%	15,745	2.4%	15,207	2.4%	14,609	2.3%
Families with children	680,775	100.0%	672,174	100.0%	661,151	100.0%	651,349	100.0%	642,848	100.0%	644,444	100.0%

* Since 1989 the group co-habiting couples has been divided into three subgroups, registered couples (homosexual couples), cohabiting couples with children that belong to both of them and cohabiting couples with children belonging to only one of the couple.

Source: Statistical ten year review 1996.

In general the characteristics of lone mothers do not differ from those of all mothers. Denmark (like France, Germany and the Netherlands) has a very low number of teenage mothers compared to some other EU countries (Ditch, Bradshaw and Eardly 1995b, p.31). This is explained by women's high labour-market participation and the rise in women's educational attainment, together with good access to birth control. The rather high average age for single parents in Denmark is similar to that of other families with children: 37 years for women and 41 for men in 1987 (Larsen and Sørensen 1994, p.144).

As in many other countries the cultural portrayal of lone mothers is positive. This is connected both with the spread of feminist ideas and with the trend towards equalising the treatment of all Danish mothers during the last 20 years. Research has documented that in most cases it is women who take the initiative to divorce (Koch-Nielsen 1993). Studies have also confirmed that divorce is often experienced as empowerment for women who wish to leave a difficult relationship and who want to live an autonomous life (Bak 1996, p.104). However, there are, broadly speaking, two different groups of women who divorce and become lone parents: at one extreme a group of university educated women in employment and at the other a group of young unskilled, unemployed women (Larsen and Sørensen 1994, p.144). The first of these groups is able to live an autonomous and independent life on the basis of their own earnings, while the other group becomes dependent on unemployment benefit or long-term public support. It is interesting that education also divides lone fathers into two groups: a minority of single-male providers have little by way of education, while the majority of lone fathers have more educational qualifications than men in other families, and compared to women. (Larsen and Sørensen 1994, p.145). Several studies have confirmed that the group of single parents is not a homogeneous social group in Denmark and they show that there are more similarities between better-off two-parent families and better-off lone parents than there are between lone parents generally (Thaulow and Gamst 1987; Larsen and Sørensen 1994, p.143).

Family and work in different family types

The dual-breadwinner model has made all families crucially dependent on married women's wage work for their income. Thus the relationship between work and family has become central not only for lone mothers, but for all mothers. In terms of wage work, however, there is a difference between lone mothers and mothers in general. The employment rate for lone mothers is lower than for all mothers, but a higher proportion of lone mothers work full time: 66 per cent of all lone mothers work full time compared to 44 per cent of mothers in families with two parents. This is especially important for lone mothers with small children (0–6), of whom 80 per cent work full time against 50 per cent of mothers in families with two children. The reason for this is probably that most lone parents cannot afford not to work full time. A 1986 survey showed that lone fathers had a longer average working week than lone mothers (42 and 38 hours per week respectively), while lone mothers had a longer total working week than mothers in two-parent families (38½ and 34 hours respectively). As a result both lone mothers and lone fathers have a higher income than men and women in two-parent families, however, the most significant wage difference is between lone mothers and lone fathers. The average earnings of lone fathers before tax was significantly higher than that of lone mothers (Larsen and Sørensen 1994, p.145).

A number of studies have concluded that the high unemployment rate in Denmark following the oil crisis in 1973 affected lone parents disproportionally. As a result the economic and social situation of lone mothers has deteriorated during the 1980s: in 1985, 25 per cent of lone mothers were unemployed, while men's unemployment rate was 9 per cent and women's 12 per cent. In 1990, the rate for lone mothers had risen to 39 per cent, whereas that of men and other women remained almost the same (LO 1991). In 1990, 40 per cent of all lone mothers received public support in the form of either unemployment benefit or social assistance, compared to 10 per cent in 1974, and another 10 per cent received state support because of long term illness or disability. Thus almost half of lone mothers are today supported by some kind of state benefits. Unemployment was highest for lone mothers with small children but there is a general tendency for mothers, compared to other groups, to be unemployed. For men it is actually the other way around; fathers with small children have a lower unemployment rate than other men (Larsen and Sørensen 1994, p.146).

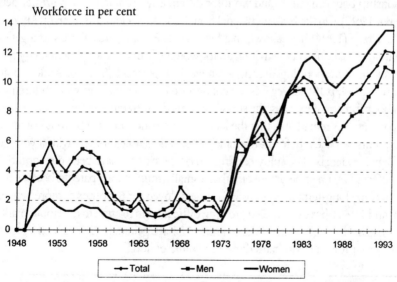

Source: 50-års oversigt, Danmarks Statistik 1995 (50-year review, Danish
          Statistical Bureau)
Figure 6.3: Unemployment, 1948–1994

A recent study of unskilled women has concluded that for lone mothers the conflict between the need for wage work and their caring responsibilities for children is acute, and that there is generally no opportunity for part-time work (Ibsen 1993, p.48). Therefore, lone mothers tend to be either full-time workers or unemployed. The study shows that lone mothers have higher unemployment rates than other mothers who have children under seven, but that they have a lower unemployment rate than other mothers when the children are older. We do not know the reason for this, and it is not possible to say whether the high unemployment rate is a manifestation of marginalisation, or whether it represents women's own attempt to solve the conflict between wage work and caring.

Since the late 1970s, Danish women have had higher unemployment rates than men, and one of the crucial questions is what unemployment means for women in the Danish system. The unemployment benefit system has until recently been described as probably the most generous in the world in terms of easy access, long periods of support, high level of compensation and little by way of surveillance. One remarkable effect of the unemployment programmes has been the fact that Denmark has the lowest proportion of long term unemployed in the EU (Goul Andersen 1996). The question is whether the high unemployment rate of lone mothers in Denmark is accompanied by social and political marginalisation. This question will be explored in the last section of this chapter on the basis of qualitative case studies of lone mothers.

The creation of a unique statistical database (IDA = Integrated Database for Labour Market Research) by the Danish Statistical Bureau has made it possible to analyse the relationship between family and work for different types of families in greater detail (Emerek 1995). On the basis of material from IDA, the sociologists Stenvig, Andersen and Lauersen (1994) have shown that between 1980 and 1987 there was a general growth in the labour force activity rates for women from all types of families by 5 per cent, and a corresponding decline for men of 1 per cent (Stenvig, Andersen and Lauersen 1994, p.38). As regards the connection between families with children and the labour force activity rates, the study confirms the difference between lone parents and couples. It is remarkable that the labour participation rate fell by four points and three points respectively for both single fathers and single mothers with a youngest child aged under six. The study confirms that lone parents have been disproportionately affected by unemployment and that a small group of lone parents, because they have become long-term unemployed (i.e. unemployed for 6 months or more between 1980 and 1987), has experienced growing difficulties in relation to the labour market. In comparison, couples with children under 12 have generally experienced a growth in the labour force activity rates during the same period.[6]

---

6   The labour force activity rate of men in couples where the youngest child is 0–6 or 7–12 years old is still the highest for men (i.e. 97% in both groups). However, there has been a significant rise in the activity rates for women in couples with children in the same age groups (from 87 to 92 and from 88 to 93% respectively) (Stenvig, Andersen and Lauersen 1994, Table 3.5).

Thus in terms of unemployment the primary difference between lone parents and two-parent families is the higher unemployment rate of lone mothers, although in general mothers with small children have a higher unemployment rate than fathers with small children. The high degree of unemployment creates serious economic problems for single mothers who need full-time work to provide for themselves and their children. The detailed study based on the integrated database (IDA 1991) has shown the position of a growing number of lone parents in the labour market is vulnerable compared to other groups. First, a large proportion of those who have been unemployed for more than six months are lone parents. Second, a large proportion of single mothers are not in the labour force, and third, the study found a growing polarisation between single mothers who are either employed or in education and those who are either unemployed, have retired early or receive social assistance (Stenvig, Anderson and Lauersen 1994, p.40).

The conclusion is that in Denmark it is not the fact of being a lone mother that in and of itself creates economic difficulties. The Danish model is premised on full employment and the growing tendency toward marginalisation of lone mothers in respect of the labour market is a result of mass unemployment during the 1980s. The key factor is a tendency towards polarisation in the group of single parents according to *education*. It has been a matter of growing public concern that it is predominantly unskilled mothers without vocational training who are either long-term unemployed, on social assistance, or live on disability pensions (Stenvig, Andersen and Lauersen 1994, pp.38–39). During the 1980s, there was a political consensus about policies to (re)integrate mothers into the labour market and society by creating active labour market and educational policies targeted toward unskilled women and lone mothers, and by increasing public services and transfers for all families with children.

Policies toward families with children

In Denmark, the general principle of the modern welfare state of *universal* benefits directed towards *all* citizens was institutionalised through legislation after 1960. This replaced the earlier system of social insurance against old age, sickness and unemployment for selected groups that had been introduced in 1922 (Knudsen 1989). There has been a dramatic increase in public expenditure on social welfare since 1960 and in spite of political attempts to reduce the scope of the public sector, social expenditure has continued to rise during the 1980s. Public expenditure on social policies grew to 33.2 per cent of Gross National Product (GNP) in 1993 and expenditure on families now makes up around 10 per cent of all social expenditure (Abrahamsen and Borchorst 1996). The decrease in total spending on families (from 18 to 10% between 1950 and 1990) took place in spite of a general rise in public expenditure per child during the 1970s and 1980s (Knudsen 1990, p.116–125). One reason for the fall is the gradual decline in the number of children born during this period. Another reason is the expansion of other areas of public care, such as that for the elderly and handicapped. Today expenditures on those with disabilities and on elderly people comprise the largest category of public expenditure (i.e. around 50%) (Knudsen 1990, p.118).

In a comparison to public support for families in the Nordic countries, Knudsen has shown that despite similarities in the general principle of universal benefits, the Nordic welfare states have historically chosen somewhat different policy solutions for families with children. From the 1950s, Finland, and to some extent Norway, granted relatively high levels of cash benefits and generous tax deductions to families, while Denmark and Sweden gave priority to the provision of child care services to families with children (Knudsen 1990, p.116). Nordic family policies have gradually converged over the last thirty years, although there is still a difference between the relative importance of cash benefits as opposed to the provision of services to families with children. In Denmark and Sweden provision of services today make up around half of all public provision for families, whereas in Norway and Finland they only make up between 23 (Norway) and 37 per cent (Finland) (Knudsen 1990, p.118).

Development of benefits in cash and kind for children and families

In Denmark the understanding of child-oriented family policies includes provision of day-care services as well as cash benefits. Family policies have been characterised as child-oriented, because the political objective has been to improve the well-being of children rather than to favour a specific family form. From 1937, Parliament regulated the obligations of unmarried fathers in such a way that their children were given the same rights as legitimate children in regard to inheritance, the right to bear the father's name, and the right to receive maintenance from their fathers (Rosenbeck 1989, Koch-Nielsen 1995). Historically, social policies were directed primarily towards low-income families, such as lone mothers, but over the last thirty years family policies have gradually become inclusive of all types of family.

The economic crisis of the 1930s gave rise to a political alliance of workers and peasant parties that emphasised the social needs of children and families. Reforms in social policy were introduced in connection with the Population Commission and population policies were introduced that were designed to improve the situation of poor and underprivileged families. The Population Commission proposed a new benefit for all mothers, including lone mothers, which was, however, rejected. Instead the voluntary organisation 'Mothers Help' that assisted young pregnant women became state funded.

Since World War II, there has been a gradual shift from *indirect* economic support for children via tax deductions, to *direct* support through cash benefits. Cash benefits were originally targeted towards specific groups of families in need, but were gradually converted to universal benefits for all families. The tax allowance for children, first introduced in 1901, was gradually increased during the 1940s, and in 1950/51 was supplemented by a small cash benefit for families, called the 'children's grant'. From 1966 a number of new family related benefits were introduced, including a special cash benefit for lone parents. The direct cash benefits for all children regardless of family income and number of children were, however, not introduced until 1970 (Borchorst and Siim 1984, pp.75–90, p.154). The explicit objective of these policy initiatives was to improve the situation of families with children in general as well as that of lone parents in particular.

From 1964, publicly provided day care for all families with children, not just for poor families, became a key element in Danish family policy. During the 1970s and 1980s, there was political agreement to expand the number of places in child care institutions for all children. The political objectives behind this policy were a mixture of; (1) *pedagogical* goals to improve the up-bringing of all children; (2) *egalitarian* ideals to integrate all children in a common programme; and (3) *employment*-related goals to increase the labour market participation rates of women (Jensen 1994).

Family obligations in social legislation

At the beginning of the 1970s new objectives for social policy were introduced that formed the guidelines for social policy during the next twenty years. The 1976 Social Welfare Act was a complex piece of legislation that set out the social services provisions for children and families and the new rules for cash benefits. The legislation was premised on the decentralisation of responsibilities for social issues from the central to the local state. The new ambitious objectives for social policy, which involved securing the safety and well-being of all citizens, were adopted during a period of expansion in the public sector and welfare services (Plovsing 1994).

Since the 1970s, the general trend towards *individualisation* has become very apparent in social policies and has also been present in family law. In respect of the public sector, section 6 of the 1976 Social Welfare Act stated a new principle: 'that every individual is obliged to provide for herself or himself, his or her spouse, and his or her children under 18 years of age' (Petersen 1994, p.43). The purpose of this obligation is to ensure that the state is not obliged to take care of individuals who can take care of themselves. As a consequence the individual, not the household or the family, became the primary unit in social policy.

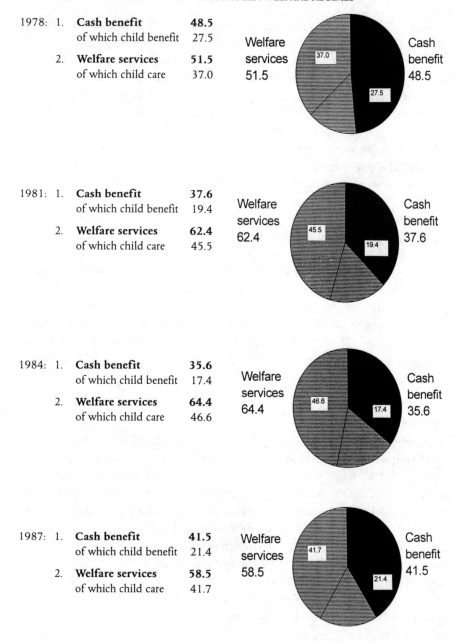

1978: 1. **Cash benefit**   **48.5**
           of which child benefit   27.5

       2. **Welfare services**   **51.5**
           of which child care   37.0

1981: 1. **Cash benefit**   **37.6**
           of which child benefit   19.4

       2. **Welfare services**   **62.4**
           of which child care   45.5

1984: 1. **Cash benefit**   **35.6**
           of which child benefit   17.4

       2. **Welfare services**   **64.4**
           of which child care   46.6

1987: 1. **Cash benefit**   **41.5**
           of which child benefit   21.4

       2. **Welfare services**   **58.5**
           of which child care   41.7

Source: Knudsen (1989) Table 8.2.4

Figure 6.4: Breakdown of family benefits distributed by the Danish Government from 1978–1987 (%)

This principle has had far reaching implications for the relationship between parents and children, and between women and men. It follows that parents are only obliged to provide for their children until they are 18; that cohabiting couples have the same obligations towards each other as married couples; that women have a double obligation (or right) to work and care; and that fathers must provide and care for children.[7] As a consequence, *informal* norms about the division of caring have become increasingly important and a space has opened up for negotiations between women and men in two-parent families.

The decentralisation of the Danish welfare state meant that most social services, such as care for the elderly, nursery schools, child protection, sickness allowances, services to disabled people, the administration of public pensions and old age pensions became the direct responsibility of 275 local governments. Health services – primary care as well as hospitals – became the responsibility of 14 regional governments (Andersen 1993, p.111). The local state has proved to be an excellent pressure point for the growing activities of citizens wishing to improve welfare services. Since local government is close to the problems and demands of citizens, it has been easier for local groups to influence the quality of services and to increase the level of service provision. The proximity of the state to citizens has also made it susceptible to public criticism of bureaucratic practices and research has shown that there is a high degree of citizen satisfaction with local services (Hoff 1993).

Public debates about family and child care in the 1980s

Mass unemployment in Denmark had negative effects on the implementation of the Social Welfare Act. During the 1970s and 1980s, the development of the welfare state was characterised both by a financial crisis and a legitimation crisis that opened up new political conflicts about privatisation and modernisation of the welfare state. From 1982 to 1992 the Conservative–Centre Government that followed Social Democratic minority Governments of the 1970s stated its desire to reduce the size of the (large) public sector. The Government started an ideological debate that challenged some of the main objectives of social policy, such as the principle of universality. The alternative policy was to direct more resources to those in need, and to rely more on the abilities of social networks in civil society to solve social problems and less on public benefits and state institutions (Plovsing 1994).

---

7   Hanne Petersen suggests that there has, therefore, been a shift in focus from marital status to maternal status. Women's obligations are today connected with motherhood and not with marriage as such. The obligation to provide 'private' care is laid down in the Danish Act on the legal effect of Matrimony, section 2. Husband and wife are obliged to help to provide for the family through money, work in the home or other means. There is still an expectation in many areas of society, including women, that the woman, as mother, provides most of what Petersen call the 'status-determined care' in the family (Petersen 1994, p.43)

The general principles of the Conservative–Centre government were *priva-tisation* and *modernisation* of the public sector. The main objective of privatisation was to save money by moving tasks from the public sector to the private market, and modernisation was an attempt to make the public sector more efficient and less costly. Privatisation was used primarily in connection with transport, communication and energy, and had no significant effect on the development of social policy (Plovsing 1994, p.82). There was some attempt to make individuals more responsible for their own lives, for example through the introduction of small user charges for prescriptions and for dental services. Despite debate about the scope of the public sector, and the level of public expenditure and taxation[8] care services have not been privatised other than for the contracting out of meals-on-wheels. There is, however, at present discussion within the Government and in the press about the interplay between public and private provision of care for the elderly; there are proposals for contracting out services for the elderly, as well for introducing charges for supplementary services (Koch-Nielsen 1995, p.42)

It is somewhat surprising that the new ideological developments did not seriously affect family and child care policies. The trend toward individualisa-tion was not challenged, and there was no attempt to bring the family back in as a legal unit in respect of financial rights and obligations. The political consensus about the principle of individualisation was explicitly confirmed by a parliamentary decision in 1987 that confirmed the independence of spouses and equal rights of cohabiting partners in social legislation and all other legislation. It was part of a political package to increase public expenditure on services for families with children as well as universal cash benefits (Koch-Niel-sen 1995, p.4).

Universal policies towards families and children

From the mid-1970s there has been a broad political debate about the conditions of children. The Family Commission was formed in 1975 in order to analyse the problems of families with small children. The main 'family' problems described in the Commission's 1982 Report were problems of *caring* and of *material resources*; (1) lack of time to care for children with two parents out at work including; (2) lack of places in child care institutions; (3) difficultly for parents to care for children when they are sick; (4) parents in low-income

---

8   In some areas of publicly provided care, such as care for the elderly and disabled, new policies of de-institutionalisation from residential care to community care were adopted in the 1980s which served to emphasise the importance of care in the home and the expansion of home help services. The underlying philosophy was not primarily to save money, although this may have been a secondary goal, and de-institutionalisation of the elderly was supported by all political parties. In other areas, such as health care, there is a stronger support for private solutions within the framework of the public health system (Koch-Nielsen 1995).

families' lack of material resources, which especially affected the children of lone parents (Plovsing 1994).

The recommendations from the Commission were put forward as policy proposals by the Conservative–Centre Governments during the 1980s, as well as by the Social–Democratic–Centre Government in the early 1990s. One of the results was the adoption of a *universal* benefit for all children in 1987 in connection with tax reform: the family allowance is a benefit for all children and young people under 18, paid irrespective of family income and of the number of children in the family (about 6600 DKK for 0–3 and 4600 DKK for 4–17 year olds in 1990). On top of this there is an extra benefit per family (of about 3092 DKK in 1990) and the children of lone parents receive an additional child benefit regardless of family income (worth about 4048 DKK per child in 1990) together with an extra benefit per family (of about 3092 DKK in 1990). In 1990 a multiple births benefit was introduced (about 5000 DKK[9] per year). The total cash benefits are an important part of the income of lone parents, who receive about 20,000 DKK per year tax free. Finally, the state also guarantees the maintenance payable in respect of children after divorce (Plovsing 1994, pp.154–159).

The growing political consensus in the 1980s about the importance of the universal principle of support for all children and families regardless of income and of marital status, and of increasing the number of places in child care centres, can be interpreted as a convergence in the family and child care policies of the Left and Right. Historically, the logic of the social policies of the Social Democratic Party has been to create equality between children in different family types by providing a safety net for low-income families regardless of family type. Contrary to this, the policy of the Right has been to increase support for all families, including high-income families, through universal cash benefits that replaced tax deductions for children. Thus, both Left and Right have promoted policies to support children.

The impact of social policies

The general aim of Danish social policies during the 1980s was to increase the economic support to all families, including single parents. The question is what has been the impact of these policies on different family types, especially for lone mothers?

In Denmark the main source of income for all mothers is wage work, but research has documented the extent to which state support via family benefits in cash and services are an important component of the incomes of a majority of families (Knudsen 1990; Thaulow and Gamst 1987). For many single parents with low incomes, cash benefits are a necessary supplement to their own wages

---

9   At the late 1996 exchange rate: £1 = 9.77 DKK

and have prevented them from falling into absolute or relative poverty. Larsen and Sørensen have looked at the poverty rates by gender, age and family type and have found that women have an above average risk of poverty and that the poverty rate of lone mothers is significantly higher than of lone fathers due to their structurally weak position in the labour market (Larsen and Sørensen 1994, p.148). They show that with a very broad definition of poverty, in the sense 'that people are more or less precluded by a lack of material resources from participating in the lifestyle and activities and enjoying the standard of living which is generally prevalent in Denmark', the poverty rate of lone parents is more than twice the average for the population as a whole, 26 per cent as opposed to 12 per cent, and the poverty rate of lone mothers is significantly higher than that of lone fathers, 28 per cent and 17 per cent respectively. Their definition contrasts with the official EC definition on poverty, according to which Denmark has the lowest proportion of households in the European Unions living below the poverty line: about 8 per cent in 1990 compared to an EU average of about 16 per cent; only some 3 per cent of the households where the head of the household in unemployed falls in the poverty category. The numbers that Larsen and Sørensen give are undoubtedly exaggerated, but the tendency for single parents to have a poverty rate that is above the average of the population as a whole is undoubtedly true (Larsen and Sørensen 1994, p.148 and Abrahamsen and Hansen 1996, p.45).

A comparison of different 'model' families, made by the Danish statistician Rita Knudsen at the request of the Nordic statistical secretariat, has shown that benefits to children have an important equalising effect on families (Knudsen 1990). In 1987 the total effect of cash benefits and tax allowances was to increase the real income of lone, working class mothers after tax by 22 per cent in Denmark (compared to 31% in Norway and Iceland). A comparison between the three model family types: (1) a two-parent working class family with two children and two employed parents; (2) a two-parent working class family with two children and one working parent; and (3) a single working mother with one child, shows that lone mothers under these circumstances receive about the same amount of real income per child as the family with two working parents and two children, and almost double their income before tax. Knudsen concludes that where parents have an income from unskilled industrial wage work, an unskilled working-class family with two children and only one income is significantly worse off than a lone mother with one child (Knudsen 1990, pp.81–90).

In practice, however, all things are never equal. We have seen that lone mothers are dependent on wage work and that, in comparison with other groups, mass unemployment has disproportionately affected unskilled lone parents. Knudsen shows that other areas of social policies, like universal health services, have been important for the welfare of lone-parent families. The general housing benefit which is a means-tested benefit for low-income families in rented homes is especially important (Knudsen 1990, p.48).

Thus, in Denmark lone mothers have packaged income from wage work, state benefits and to a smaller degree from husbands. They have also profited from the generous Danish social wage in the form of child care. In spite of an increase in state benefits unskilled lone mothers remain an economically vulnerable group, with the result that a growing group of lone mothers have come to rely heavily on transfers in the form of unemployment benefits or social assistance. Active and passive labour market policies[10] have been important for lone mothers and over the last five years there have been relatively generous leave arrangements and new opportunities to withdraw from the labour market have been introduced. Since August 1994, unemployment figures have started to decline but women's unemployment rates are still higher than men's (13.6 against 10.8% in 1994), and there is not yet any clear indication of what the consequences of the new leave policies will be for mothers and for lone parents.

Recent debates about public child care

Since the mid-1960s, public child care institutions have been a universal social service for all families and are arguably the key element in the caring dimension of the Danish welfare state.[11] During the last fifteen years the provision of public child care has achieved a high degree of political consensus and has increasingly been justified in terms of securing gender equality (Borchorst and Siim 1984; Jensen 1994). As early as 1964, the idea of child care as a private responsibility was rejected, and during the last twenty years the trend has been for more and more children to attend public day-care, either in the form of day- care centres, local authority family day care, or after-school schemes. Private arrangements, with kin or childminders ('mothers' help'), are declining (Jensen 1994, p.105).

Today public day care is exclusively a local government responsibility and there is considerable variation in how the municipalities tackle the issue. According to the 1976 Social Welfare Act the municipalities must provide the

10 Recently a number of generous leave arrangements (education leave, parental leave and sabbatical leave introduced in 1992/93) have be introduced, as well as opportunities to withdraw from the labour market at an early age (early retirement allowances for 60–66 year olds were introduced in 1979; transitional allowances – at 80% of maximum benefits – for long term unemployed aged 50–59 were introduced by 1992/93). The programmes have been open to the unemployed. Roughly half of the people on parental leave were unemployed, and 90 per cent of them were women.

11 There has traditionally been a difference between the parties on the Right (the Liberal Left, the Progressive Party and the small Christian Party), who want to increase the power of families to choose their own solutions for child care, and the parties on the Left (the Social Democratic Party and the Socialist Folks Party) who support an increase in publicly provided child care and greater equality between families. In Denmark these differences have diminished during the 1980s and during the last 25 years, there has been cross-party support for social policies toward women, children and families. (Borchorst 1989).

number of places that is needed, but this is left for them to evaluate.[12] This right to a place in a day care institution is not a social right that can be pursued through the courts, but the law is used by parents to put pressure on local governments. Day care institutions are not free. Parents have to pay a maximum of 30 per cent of the costs, but there is a great difference between municipalities regarding the fees charged. Although Denmark has the highest day care coverage of all European countries, demands from parents have been growing. The result has been long waiting lists for child care places during the 1990s. In 1992, between 20,000 and 30,000 0–6 year olds were in acute need of a place, the majority of them aged between 0 and 2 (Jensen 1994, p.106). One reason for the growing need to create extra day care places is the rise in the birth rate since the 1980s.

The political consensus on child care has been promoted by the growing organisation of parents as a cross-party pressure group on local governments. Since 1992, the official national policy has been to abolish all waiting lists and in 1994 the government announced that there would be a 'child care guarantee' for children aged between 0–5 years by 1996. It has, however, been difficult for the municipalities to live up to these promises because of the rise in the birth rate. Bringing down waiting lists is currently high on the political agenda, but abolishing them will involve major expenditures for the municipalities and will increase the problem of balancing their budgets. There is a growing difference between municipalities on child care policies and several have announced that they cannot live up to the child care guarantee. However, some municipalities guarantee child care provisions for all families in order to attract young families to the municipality. Parliament has tried to solve the problem of waiting lists in different ways: by giving the unemployed work as 'social care leaders' and child care assistants; and by introducing parental leave, whereby parents of children under nine have the opportunity of taking 13–36 week leave at 80 per cent (reduced to 70% in 1995) of the maximum unemployment benefits[13] (Jensen 1994, p.108). In general, more flexible measures have been advocated to accommodate more children within the existing schemes.

In Denmark, parents have become an important group of participating citizens. They have organised themselves locally and nationally to tackle waiting lists, and as users of social services they have shown an active involvement in

---

12 The 'municipalisation' of the welfare state has led to geographical variations in the level of provisions of child care. Provision for the 0–2 year olds thus varies between 23 per cent in the municipality with the lowest coverage and 74 per cent in the municipality with the highest coverage. Each local authority determines the objectives and organisational conditions (e.g. staffing) of the services. However, the National Ministry of Social Affairs has put forward five broad principles on which the social and pedagogical objectives of the services should be based (Jensen 1994, p.106).

13 One possible way of reducing waiting lists would be to extend maternity and paternity leave. It has been calculated that for each month the leave is extended, waiting lists are reduced by 2600 places, resulting in the fact that 75 per cent of all mothers or fathers extend their leave.

their children's day care. Since 1993, all municipalities have had to establish parental boards with majority parental representation. The board has the power to influence the principles and budgets of the day-care centres and are able to appoint new employees. The institutionalisation of parents' participation in this way is important for gender relations as well as from a more general perspective of citizenship. Will mothers become more involved than fathers, or will the institutionalisation of participation strengthen the participation of fathers? Will the power of parents, as citizens, to influence child care policies be strengthened?

The strategies and values of lone mothers

Part-time work is traditionally a strategy used by women to reconcile the problem of balancing work and care for children. In families with two working parents, mothers often choose to work part time, and their husbands work overtime to compensate for lost wages. A day-care survey (from 1989) shows that in fact a large group of both mothers and fathers with small children would actually prefer to work part time (Jensen 1994, pp.112–114). Part-time work is generally not a strategy open to lone mothers (80% work full time). These women may be forced to choose between full time work and unemployment when the children are young. In addition, lone mothers can only share caring responsibilities with the other parent to a limited extent, for example, through mutual agreements between divorced couples about dividing child care (Stoltz 1995). The question, then, is what strategies are open to single mothers in order to balance wage work and caring for children.

Studies of lone mothers using interviews, or case studies of local communities, have given a more detailed picture than have surveys of single mothers' strategies, values and priorities in relation to wage work and caring for children. Thaulow and Gamst's 1985 study was based on intensive interviews with 19 lone mothers, all of whom received public assistance, and Bak's 1990 study was based on intensive interviews with 25 lone mothers. Half of the group of 25 were working and the rest were unemployed, in low paid or part-time work, or in irregular jobs, but only four were on social assistance (Bak 1996). Both investigations show that lone mothers actually prefer to have wage work and do not express any wish to become full-time carers, which is in accordance with public policies that expect lone parents to earn (Thaulow and Gamst 1987; Bak 1996).

The focus of Bak's study was the situation of ordinary lone-mother families (*enemorfamilier*). On the basis of her interviews, she differentiated between two types according to their overall goals:

(1) Traditional; where the aim of the women is to recreate a nuclear family with two parents.

(2) Late modern; where the aim of the women is to support themselves and their children as lone mother.

According to Bak, the majority of the 25 lone mother families belonged to the second group. The women used three different strategies to gain autonomy in their own lives:

(1) The adoption of strict economic discipline.

(2) The careful construction of a daily life with their children.

(3) The development of resources through the creation of social networks.

The investigation illustrates two general points: first, while there is an important difference in economic resources between lone mothers, the majority being dependent on public transfers, not only those on social assistance but also those on low and medium incomes. This indicates that *secondary economic transfers* provided by state benefits make up an important part of the budgets of lone mothers and that without them half the mothers would be in a situation that could be described as near poverty. There is a poverty-trap in the sense that there is not much difference between living on social assistance or on unemployment benefits, and living on low wages. Notwithstanding this, Bak found that none of the women interviewed wanted to give up their jobs and live on unemployment benefit or social assistance. The four women on social assistance all wanted to enter education and get a job.

Second, *time* becomes one of the crucial resources for lone mothers, who are generally more time-poor and exhausted than mothers in two-parent families. In Bak's study more than half of the women (14 of 25) worked 37 hours or more, while eight women managed to work three-quarters time, that is, 30 hours a week. Other studies have confirmed that single women do not in general spend less time with their children than other parents, their strategy is to cut down on housework. Bak suggests that for single mothers time is an important consideration that can be seen both as freedom to determine the time they spend with their children, and as a restraint because of their tendency to work full time (Bak 1996, p.25).

The qualitative studies of Thaulow and Gamst (1987) and Bak (1996) have shown that in Denmark lone mothers perceive themselves to be part of the work force and want to provide for themselves through wage work. They confirm the general hypothesis that single mothers experience more acutely the general problems that all mothers have reconciling work and care. Lone mothers in employment are time poor because they work more hours than other women. Equally a large group of lone mothers with small children have economic problems because they experience a higher degree of unemployment and marginalisation from the labour market than do other mothers.

The studies further confirm that the difference in income between lone mothers makes it difficult to generalise about their economic conditions as a group. In Bak's study state support in the form of family benefits for children and housing benefit for lone mothers with low and middle incomes proved to be at least as impotent as in Knudsen's analysis of model families. These benefits made up a larger percentage, between 20 and 30 per cent, of their income and may therefore be seen as an economic safety net that keeps them out of poverty. The minimum wage is not enough to ensure that single mothers and their children can provide for themselves. It is necessary, even in Denmark, to supplement it with state support, such as the child/family and housing benefits in order to enable single mothers to live an autonomous life (Bak 1996, p.32).

Bak's study suggests that in Denmark structural vulnerability in the labour market does not necessarily lead to social marginalisation. There is a space for women to exercise agency through social networks and through their own strategies designed to cut down on housework and save time. It is remarkable that the majority of the 25 lone mothers in the study felt empowered, in the sense of making decisions for themselves in a way that other women cannot always do. This shows that there is an important difference between the socio-economic position of lone mothers and their socio-cultural position, between unemployment and social marginalisation.

Conclusion – the policy logic of the Danish case

Since the 1970s, the universalist Danish welfare system has moved from a male-breadwinner to a dual-breadwinner model with far reaching implications for women's situation as workers, mothers and citizens. In Denmark lone mothers were originally perceived as low-income families, but with the move toward a dual-breadwinner norm, lone mothers have increasingly been perceived in the same way as other mothers. Lone mothers have historically packaged their income from three different sources: the labour market, the state and fathers. In the Danish welfare system, the labour market, as opposed to the state and fathers, has historically been perceived as the most important source of income for poor lone mothers. The intervention of the state was limited to supporting those who could not provide for themselves. Since the dual-worker model has become the norm, the labour market has, in principle, come to play the primary role for all mothers. However, research shows that, in practice, state benefits and services have played a crucial role in determining the social and economic situation of lone mothers. The comparison of model families as well as qualitative studies show that state support is a crucial contribution to their income and in addition has an equalising effect between lone mother and two- earner families.

During the last 15 years mass unemployment has created economic problems for a large group of lone mothers. Unemployment is a problem for all low-income families, but it is arguably a particular problem for unskilled lone parents, because they cannot, like couples, compensate for the unemployment of one parent by the other parent undertaking extra work. Therefore social services and transfers in the form of family allowances and child/family benefits are crucial for lone mothers. The latest figures show that about 40 per cent of lone mothers live on either unemployment benefit or social assistance. Social policies in Denmark were based on the presumption of full employment and the growing number of lone mothers dependent on transfers has been the subject of growing political concern, but there has been no attack on family allowances or the extra child/family benefits to lone mothers.

From the perspective of *gender*, the Danish case shows both strengths and weaknesses in relation to mothers in general, and to lone mothers in particular. Women's employment can be perceived both as a positive option and as an obligation that has today become an economic necessity for families with children. In the Danish welfare state women's wage work has been paralleled by an expansion of state provision that includes both a system of direct cash benefits for families with children, including lone parents, and a high level of social care for children, the elderly, sick, handicapped and disabled. The dual-breadwinner norm has on the one hand been positive, because it has equalised the situation of all mothers in relation to the labour market. On the other hand, labour market dependency is a problem for mothers with young children, because it is combined with an unequal, gendered obligation to care for children. From the perspective of lone parents, the problems of combining wage work and caring for children are acute, because they normally cannot afford to work part time.

It can be argued that the high degree of universality in welfare services for children and the elderly has been a key factor enabling lone mothers to support themselves and their children. The development of welfare services has been the result of a combination of institutional factors, policies and political participation, including:

(1) A high degree of decentralisation of the welfare state that has made the demands of citizens for an expansion of social services for the elderly and children extremely effective.

(2) The principle of universality that has made it easier to form alliances among citizens at local level around issues of child care, schools, care for the elderly and hospitals.

(3) A high level of women's participation as providers of social services, as users, as policy makers and as concerned citizens that has enabled them to play an important role in the debates and campaigns to expand social programmes and to stop cuts in existing programmes.

In terms of public policy, it is crucial that there has been no political attempt in Denmark to make mothers full-time carers and there has been no serious attempt to challenge the publicly funded day care system. Since 1992/1993, the new Social–Democratic–Centre Government has intensified the active labour-market programmes targeted towards unskilled women and lone parents. The new leave programmes for education and child care can be interpreted as innovative labour-market policies with aim of creating more jobs as well as of expanding the caring and educational dimensions of the Danish welfare state. Notwithstanding the intentions, women make up the largest group of participants on leave schemes, and unemployed women and lone mothers make a large group of the participants on child care leave. This points toward a real dilemma: on the one hand, there is a need for women to have more time to care for young children, on the other, it has been suggested that women's demand to have more time for children is problematic from an equality perspective at a time when competition for jobs is severe. Educational schemes to improve the qualifications of the unemployed and directed explicitly toward unemployed, unskilled groups of women may be an alternative, but they do not solve the dilemma posed by full-time work and caring responsibilities. Since 1994, unemployment figures have gradually been reduced but mostly for men. Even if women's unemployment rates start to fall, full-time employment is neither a realistic nor a preferred solution for unskilled lone mothers with small children.

References

Abrahamsen, P. and Borchorst, B. (1996) *EU og socialpolitik* (EU and Social Politics). *Rapport givet til Rådet for Europæisk politik* (Report to the Council of European Politics), *March 1996.*

Abrahamsen, P. and Hansen, F.K. (1996) *Poverty in the European Union.* European Parliament: Centre for Alternative Social Analysis (CASA).

Andersen, B.R. (1989) 'Den offentlige vækst' (Public growth) *Politica 2,* 120–131.

Andersen, B.R. (1993) 'The Nordic welfare state under pressure: the Danish experience.' *Politics and Policy 21,* 2, April 1993.

Bak, M. (1996) *Enemorfamilien som senmoderne familieform* (Lone-parent families as postmodern family form). Ph.D. dissertation, Aalborg University: Institut for sociale forhold og organisation.

Bergquist, C. (1994) *Mäns makt och kvinnors intressen* (Women's and men's interests). Uppsala: Acto Universitatis Upsaliensis.

Borchorst, A. (1989) Kvinderne, velfærdsstaen og omsorgsarbejdet (Women, the Welfare State and Care Work) *Politica 2,* 132–148.

Borchorst, A. (1994) 'Working lives and family lives in Western Europe.' In S. Carlsen and J. Larsen (eds) *The Equality Dilemma. Reconciling Working Life and Family Life, Viewed from an Equality Perspective – the Danish Example.* Copenhagen: Munksgård.

Borchorst, A. (1995) 'Welfare state regimes, women's interests and the EC.' In D. Sainsbury (ed) *Gendering Welfare States*. London: Sage Publications.

Borchorst, A. and Siim, B. (1984) 'Kvinder i velfærdsstaten. Mellem moderskab og lonarbejde i 100 år' (Women in the welfare state). *Serie for kvindeforskning 14*, Aalborg Universitetsforlag.

Carlsen, S. and Larsen, J.E. (eds) (1994) *The Equality Dilemma. Reconciling Working Life and Family Life, Viewed from an Equality Perspective – the Danish Example*. Copenhagen: Munksgård.

Christoffersen, M.N. (1996) *En undersogelse af fædre med 3–5årige born* (An investigation of fathers with 3–5 year olds). Copenhagen: Socialforskningsinstituttet.

Ditch, J., Bradshaw, J. and Eardly, T. (1995a) *Developments in National Policies in 1994, European Observatory on National Family Policies*. University of York: Social Policy Research Unit.

Ditch, J., Bradshaw, J. and Eardly, T. (1995b) *A Synthesis of National Family Policies in 1994, European Observatory on National Family Policies*. University of York: Social Policy Research Unit.

Emerek, R. (1995) *On the Subject of Measuring Women's (and Men's) Participation in the Labour Market*. Feminist Research Centre in Aalborg, paper no.20.

E.S.C.R. Cross-National Research papers, Fourth Series. In L. Hantrais and M.-T. Letablier (eds) *Concepts and contexts in International Comparisons of Family Policies in Europe no. 1–4*.

Fifty Year Review 1995 (50-årsoversigten, 1995). Copenhagen: Danmarks statistik.

Goul Andersen, J. (1996) 'Marginalization, citizenship and the economy. The capacities of the universalist welfare state in Denmark.' Forthcoming in E. Eriksen and J. Loftager (eds) *The Rationality of the Welfare State*. Oslo: Universitetsforlaget.

Halskov, T. (1994) *Liden tue kan vælte et stort læs. Om enlige modre i EU. Tre eksempler: Tyskland, Italien og Danmark*, (Lone parents in the EU: Germany, Italy and Denmark). Copenhagen: Socialpolitisk Forening og forlag.

Hausen, F.K. (1990) *Børnefamilierness Økonomi* (The economics of families with children). Copenhagen: The Danish National Institute of Social Research.

Hernes, H. (1987) *Welfare State and Women Power*. Oslo: Norwegea University Press.

Hirdman, Y. (1989) *Att lägga livet till rätta. Studier i svensk folkhemspolitik* (Regulating Life). Stockholm: Carlssoms.

Hobson, B. (1995) 'Solo mothers, social policy regimes and the logic of gender.' In D. Sainsbury (ed) *Gendering Welfare States*. London: Sage Publications.

Hoff, J. (1993) 'Medburskab bruggerole.' In B.R. Anderson (ed) *Democracy and Political Participation*. Copenhagen: Munksgård.

Holt, H. (1994) 'The influence of work place culture on family life.' In S. Carlsen and J.E. Larsen (eds) *The Equality Dilemma. Reconciling Working Life, Viewed in an Equality Perspective, The Danish Example*. Copenhagen: The Danish Equal Status Council, Munksgård.

Ibsen, S. (1993) *Kvindelige arbejderes arbejdstid* (The Working Time of Female Workers). Copenhagen: Center for Alternativ Samfundsanalyse.

IDA (1991) Arbejdsnotat nr. 14. 1991. 'Kilder til personoplysninger om IDA vedroreende demografiske forhold, samliv og familie' (Sources of Information on persons in IDA concerning demography, cohabition and families). Rapport fra IDA-projektet. Copenhagen: Danmarks Statistik.

Jensen, J.J. (1994) 'Public child care in an equality perspective.' In S. Carlsen and J.E. Larsen (eds) *The Equality Dilemma. Reconciling Working Life, Viewed in an Equality Perspective, The Danish Example.* Copenhagen: The Danish Equal Status Council, Munksgård.

Knijn, T. (1994) 'Fish without bikes: revision of the Dutch welfare state and its consequences for the (in)dependencie of single mothers.' *Social Politics. International Studies in Gender, State and Society 1*, 1.

Knijn, T. and Kremer, M. (1995) 'Towards Inclusive Citizenship: Gender and the Caring Dimension of Welfare States.' Paper for the first expert seminar of the EC programme: 'Gender and Citizenship' Engendering Citizenship, Work and Care for Gender and Citizenship, Netherlands Institute for Advanced Studies, Wassenaar, July 3–5, 1996.

Knudsen, L.B. (1993) 'Fertility trends in Denmark in the 1980s.' *Danmarks Statistik* (Danish Statistics) 1993.

Knudsen, R. (1989) 'Social security in the Nordic countries.' *Norden förr och nu. Et sekel i statistisk belysning. 18.* Stockholm: Nordiske statistikermode.

Knudsen, R. (1990) *Familieydelser i Norden 1989* (Family Benefits in the Nordic countries 1989). Stockholm: Nordisk Statistisk Secretariat.

Koch-Nielsen, I. and Rostgaard, T. (1995) *Family Obligations in Denmark.* Socialforskningsinstituttet (Danish National Institute of Social Research) Working Paper, Copenhagen.

Larsen, J.E. and Sørensen, A.M. (1994) 'Lone parents.' In S. Carlsen and J.E. Larsen (eds) *The Equality Dilemma. Reconciling Working Life and Family Life, Viewed from an Equality Perspective – the Danish Example.* Copenhagen: The Danish Equal Status Council, Munksgård.

Leira, A. (1992) *Models of Motherhood. Welfare State Policy and Scandinavian Experiences of Everyday Practices.* Cambridge: Cambridge University Press.

Levevilkår i Danmark. Statistisk oversigt 1992, Socialforskningsinstituttet (Living Conditions in Denmark, Statistical Compendium). Copenhagen: Danish National Institute of Social Research.

Lewis, J. (ed) (1993) 'Introduction. Women, work and social policies in Europe.' In *Women and Social Policies in Europe. Work, the Family and the State.* Aldershot: Edward Elgar.

Lewis, J. and Ostner. I. (1994) *Gender and the Evolution of the European Social Policies.* Bremen: Centre for Social Policy Research, Arbeitspapir no.4. University of Bremen.

LO, The Danish Federation of Trade Unions (1991) *Bornefamilieredegrelse* (Family Review). Copenhagen: LO.

Orloff, A. (1993) *Gender and the Social Rights of Citizenship: The Comparative Analysis of Gender Relations and the Welfare States.* IRP Reprint Series, University of Madison.

Ostner, I. (1994) 'Independence and dependence – options and constraints for women over a life course.' In *Womens International Studies Forum 1994.* USA: Pergamon Press.

Petersen, H. (1994) 'Law and order in family life and working life.' In S. Carlsen and
    J.E. Larsen (eds) *The Equality Dilemma. Reconciling Working Life, Viewed in an Equality
    Perspective, The Danish Example.* Copenhagen: The Danish Equal Status Council.
Plovsing, J. (1994) *Socialpolitik i velfærdsstaten* (Social Politics in the Welfare State).
    Kobenhavn: Munsgård.
Qvortrup, J. (1994) 'The consequences of equality for children.' In S. Carlsen and
    J.E. Larsen (eds) *The Equality Dilemma. Reconciling Working Life, Viewed in an Equality
    Perspective, The Danish Example.* Copenhagen: The Danish Equal Status Council.
Rosenbeck, B. (1989) *Kvindekon. Den moderne kvindeligheds historie 1880–1960.* (The
    History of Modern Femininity). Copenhagen: Gyldendel.
Siim, B. (1988) 'Towards a feminist rethinking of the welfare state.' In K. Jones and
    A. Jonasdottir (eds) *The Political Interests of Women. Developing Theory and Research
    with a Feminist Face.* London: Sage Publications.
Siim, B. (1993) 'The gendered Scandinavian welfare states: the interplay between
    women's roles as mothers, workers and citizens in Denmark.' In J. Lewis (ed)
    Women and Social Policies in Europe. Work, the Family and the State. Aldershot: Edward
    Elgar.
Skjeie, H. (1992) 'Den politiske betydningen av kjönn. En studie av norsk
    topp-politik' (The Political Meaning of Gender). *Institut for Samfundsforskning, 92,*
    11.
Sommer, D. (1994) 'Fatherhood and caring. Who cares?' In S. Carlsen and J.E.
    Larsen (eds) *The Equality Dilemma. Reconciling Working Life, Viewed in an Equality
    Perspective, The Danish Example.* Copenhagen: The Danish Equal Status Council.
Statistisk 10-års oversigt, 1995 (Statistical ten year Review). Tema om
    befokningsudviklingen siden 1960 (Theme about the Population Development
    since 1960), Copenhagen: Danmarks Statistik.
Statistisk 10-års oversigt, 1996 (Statistical ten-year Review). Tema om
    befokningsudviklingen siden 1960 (Theme about the Population Development
    since 1960). Copenhagen: Danmarks Statistik.
Stenvig, B., Andersen, J. and Lauersen (1994) 'Statistisc for work and the family in
    Denmark and the EC.' In S. Soren Carlsen and J.E. Larsen (eds) *The Equality
    Dilemma. Reconciling Working Life, Viewed in an Equality Perspective, The Danish
    Example.* Copenhagen: The Danish Equal Status Councuil.
Stoltz, P. (1995) *Single Mothers in Denmark,* Working paper of the Gender and
    European Welfare Regime of the Human Capital and Mobility Programme of
    DGXII of the European Commission. LSE.
Ten Year Review 1995 (10-års oversigt, 1995) Copenhagen: Denmarks statistik.
Thaulow, I. and Gamst, B. (1987) *Enlige forsorgere mellem selvforsorgelse og bistandshjælp*
    (Single providers between wage work and social assistance). Copenhagen:
    Socialforsknings-institutet, The Social Research Institute.

CHAPTER SEVEN

Lone Mothers in Italy: a Hidden and Embarrassing Issue in a Familist Welfare Regime

Franca Bimbi

Introduction

In Italy the subject of lone mothers is one which has received little attention from sociologists and which remains outside political discussion. As far as existing welfare provisions are concerned, lone mothers are neither seen or heard. In part, this is easy to explain: there are few lone mothers (*see* Table 7.1), and even fewer lone fathers, few children under 14 or youngsters under 18 live with a lone parent (*see* Table 7.2) or in an institution[1] (Centro nazionale per la tutela dell'infanzia 1996). Moreover, as a group, lone mothers would not appear to be particularly exposed to the risk of poverty (Pressman 1995; Zanatta 1996; Commissione d'indagine sulla povertà e l'emarginazione 1996; Centro nazionale per la tutela dell'infanzia 1996) (*see* Table 7.2). Neither their behaviour nor that of their children appears to give rise to an acute social problem; nor are woman-headed families or children born out of wedlock seen as a moral threat to society.

Nevertheless, the case of lone mothers illustrates the contrast between a predominantly familist national culture and a welfare state which is virtually inactive as regards family policies (Saraceno 1994; Palomba and Menniti 1994; Menniti 1995; Bimbi 1995a).

---

1 In 1983 there were 202,000 lone fathers; the figures increased to 244,000 in 1988 and 272,000 in 1990. They represented respectively 14.7, 15.8 and 17.2 per cent of all lone parent families. As regard children, according to the 1991 Census, 90.2 per cent of minors were living with both parents (10,374,076 children overall), 7.9 per cent with only one parent (912,525 children) and 1.9 per cent with neither. In the same year, 9885 children under 14 years of age (1.10% of all children in that age-group) were living in institutions (Centro nazionale per la tutela dell'infanzia 1996).

Table 7.1 Lone mothers in Italy 1983–1990 (000 and %)

	1983	1988	1990
Numbers of lone mothers	1169	1302	1319
Lone mothers with dependent° children % of all families* with dependent° children	6.3**	6.5	8.0
Lone mothers with children <18 years % of all families* with children <18 years	4.7	5.4	5.9
Lone mothers with children >18 years % of all families*with children >18 years	22.3	29.5	28.1
Lone mothers % of all lone-parent families*	85.3	84.2	82.9

* Percentage is calculated on number of family nuclei regardless of the presence of other relatives in the household.

** Cohabitant children < 25 years.

° Children depending on parents' income, irrespective of the children's age.

Source: Istituto Nazionale di Statistica (1985) and Istituto Nazionale di Statistica (1993)

Table 7.2 Children in lone-parent families and poverty 1991 (%)

	Italy	North	Centre	South and Islands
Children <18 in lone-parent families*	7.9	15.7	8.4	15.5
Children <18 in lone-mother families*	5.2	11.7	5.6	9.2
Children <18 in poverty living** with lone parents	8.4	4.8	3.1	21.6
Children <18 in poverty living** with lone mother	10.8	5.9	3.7	24.1

* Percentage is calculated on number of children <18 living in families in the area regardless of the presence of other relatives (not parents or mother) in the household.

** Percentage is calculated on number of all Italian children <18 living with lone parents regardless of the presence of other relatives (not parents or mother) in the household.

Source: elaboration of data in: Centro nazionale per la tutela dell'infanzia, Dipartimento Affari Sociali (1996)

The fertility rate in Italy is among the lowest in the world (Lesthaeghe 1992). Abortions are decreasing (*see* Table 7.3) and births out-of-wedlock are relatively few among all age groups (*see* Table 7.4 and Table 7.5), despite the lowering of the age at which teenagers first have sexual intercourse (Castiglioni and Dalla Zuanna 1995). For the most part, children in Italy are mainly born within marriage, even when they are conceived before the wedding takes place (Pinnelli and Prati 1994). Given that the divorce rate is the lowest in the European Union and that the number of divorces and separations is rising slowly (*see* Table 7.6), it is easy to understand why there are relatively few lone mothers. At present, the majority of lone mothers are, in fact, widows (*see* Table 7.7).

Table 7.3 Abortions of non-married and married women, per 1000 women 1980–1991

Year	Non-married women	Married women
1980	12.4	20.8
1983	14.2	22.3
1988	10.8	16.3
1991	10.0	14.0

Source: Pinnelli, A. and Prati, S. (1994)

Table 7.4 Marital and extra-marital births 1950–1991
Fertility rate per 1000 women 15–44 and % never married women

Years	Legitimate births	'Natural'* births	Never married women
1950–1951	121.0	9.2	44.4
1961–1962	129.7	6.4	49.8
1971–1972	102.7	5.3	42.8
1980	83.6	6.2	38.5
1985	76.4	6.0	41.6
1991	77.0	6.0	46.0

* After the 1970 family law the term 'illegitimate birth' was changed to 'natural birth'.
Source: Pinnelli, A. and Prati, S. (1994)

Table 7.5 'Natural'* births and registration of births outside marriage 1951–1991

Years	Natural births per 1,000 live births	% of joint registrations
1951	35.2	13.2
1961	22.0	12.9
1970	19.5	16.2
1973	25.3	20.1
1980	42.9	64.9
1983	48.7	70.4
1988	58.5	76.7
1991	62.3	84.6

* After the 1970 family law the term 'illegitimate birth' was changed to 'natural birth'.
Source: Pinnelli, A. and Prati, S. (1994)

Table 7.6 Separation rates and divorces rates 1921–1991 (rates per 10,000 population)

Year	Separation rate	Divorce rate
1921–1930	0.3	–
1931–1940	0.3	–
1941–1950	1.1	–
1951–1960	0.9	–
1961–1970	1.2	–
1971–1980	3.6	2.8
1981	5.4	2.2
1991	6.0	3.0

Source: Golini, A. (1988)

Table 7.7 Distribution of lone mothers by marital status 1983–1990 (%)

Lone mothers	1983	1988	1990
Never married	6.0	7.0	6.3
Separated	18.6	18.5	20.7
Divorced	4.0	5.0	5.3
Widowed	71.4	69.5	67.7

Source: elaboration of data in: Istituto Nazionale di Statistica (1993)

Another characteristic peculiar to Italy is that children live with their parents until they get married (De Sandre 1988; De Sandre 1991; Bimbi 1991), and are maintained by them so long as they stay in the family. It is therefore extremely difficult to distinguish lone mothers with dependent children by referring only to the legal age of 18 years (the average age at marriage is 26 years for women and 29 years for men).

Despite the fact that the responsibility for maintaining and caring for children continues for so long, even in families with a single breadwinner, there is, nevertheless, no national policy of support for lone mothers. There is a patchwork of local policies which, for the most part, are means-tested and aimed at minors or families in difficulty. They have developed since the second half of the 1970s and are provided by the *comune* (local council) or local health board. The *provincia* (regional government), on the other hand, is responsible for highly discretional and categorical policies, mainly financial assistance, that give support to never-married mothers and children born out-of-wedlock. These are based on legislation to encourage population growth dating from the Fascist period.

The absence of both political debate on the subject of lone mothers and welfare policies concerning them should be placed within the framework of the general lack of family policies which is a persistent feature of post-war Italy. The causes of this are to be sought in three directions. First, we must remember that there still exists a profound reaction to Fascism, which, for the first and only time in Italian history, produced explicit family policies and categorical policies for lone mothers. Second, the Mediterranean model of welfare has, since the post-war period, featured a long period of family care for children and relatives, alongside residual state responsibility for family welfare. This means that the welfare state consistantly recognises the legitimate priority of the family group to mediate individual rights. Third, the co-existence of profound demographic changes alongside the equally strong traditional forms of matrimonial and intergenerational bonds, points to the hegemony of a shared cultural model marked by the importance of the family group.

As elsewhere, in present day Italy, sex and marriage and marriage and family do not necessarily coexist, just as marriage and parenthood may be separated. Nevertheless, the family, however defined at various stages of the life cycle, continues to be seen as the primary system of social protection, irrespective of the individual's relationship to the labour market and the rights of individuals recognised by the welfare state. This cultural model structures the gendered nature of the welfare regime and the way in which lone mothers package income.

Lone mothers may derive their income from several sources: waged labour (*see* Table 7.8), maintenance payments (for divorced or separated women), survivors' pensions (for widows and divorcees with maintenance rights), financial help or services provided by the family of origin, and public assistance. The labour market and the family of origin provide the most important support for lone mothers (La Mendola and Neresini 1995). Lone mothers who turn to public assistance are also dependent on waged labour and the family. Only some widows receive a survivor's pension which, when added to the benefits received by their children, provides enough to live on. Receiving benefits from social assistance does not rule out other sources of income such as wage income, pensions, derived pensions and maintenance payments. On this count, the Italian welfare system would appear to have a neutral attitude to the presence of women in the labour market or even to be facilitating a dual-breadwinner norm for couples.

Table 7.8 Lone mothers, mothers in couples and employment from the 1980s to the 1990s (%)

	1980	1990
Employed mothers in couples	32.1 (ISTAT 1988)	32.6 (ISTAT 1990)
Employed lone mothers	34.8 (ISTAT 1988)	37.0 (ISTAT 1990)
Unemployed mothers in couples with children under 5	19.1 (Rubery and Fagan 1989)	
Unemployed mothers in couples with children 5–9	14.4 (Rubery and Fagan 1989)	
Unemployed lone mothers with children under 5	22.3 (Rubery and Fagan 1989)	
Unemployed lone mothers with children 5–9	13.8 (Rubery and Fagan 1989)	
Employed lone mothers with children <18	53.8 (Menniti and Palomba 1985)	67.6 (Zanatta 1993) 71.9 (Eurostat 1993)
Unemployed lone mothers with children <18		13.9 (Eurostat 993)
Unemployed lone mothers with dependent° children	46.6 (ISTAT 1988)	48.5 (ISTAT 1990)

* Percentage is calculated on number of families regardless of the presence of other relatives in the household.

° Children depending on parents' income, irrespective of the children's age.

Sources: EUROSTAT (1995), Istituto Nazionale di Statistica (1985), Istituto Nazionale di Statistica (1993), Menniti, A. and Palomba, R. (1988), Rubery, J. and Fagan, C.(1993) and Zanatta, A.L. (1996)

The family of origin has the important role of helping the lone mother look after her children, thus enabling her to work full time. In Italy, support from the family network is a necessary pre-condition for women's presence in the labour market; they mostly work full time (European Community Commission 1995).

Relatively few lone mothers depend on men's incomes for support. Maintenance payments from former husbands (but not those paid in respect of the children) are subject to taxation as are the pensions of widows and orphans. These provisions, like all social provisions in Italy (except for maternity leave), are not specifically for women (Gauthier 1995; Bimbi 1995b).

For the most part, the Italian welfare system regards lone mothers as workers who happen to be mothers rather than mothers who also work. Their major source of income, as well as social rights and status, is derived mainly from paid work. From this point of view, in a country which has one of the lowest levels of women's employment in the European Union (33.6% in 1993: Eurostat 1995), lone mothers appear to be a prototype of the modernisation of women's roles and the gender system.

As regards employment among lone mothers and their exposure to the risk of poverty and relation to public assistance, a distinction must be made between the situation in the South of Italy and that of the rest of the country (*see* Table 7.9). A strong economic dualism exists in Italy. Among southern families, the traditional male-breadwinner regime prevails (*see* Table 7.10), marked by the very limited presence of women on the labour market and high male unemployment (Commissione d'indagine sulla povertà 1996a). In Northern and Central Italy, the prevailing image of modernity is, however, contradicted by working women's dependence on their family of origin, particularly on grandmothers, for childcare, which constitutes a moral duty and a traditional tie.

Table 7.9 Distribution of lone-mother families* in different areas, 1983–1990 (%)

	1983	1988	1990
North	51.0	49.3	50.5
Centre	18.1	18.4	19.9
South and Islands	30.9	32.3	29.6
ITALY	100	100	100

* Percentage is calculated on number of families regardless of the presence of other relatives in the household.

Source: elaboration of data in: Istituto Nazionale di Statistica (1993)

**Table 7.10 Lone mothers and breadwinner regimes in couples.
Families* with children <18, 1991 (%)***

	North (weak dual-breadwinner regime and strong labour-market orientation for lone mothers)	Centre (weak male-breadwinner regime and labour-market orientation for lone mothers)	South and Islands (Strong male-breadwinner regime and familist-breadwinner regime for lone mothers)	Italy
Children <18 living with two parents, both employed	51.2	49.8	43.8	47.8
Children <18 living with employed lone mothers	62.1	55.6	34.9	50.1

* Percentages are calculated on number of children <18 living with two parents (in the first row) and on number of children <18 living with lone mothers (in the second row), on the basis of families in the area regardless of the presence of other relatives (not parents or mother) in the household.

Source: elaboration of data in: Centro nazionale per la tutela dell'infanzia, Dipartimento Affari sociali (1996)

Furthermore, the particular difficulties faced by lone mothers which distinguish them from mothers forming part of couples have not been tackled. In the case of separation or divorce, there is no assumption of responsibility, either by way of compensation or substitution, by the state to make up for the lack of maintenance from fathers.

Paradoxically, in the land of mamma and bambini, where mothers and children are high profile, lone mothers, whether waged workers or housewives, end up as madri-ombra (mothers in the shadows). In this chapter, we will attempt to explain this paradox.

Lone mothers: structural and cultural aspects of the Italian demographic model

In Italy in 1991, the fertility rate per woman was 1.3, giving a birth rate of 9.9 per 1000 inhabitants. Children born out-of-wedlock accounted for 6.6 per 100 births, almost five times less than in the UK and France, and seven times less than in Denmark (Golini 1994). In Italy there is a sharper separation between sex and reproduction than in other industrialised countries, but reproduction takes place within marriage. At present, it seems that most couples prefer to have an only child and that this trend is on the increase (Santini 1995a; Bimbi 1996a). However, a child is still considered necessary for 'having a family' (Palomba 1987). There are fewer women with no children among those born after World War II than among women born in the interwar years (Egidi and Zaccarin 1995). On the other hand, two typical features of modernity, the separation of sex and marriage and the link between sexual liberalisation and out-of-wedlock births, are less marked in Italy than elsewhere.

These forms of behaviour reflect the cultural aspects of the Italian demographic model and shape the context of lone motherhood. At the start of the demographic transition, in the 1920s and 1930s, the birth rate began to fall but was still higher than many other European countries (Livi Bacci 1980). The post-war years saw a sharper drop in the birth rate than elsewhere, but births occurred more often within wedlock than in the past (Golini 1988; Santini 1995b). The 'contraceptive revolution', prior to the contraceptive pill, took place within marriage. Until the 1970s, the gender system still attached great importance to women's virginity and the right of men to demand what the law itself termed *debito coniugale* (conjugal debt or duty). Throughout the 1980s, the most frequently used contraceptive method was *coitus interruptus*, chiefly a male decision, while that used least was the contraceptive pill (sterilisation is not allowed by the law). In the 1980s and 1990s, the effects of the separation between sex and reproduction are to be seen chiefly within marriage (Giacobazzi *et al.* 1989; Blangiardo and Bonarini 1988; Menniti and Palomba 1994). Even abortions involve chiefly adult, married women.

We can explore these changes by observing the sexual behaviour of younger women. Research into the age of first sexual intercourse for women born between 1960 and 1965 shows that among Italian teenagers the separation of sex and marriage took place later than in other European countries. At the beginning of the 1990s, the mean age for first sexual intercourse was 18 years for males and 19 years for females (Castiglioni and Della Zuanna 1995). Even though sexual intercourse almost always precedes marriage, women especially seem to maintain a monogamous orientation in pre-marital sexual intercourse.[2] As regards the connection between sex and out-of-wedlock births, there is substantial continuity in terms of the rate of pre-marital conceptions (PMC) and out-of-wedlock births throughout the 1950s and early 1960s[3] (Castiglioni and Della Zuanna 1995; Golini 1988).

---

2   In the course of interviews we carried out (Bimbi and Castellano 1990; Bimbi 1996b; Nava 1996) on two groups of couples, the first with children under 3 years of age and the second with children under 12, the women (unlike their partners) reported first having sexual intercourse with their spouses.

3   For the 1950s and 1960s Castiglioni and Della Zuanna (1995) reported 14 PMC per 1000 never-married women aged 15–44, about 18 PMC per 100 marriages. In the 1990s there were 7 PMC per 1000 never-married women aged 15–44, 14 PMC per 100 marriages. Out-of-wedlock births decreased throughout the 1970s; by 1986 there were the same number of out-of-wedlock births as a century before (5.6 per 100 births; Golini 1988). We should, however, bear in mind that no statistics exist prior to 1978 for abortions.

Researchers agree that the changes in sexual, reproductive and matrimonial behaviour began to intensify from the second half of the 1960s onward (Barbagli 1990; Livi Bacci and Breschi 1992). It is interesting to observe that many indications of a transition in behaviour preceded a change in the law (Bimbi 1993). Divorce was made legal in 1970 and in 1975 the new family law code came into effect. The ban on publicity for contraceptives was lifted in 1971, family planning policies aimed at securing freedom of choice for women were introduced in 1975, and 1978 saw the legalisation of abortion. From 1971 to 1981, the number of separations, divorces, cohabitations, out-of-wedlock births and non-religious weddings all increased sharply. There was a fall in the number of weddings in general and in church weddings in particular and the number of children per woman also decreased (Golini et al. 1988; Santini 1988). However, while these changes moved in the same direction as those in other countries, they were much less intense, apart from the fall in the birth rate.

Overall, the liberalisation of sexual and reproductive behaviour which has taken place has so far maintained the connection between marriage and reproduction. For the time being, the secularisation of values related to sexuality has not threatened the institution of marriage.

Cohabitation rarely occurs in Italy and when it does it is very often for a limited period, prior to marriage, and seldom involves the birth of children (Barbagli 1990; Sabbadini 1991a; Sabbadini 1991b; De Santis 1992). Nevertheless, the figures are probably underestimates because unmarried couples have no particular legal standing and become visible only when they have children.[4]

Lone-parent families in Italy have only been the subject of study since 1983 (ISTAT 1985; Golini, Menniti and Palomba 1987; Menniti and Palomba 1988; Rossi Sciumé and Scabini 1991; La Mendola and Neresini 1995; Zanatta 1996). In 1990, they numbered 10 per cent of families, but this figure falls to 5.5 per cent if we consider only those with children under the age of 18. The only feature they have in common with lone-parent families in other countries is the great predominance of lone mothers over lone fathers. Since widowhood is the most common marital status among Italian lone mothers, and because children tend to stay at home longer, it follows that Italian lone mothers are older than elsewhere. The number of very young lone mothers is extremely low.

Thus we see that lone motherhood in Italy keeps its traditional aspects for the time being. We should, however, bear in mind that it is only since 1970 that women have been exposed to the idea that the separation of sex, reproduction and marriage is legitimate. The severance of sex and reproduction

---

4   In the 1960s, 2 per cent of marriages were preceded by cohabitation. By 1980, 8 per cent of couples were living together. Between 1983 and 1990, unmarried couples remained steady at about 1.3 per cent of the total number of families. In 1931 the figure was 2.4 per cent (Golini 1988). Over two-thirds of those living together are 45 years of age or more.

within marriage has been the most important innovation for women born in the post-war years. The separation of parenthood and marriage could become more manifest in the next generation, for example among those women reaching the reproductive stage from the mid-1980s onwards. There will probably be an increase in never-married mothers since it was in the 1980s that women began to have sexual intercourse at a younger age and pre-marital sexuality became more widespread. Furthermore, this happened at a time when there was no policy of contraceptive information aimed at the younger generation and legalised abortion was again being called into question.

Today in the 1990s, the conflict between the traditional paradigm of sexuality, which envisages reproduction within wedlock, and the secular paradigm, which holds that the separation of sex, reproduction, marriage and parenthood is legitimate for women as well as for men, is strikingly evident in the re-emergence of certain phenomena that were typical of the past (Pomata, 1980; Kertzer 1993), such as infanticide and the abandonment of children. Though the cases are few, they nevertheless deserve attention. Statistics show that the severance of sexuality, reproduction and marriage is more intense in Northern and Central Italy, where contraception is under women's control to a greater extent (the use of the contraceptive pill predominates and is on the increase), and where the proportion of separated and divorced women has always been greater. In the country as a whole, from 1983 to 1991 there has been an increase in the number of lone mothers (*see* Table 7.1 and Table 7.7), especially among those separated either legally or *de facto*.

The presence and absence of lone mothers in the social construction of the Italian welfare regime

1922 to 1945. The Fascist Regime: the first and only welfare policy for lone mothers

The Fascist period saw the first and only systematic attempt at a welfare policy for lone mothers in Italian history (Saraceno 1988; Saraceno 1991a; Saraceno 1992; Bock 1992; De Grazia 1992a; De Grazia 1992b; Simoni forthcoming). The Fascist policies for the family, sexuality, reproduction and motherhood were shaped within an authoritarian and patriarchal framework, and were directed to ends such as nationalism and expansionism, increasing the population and defending the race. The Fascist policy on women had three basic points:

(1) A strong tendency toward state intervention on reproduction, in contrast to the *laissez-faire* attitude of the liberal state.

(2) The differentiation of women by emphasising the maternal role, excluding them from political citizenship and discriminating against them in the labour market and in education.

(3) The definition of marriage and reproduction as matters for public concern (Ipsen 1993; Stiglitz 1993), guaranteed by the legal authority of the husband and father, and directed towards achieving the demographic aims of the regime.

All of this contrasted with Catholic doctrine, which saw the family as an institution set up according to natural law, pre-existing the state, and bearing rights that were justified by the intrinsic relationship between natural morality and religious morality. The Fascist regime's social policies were reformatory compared to those of the previous liberal state, but reactionary as regards women's citizenship and weak in practical and ideological terms compared to the influence of the Catholic Church on the private life of the individual.

The social construction of motherhood under Fascism was based on four pillars:

(1) The setting up of the National Institute for Motherhood and Childhood (ONMI) in 1925.

(2) The protection of working mothers within an increasingly rigid male-breadwinner regime (1923 and 1934).

(3) The regulation of prostitution (1929).

(4) The Concordat with the Catholic Church of 1929 (which, among other things, redefined children born of marriages celebrated only in church as legitimate), together with the new Civil Code of 1942, which defined abortion and contraception as crimes against the race and rape as a crime against public morals and decency.

With these tools, the Fascist regime was able to twin mothers into social group and reproduction into a privileged issue for social policy (Cappiello *et al.* 1988). This was done by means of the separation and differentiation of women into various categories: 'fallen' or 'seduced' women (Terragni 1996) incapable of motherhood (that is prostitutes or mothers who abandoned their children or who did not wish to bring them up); lone mothers and poor nursing mothers (aided by ONMI); married mothers or widows not at risk (dependent on their husband's income, benefits or pension); and working mothers, for whom, apart from compulsory maternity leave, there were benefits paid mainly to their husbands (bonuses for marriage and childbirth, and family allowances).

It was mainly pregnant women, never-married women and widows who were assisted by ONMI, but it also helped married women, deserted by their husbands and those whose husbands were in prison or unable to maintain the family (according to the ONMI's law of 1926). A series of measures aimed at mothers, irrespective of their relationships with the father of their children, were passed with two conditions, namely that the mothers lacked the means of support for their children and that they did not give the babies to a wet nurse. Lone mothers were both privileged and stigmatised at the same time in national social policy, which was directed towards safeguarding the health and morals of the younger generation. A system of social services and financial benefits (housing for the mothers, crèches and free school meals) covered the period from the final weeks of pregnancy to the child's coming of age. This type of action was designed to rescue as many mothers as possible in both physical and moral terms. 'Fallen' women and girls 'at risk' were helped to at least nurse their children, even if they could not raise them; illegitimate children could become legitimate, a special dowry being offered to the 'seducer' if he married the mother.

ONMI pursued both a pro-natalist policy for the nation and a normalising and controlling one for the individual's private life; promoting the restoration of the legitimate family, the moralisation of women and the prevention of abandonment of children. The idea was that 'fallen women' or unsuitable mothers could be changed into nursing mothers, or even raise their own children and become wives if they co-operated with the public assistance authorities. Legislation on public assistance and on the control of prostitution were complementary, aiming at dividing women and differentiating them according to social and moral categories. The mother became a rhetorical figure for the strength of the nation and the health of the race. Ideally she was a housewife, mother to a brood of children (all legitimate), and totally dependent on her husband. It is no coincidence that the protection of working mothers, though well developed and financially supportive, was accompanied by legislation giving men preferential access to education, jobs, careers, family allowances and bonuses for marriage and births.

The Concordat of 1929 and the new Civil Code of 1942 gave a public and political significance to private life which, for women, stressed the ideal model of the mother with no financial autonomy. Furthermore, the legislation emphasised at a symbolic level and as far as public morals were concerned, women's lack of decision-making capacity as regards sexuality, reproduction, contraception and abortion. However, the Fascist regime failed in its attempt to define marriage and reproduction as public goods. The Concordat effectively limited the attempt to render motherhood and family an affair for the state alone, by bringing marriage ceremonies celebrated in a Catholic church back within the Italian legal system. This served to connect Fascism's redefinition of patriarchy and the male-breadwinner family model to religious ideology. The Church achieved its objective of bringing the public definition of the individual's private life within its moral and doctrinal perspective. Furthermore, the drop in the birth rate and the rise in women's employment show the practical limits of Fascist policies aimed at strengthening women's maternal role and the male-breadwinner regime.

*From the post-war years to the 1980s. The eclipse of lone mothers: from
moral censure of atypical families to the mild decommodification of welfare
policies*

At the end of the war, the directly pro-natalist policies of the Fascist regime
were abolished. Moreover, every direct intervention by the state into the private
life of the individual was delegitimised. Nevertheless, public welfare policies
continued to be shaped by two strands:

(1) Catholic social doctrine which defined the family, organising it
hierarchically around the authority of the husband and father, as a
unit endowed with independent political capacity that in some
circumstances could prevail over that of the state.

(2) Catholic sexual morality which guaranteed the control of women's
sexuality by the family.

These were expressed through the school system and social legislation. After
the Fascist period the Church regained its hegemony in the field of public
assistance and its leading role in the public debate on the family and reproduction. Until the end of the 1960s the ruling Christian Democrat Party (DC)
guaranteed the hegemony of the Catholic ideology giving considerable financial support to the welfare and educational activities of the Church. The Church
played a particularly active role in running institutes for abandoned children
and in primary and pre-school education.

At the national level, public welfare policies were moving towards commodi-
fication, with, for example the implementation of the contributory insurance
system for workers. As far as lone mothers were concerned, there was a fairly
uniform development up to the second half of the 1960s. Government policy
supported a welfare system based on the male-breadwinner regime. The most
important measure was dependants' allowances (*assegni familiari*) paid to heads
of households (1955 and 1961). Working women with dependent children or
relatives could only receive these if they were widows; women separated from,
or abandoned by, their husbands; married to a permanent invalid; or never-married mothers with children not recognised by the father. Since 1948, survivors'
pension entitlements have been gradually extended to widows, widowers,
orphans under 18 years and to those adult children with no income (however
married daughters were excluded as indeed were non-invalid husbands). Up to
the 1980s at least, the system of dependants' allowances and survivor's pensions
gave husbands an advantage over wives, widows over widowers, and lone
working mothers over married ones.

The 1970s marked a turning point in welfare policy and the social
construction of women and motherhood. As regards welfare policy, the shift in
responsibility from the centralised state to local authorities was of crucial

importance (Bimbi 1995c). Between 1970 and 1977, regional governments and local councils were given most of the responsibility for the majority of welfare policies, including financial support as well as social services. Since this shift, there has been a mixture of an institutional welfare system, organised by regional governments and, in particular, local councils, on the one hand, and insurance-based welfare, on the other. However, a tendency, albeit a mild one, did emerge towards a decommodification of assistance, chiefly in respect of mothers and children. Regional and local social provision includes free health-care during pregnancy and childbirth, free preventative medicine for children, free nursery schools and crèches for working mothers, community health centres, and basic council social work services. These policies were based on a universalist concept of citizenship rather than insurance contributions, and avoided categorical benefits. It goes without saying that this process of decommodification and universalism exists mainly where employment is high, in Northern and Central Italy, and not in the South where unemployment has always been high and is likely to remain so.

The growth of public welfare policies reduced the space in which the Catholic Church and other religious associations could operate. The 1970s saw the gradual decline of the Church's hegemony over the customs and legal definition of the family and sexuality (Guizzardi 1976; Guizzardi 1982). The fall in the birth-rate within marriage highlights the Church's loss of control over sexual morality, even among those who continue to get married in church and declare themselves Catholics.

In both the conservative early 1960s and the innovatory and conflictual 1970s and early 1980s, lone mothers did not get a mention. This silence on the subject of lone mothers has an absurd side to it since, in actual fact, the policies begun under Fascism were still partially in existence, and lone mothers – again partially – benefitted from the new provisions introduced by local government. However, even since 1983 and the revival of interest in types of lone-parent families, no political party or social researcher has inquired into the provisions for lone mothers. The continuing silence on the subject may be explained in the light of both the dominant representation of the woman-as-mother and the trends in the Italian welfare regime.

Up to the 1970s, two figures emerge from the critical debate on Italian social policy, that of the working woman and that of the housewife. The institution-alisation of women's lives around marriage (Saraceno 1991b) sees these two possibilities as mutually exclusive. It is as if working women did not do unpaid housework and all housewives remained housewives for life. The conflict which centred on these two roles completely silenced any mention of lone mothers. Furthermore, in the politically conservative climate of the 1950s and 1960s, lone mothers were morally embarrassing for all political parties. Catholics felt the need to censure any deviation from the norm of the legitimate family, while the Left partially shared these Catholic prejudices while also fearing their attacks. Out-of-wedlock pregnancies and unmarried mothers were often held up as examples of the undesirable effects of the presence of women in the labour market. From the 1970s onwards, the social rights of mothers have been subsumed under measures aimed at the families of employees, in industry or the pubic sector, and women workers. Thus, the working mother in the nuclear family became the subject of new policies in local welfare administrations.

During the post-war years, the central focus of public assistance on poor mothers has changed dramatically. In the period up to the 1970s, the emphasis shifted from the mother to the child in danger of being abandoned or orphaned. Later, it shifted again: the needs of mothers and children were supported, while taking into consideration the nature of the parents' relationship and the family network (Bimbi 1996c). This does not mean that the mother and child were assisted only if the father and family network did not help. Nevertheless, when determining the amount and duration of provision, the support offered by the father and family of origin was taken into account.[5] The various measures adopted also contain shifts of emphasis: from assisting unemployed mothers, to supporting mainly working mothers with low incomes, based on the assumption that work is a right-cum-duty for all women; and from public responsibility for only the very poor, to the sharing of responsibility for the mother and the family with the public assistance authorities. The shift of interest from mother to child, mother to working woman, and mother to parents and family network provided the legitimation for the removal of lone mothers from the political debate, even though they continued to be the main beneficiaries of certain public welfare policies.

The outcome: lone mothers in welfare practice and the debate on the family

The different trajectories of lone mothers in the welfare system: integration without recognition

Lone mothers go unnoticed in the welfare system for several reasons. To some extent, it is because their entitlement to certain provisions has subsequently been re-allocated to out-of-wedlock children (called 'natural' children after 1975). In part, it is because certain categorical benefits originally reserved for lone mothers are interpreted by local bodies as part of a gender neutral assistance system and used more generally to support children in poor families. Finally, it is because lone mothers are integrated into the system of benefits and social services reserved for women workers (créches), or organised on a

---

5   It should be borne in mind that there is still no national legislation on welfare assistance and that even the national law for ONMI varies considerably in its application depending on regional and local rules.

universalist basis (nursery schools and health services). In practice, the small numbers of Italian lone mothers are distributed within the entire system of welfare, both insurance based and assistance based. On the one hand, they have been urged to integrate into the broader system of citizenship through paid work and, on the other, they have disappeared as a social group precisely at the time when the Feminist Movement was making strong demands for social citizenship (Calabrò and Grasso 1985; Boccia *et al.* 1987; Del Re 1996). This makes it easier to understand why the post-war continuation of policies set up under Fascism go unnoticed (and have so far not been studied).

Let us now trace the more salient changes in welfare measures. All traces of Fascist ideology have been removed from legislation. However, funding for ONMI was increased in 1950 and categorical benefits for lone mothers were left intact. After the war, some institutions, financed by certain categories of workers and the state to serve widowed mothers, were set up or reorganised. For example the National Assistance Institute for Italian Workers' Orphans (ENAOLI), established in 1948 and the National Assistance Institute for Orphans of Italian Medical Personnel (ONAOSI) which was reorganised in 1957.

Some idea of the extent of ONMI's activities can be had from the fact that in 1968 ONMI crèches numbered 562 and covered 2.2 per cent of eligible children in the whole country and 3 per cent in the North (*see* Table 7.11). ONMI, however, was abolished in 1975. Between 1971 and 1975, its responsibility for welfare assistance was separated from that for the social services. Generally, in this period, its responsibilities and funds were passed to the regional, provincial or local authority. No uniform criteria were used when devolution took place and, to make matters worse, the various regions transferred funds and responsibilities in different ways according to different welfare frameworks and policy principles. Even provincial and local authorities within the same region developed different criteria and means-tests for the allocation of benefits and services.

Table 7.11 Pre-school provisions: crèches (children 0–3) and nursery schools (children 3–5) from the 1960s to the 1990s

	1960s	1970s	1980s	1990
Children in crèches, % of children 0–3	2.2 (1963)	2.1 (1976)	5.2 (1986)	5.5 (1990)
Children in nursery schools, % of children 3–5	48.5 (1962–1963)	56.8 (1970–1971)	77.8 (1980–1981)	91.1 (1991–1992)

Source: elaboration data in: ISTAT, Welfare statistics, various years.

In 1975 the running of crèches was transferred to local authorities and there was immediately a dramatic change in the type of service users. All children under the age of three whose mothers are at work now have the right to a place, on payment of a fee which varies according to family income. The policy on crèches is an example of the integration of lone mothers into the institutional system of social services for working mothers. If the lone mothers are at work, their children have priority; if they are poor and receive benefit, they may not have to pay fees. After ONMI had been abolished, responsibility for cash assistance passed to the provincial authorities, but the national laws (dating from 1926 and 1934) which defined categorical criteria for benefits in respect of lone mothers remained in force. However, the application of their general rules produces very different results since the policies operate within different regional welfare models. The Italian local welfare system may be seen as an attempt at a federalist administrative model with no national co-ordination and few certainties as regards the rights of citizens (Bimbi forthcoming). Thus, the outcomes for lone mothers in a fragmentary welfare system were extremely varied. The case of ONMI is paradigmatic.

The wide variation in outcomes has been confirmed by some exploratory investigations carried out on 50 of the 95 Italian provinces (Bordin 1996).[6] The basis for the amount of financial assistance is normally '*il minimo vitale*' (the minimum necessary for subsistence), worked out on the basis of the lowest pension available in the contributory insurance system (INPS) on the first of January of each year. However, the amounts allocated vary, as do the requirements for means-testing; priority categories may be different; and benefits may be, to a greater or lesser extent, integrated with those of the local authority or health board, or their administration delegated to these institutions. For the most part, assistance is aimed at never-married mothers, whose children may or may not be recognised by the father. It is mainly the child, rather than the mother, who is considered to have the right to such benefit, although it is almost always the mother who actually receives it. The Emilia Romagna region has a more universalist, institutional and comprehensive approach. Here the provisions are generally directed towards any lone mother in difficulty. A broader interpretation of the concepts of need and lone motherhood has enabled this

---

6   The aim of the study, directed by the author, is to build up a picture of the various models of assistance at the disposal of lone mothers within local government. So far, the policies of 50 provincial authorities have been examined (Bordin 1996). In addition, cases of social assistance for lone mothers in the local council of Treviso (Bordin 1996) and Venice (Giullardi 1996; Kyllonen 1996) have been studied. In Florence, Trifiletti conducted a survey into the life course of lone mothers using in-depth interviews. La Mendola and Ruspini are the methodological consultants. The preliminary results of the study were presented to the annual Conference of the Italian Sociological Association, 'Everyday-life' Committee, October 3–5, 1996, University of Padua (*see* Bordin 1996; Giullari 1996; Kyllonen 1996; Ruspini 1996; Sutter 1996; Terragni 1996; Trifiletti 1996).

region to abandon the preferential assistance for the category of never married-mothers (Sutter 1996).

These ex-ONMI benefits and services highlight the differences in the treatment of different kinds of lone mother by local welfare authorities (local council, provinces, health system), and also reveal the contradiction between national and regional laws. The social service philosophy, which combines financial assistance with social work for the woman and the family network, is directed towards 'solving' the case rather than responding exclusively to financial need. This leads to some interesting consequences. Intervention is discretional and varies with the professional style of the services involved. Financial support is not defined exclusively by objective rules but also depends on the woman's ability to interact with the service, and action is directed towards keeping the woman in the labour market. In Northern and Central Italy, the linking of the provision of benefits to encouraging women to enter the labour market would seem to offer a dynamic model of welfare to lone mothers legitimately seeking a means of support. However, some of those assisted continue to draw benefit for five years or more and are dependent on a number of services. Overall, the social work intervention is designed mainly either to prevent unemployment or to support marginal employment.

How far, then, does assistance to lone mothers function as an indirect labour policy for women? The answer to this question is difficult to come by since local bodies do not normally list lone mothers, lone-parent families, or the type of families assisted among the three traditional categories entitled to benefit: minors, the elderly and the disabled. The National Report on the Condition of Minors (Centro Nazionale per la tutela dell'infanzia 1996) estimates that approximately 11 per cent of families consisting of a lone mother and dependent minors live in poverty. However, we do not know how many of them receive public assistance. Empirical studies in progress on local and provincial authorities (*see* footnote 6) show an increase in separated and divorced lone mothers compared to widows and a slight increase in the number of never-married lone mothers. Those marginally employed are more numerous than housewives and the unemployed.

From our analysis of the post-1975 ex-ONMI policies, four partially contra-dictory features emerge. First, lone mothers as the recipients of benefits and services are 'invisible'. Second, they are included within the categories of poor people at the outer edges of the insurance system. Third, there is pressure on them to take on the role of working mother and head of the household, rather than being dependent on public assistance or on a male breadwinner. Finally, there is financial and psychological pressure on lone mothers to turn to their family of origin.

In the post-war period, another provision to which lone mothers have access has developed and expanded. This is the survivor's pension for widows, orphans and relatives of a deceased worker. The overall amount depends on the length of time the deceased paid insurance contributions. The sum received by each beneficiary depends on the degree of kinship and the number of surviving relatives who may benefit. It was originally a provision typical of the male-breadwinner regime but it later developed along Mediterranean familist lines (Trifiletti 1995). Since the 1977 law on parity, direct and explicit discrimination in the various pension schemes has been progressively eliminated. At present, the survivor's pension provides for, in descending order of priority of claim and amount of benefit: widows (and widowers) and former spouses, both separated and divorced (if in receipt of maintenance payments); children under 18 years and adult children if they have no income, or are students or invalids; and finally, other dependent relatives. As regards the first category (widows and ex-spouses), the benefit is for life, is not means-tested (since 1993), is paid whether the beneficiary is working or unemployed, whether she/he has or has not got children and stops only if the beneficiary re-marries.

Since most lone-parent families have a widow as head of household, the survivor's pension is the measure which perhaps provides for the greatest number of lone mothers and children of lone mothers, given that orphans have entitlement even when the parent with whom they are living is ineligible. The pension is more a recognition of the economic value of marriage (even broken marriages) than of the financial obligations towards children. On the other hand, it does not take into account the real financial situation of mothers, fathers and children. Under-age children or those who have reached majority but have no means of support receive much less benefit than widows (or widowers) irrespective of whether the latter are living with the children or not, whether they maintain them or not, or what financial means they have. However, if the children are still dependent on the parent, the latter, even though she/he may not be entitled to a share of the benefit, may be taxed on the benefit received by the children. This provision has the symbolic and practical effect of strengthening the children's dependence on the family, while at the same time penalising both the children and the parent. The parent is regarded as the executor of the children's income, even when she/he is not entitled to benefit. The survivor's pension is indicative of Italian familism, which permeates both the insurance-based system and the assistance-based one. Several features emerge: prolonged dependence of children on their parents; little attention paid to the real costs to parents of maintaining children; and finally, no protection for mothers who combine the status of divorced-without-maintenance (a growing number) with having dependent children.

The role of fathers: shared legal responsibility and limited financial responsibility

There is a hierarchy in respect of the sources of income available to lone mothers, in which the role of the father is given little importance. Yet fathers would appear to make an important contribution. If separated or divorced, with or without a new family, they are still obliged to maintain their legitimate children or any out-of-wedlock children they recognise. In fact, however, only a small proportion of separated or divorced lone mothers or never-married mothers with children recognised by the father actually receive maintenance for themselves and their children. Not even the courts can oblige the father to pay up.

The principle of the parents' responsibility to 'maintain, raise and educate their children, even those born out-of-wedlock' was enshrined in Article 30 of the 1947 Constitution. Family law and the new divorce law provided for the equal treatment of legitimate and illegitimate ('natural') children. In legal terms, this produced a complex pattern based on three points:

(1) More opportunity to file a paternity suit, with limitations for married women with children born out of wedlock.

(2) Equal parental responsibility, but with no effective sanctions in respect of maintenance outside of marriage.

(3) The equal rights of children as far as inheritance is concerned, with fewer guarantees in practical terms for out-of-wedlock children and those with divorced parents.

As a consequence, there is a marked distinction between the various types of parental responsibility which is reflected in policies. In most cases of divorce, the mother is given custody of the children and responsibility for child care is attributed to women throughout the family network. It is assumed that the father will take financial responsibility for both his first and second families. However, the emphasis placed on the shared responsibility of both parents is not accompanied by any effective means to enforce the 'natural' or divorced father's responsibility. In the case of unmarried couples in particular, lone mothers have very few financial guarantees if cohabitation ceases or their partner dies.

Fathers are also noticeable by their absence from the debate on welfare policy. The National Association for Divorced and Separated Fathers presses for more male responsibility in respect of child care. There is no pressure, however, to stimulate paternal financial responsibility, which has been decreasing over the years. The problem is also concealed by the gender neutral welfare system and a family system orientated towards marriage. By contrast, the responsibility of the father is a major issue in discussions on reproduction. Whether the topic is abortion (especially with regard to never-married women) or artificial reproduction, we are seeing attempts to make the right to abortion a decision of the couple and to establish a statute of rights for the biological father. The debate has assumed the strident tones of ideological conflict because of the problem of re-defining social and biological relations in the family.

Basic questions and trends in the re-legitimisation of family policies

In the 1980s and 1990s, discussions on the need for, and possible direction of, family policies were taken up again (Gorrieri 1983; Comitato per l'anno internazionale della famiglia 1994). The merest mention – or lack of it – of 'the family' or 'families' in the drafting of a law triggered heated arguments among the various political and cultural movements involved, even before the effects of the proposed measure could possibly be assessed. This difficulty in distinguishing the rhetorical aspects of a law from the real impact of its implementation is characteristic of the Italian welfare system. Moreover, the Italian welfare system seems to be unable to separate public responsibility for care and benefits from that of the family and the non-profit sector (which is, in any case, mostly subsidised by public funds). One of the most deep-rooted reasons for the absence of a coherent national assistance policy is basic uncertainty as to the political approach. There are two underlying questions. First, which definition of the family should inform policies? Second, how far should women be able to exercise independence in regard to reproduction and motherhood? The definition of lone mothers in political debate and welfare practice depends on the answers to these two questions.

At the national level, the Minister for Social Solidarity is responsible for family policy, with topics ranging from issues associated with minors and young adults to the elderly and disabled, immigrants and the voluntary sector. However, the Department has no independent budget. Prior to 1990, there was no Ministry for Social Affairs in Italy. It was set up in the wake of emergency situations linked to immigration and drug addiction. In just a few years, there have been three name changes. In 1994, it became the Ministry for the Family and Social Solidarity, now shortened to the Ministry for Social Solidarity. Throughout this period, three characteristics of the Ministry have remained constant despite changes in political orientation. First, it has responded to emergency situations rather than tackling the institutional policy structure. Second, on family policy themes such as benefits for caregiving, adoption, abortion and poverty, it has produced a moral discourse (on the behaviour the citizen should adopt) rather than a political one (on which policies to implement). Third, it has proposed interventions orientated more towards the compulsory solidarity of the family or the spontaneous solidarity of voluntary groups, rather than ones directed towards redefining the confused patchwork of responsibilities of public bodies as regards welfare.[7]

In the 1980s and 1990s, the issue of women's independence in respect of reproduction has been eclipsed by this new interest in the family. The debate

---

7   Since May 1996 two well-known feminists have held posts in the new government (the Ministers of Social Solidarity and Equal Opportunity), but it is too early to predict the effect this will have on welfare policy.

over which family model should underpin welfare policies was taken up again at the beginning of the 1980s. The debate goes back to the question of whether or not it was necessary to have specific family policies. The main points under discussion are these:

(1) How public assistance should be limited.

(2) How the social actions of non-profit organisations (mostly belonging to the Catholic sphere of influence, state-financed and run by religious associations) should be encouraged.

(3) How to place greater responsibility on the family and which families should receive extra financial help.

(4) Whether greater importance should be given to the family group than to the individual when deciding entitlements.

(4) Whether caring activities should be considered as having economic value, and whether women's employment should be seen as an individual 'choice' or as a right.

This ongoing debate is now producing some practical results: the setting up of a preferential tax system for non-profit organisations; larger benefits in respect of dependent spouses than for dependent children in order to promote the traditional family; tax deductions of a pro-natalist nature for children (with preferential treatment for poorer families after the third child); cuts in state funding for crèches; no expansion of part-time employment, not even in areas of high unemployment for women; and the revival of the idea of pensions for housewives, now called, in gender neutral language, pensions for 'persons who perform unpaid caring activities in connection with family responsibilities'. In respect of the last, a law proposed in August 1996, resuscitates the male-bread-winner model. The pension covers time spent caring for both dependent people (young children, the elderly and disabled) and self-sufficient relatives (husbands and grown-up children). This measure favours the 'servile economy' of the family and reinforces the gender imbalance in the division of unpaid work. It should be remembered that Italy is one of the European countries where the gender imbalance in the use of paid and unpaid time is highest (Sabbadini and Palomba 1994; Bimbi 1995d).

Due to the small sums involved and the low thresholds envisaged, the impact of all these laws will be more symbolic than real. If the embryo of a family policy is forming at the national level, it would appear to have the hallmarks of the male-breadwinner model. This becomes more important if we consider women's low labour participation rate, the inflexibility of the labour market and the sharp division between North and South. The trend towards a preference for the family with a male breadwinner and the woman as housewife is on the increase. Thus, despite new research that has revealed the existence of lone mother families, they have continued to be ignored by national policy makers.[8]

However, the issues raised by lone-mother families have met with some tangible response at the regional level. Between 1989 and 1995, six regions (Emilia-Romagna, Trentino-Alto Adige, Friuli-Venezia Giulia, Liguria, Marche and Abruzzo) passed laws on family policy and others are under discussion. Some limit action to married couple families, but others, going beyond the terms of the Constitution (Article 29), include families not founded on marriage. All these regional laws, whether explicitly or implicitly, pursue a generally pro-natalist objective. However, the distribution of rights and responsibilities varies greatly. There are at least three different models. The first favours the male-breadwinner regime by giving financial incentives to extend women's responsibility for care giving. The second model is directly pro-natalist, giving financial support for new marriages and childbirth. The third aims to support family solidarity by extending individual rights and encouraging measures to redress gender inequalities. The third model, which combines Italian familism, institutional welfare and feminism, is to be found in the first law on family policy, passed by the Emilia-Romagna region in 1989. There are two premises on which this law bases its welfare interventions: the individual's freedom of choice in the field of sexuality and reproduction, and equal recognition of all family forms. The law specifically identifies lone mothers as rights-bearing individuals, rather than as social problems. Some provisions such as unguaranteed loans and Family Centres, may, in practice, be used more often by poor lone mothers, but on the whole lone mothers appear to be included in a common model of citizenship. Even in the case of Emilia-Romagna, although it is not set up as the ideal, the married couple is still envisaged as the typical family. However, policies are not exclusively limited to families founded on marriage.

The Catholic Church claims that legislation on the family and reproduction should conform strictly to its doctrines and exerts pressure to this end. An information campaign by the Government Ministry for the Family and Social Solidarity (1995) proposed that unmarried women should put their children up for adoption as an alternative to abortion, without mentioning any provisions for the aid of lone mothers. The most explicit message to pregnant never-married women urges them to abandon the baby at birth. However, the

---

8   The National Statistics Institute (ISTAT) in its multi-purpose study on families (ISTAT 1985; ISTAT 1993), the National Institute for Population Studies (IRP) in its report on demographic trends (IRP 1985; Golini *et al.* 1988; Golini 1994), as well as government reports on poverty (Gorrieri and Saraceno 1986; Commissione d'indagine sulla povertà e l'emarginazione sociale 1996 and 1996b), family policy (Comitato per l'anno internazionale della famiglia 1994) and minors (Centro nazionale per la difesa dell'infanzia 1996), have all contributed to our knowledge of new family structures and trends.

influence of the Catholic Church on the political system seems to be stronger than its ability to affect the behaviour of the individual.

In late 1996 the focus of the public debate shifted to the crisis of individual morality. Discussion of cases indicating a mild resurgence of infanticide and abandonment of new-born babies (left in hospitals or in the street), drew attention to the moral responsibility of women. By contrast, there is silence with regards to public responsibility and the living conditions of lone mothers and their children. At the same time, the financial commitment of the state to the provision of child care and health care for young children is being withdrawn.

The lowering of the age of first sexual intercourse and with it girls' earlier exposure to the risk of unwanted pregnancies have brought out the conflict between two moral positions and welfare perspectives, which seem more polarised in Italy than elsewhere. Those who stress the moral independence of women as regards childbirth tend to favour public intervention which does not penalise contraception, abortion in the case of unwanted pregnancies, families not founded on marriage, and lone motherhood. However, this view is increasingly delegitimised and silenced in the public debate. The emphasis placed on the morality of the couple and the defence of life from the moment of conception is accompanied by resistance to information on contraceptive methods and a 'preference' for pre-natal decision to adopt.

Conclusions

In the global context of Italian social policy, lone mothers are, in the first place, *invisible*. They are included in the labour market, the economic network of the family, the welfare system and in the legal guarantees of equal responsibilities between parents, although this does not lead to real parity and equal opportunity as regards income and social protection. Second, when lone mothers receive benefits directly, they are *hidden* behind the rights of their children, although in practice the protection given to minors depends on the legal and social status of their mothers. Third, when lone mothers do emerge they become an *embarrassment* to public officials.

At the present moment, mainly at the national level, public discourse presents the choices and conditions of motherhood in terms of either the highly asymmetric 'normal' married couple (with the 'choice' of becoming a house-wife), or morally deviant behaviour (abortions and infanticide). National policy seems to be moving in two directions: first, financially limited but ideologically important action to support families where the woman is a housewife and where there are more than three children; and second, action involving social control and moral censure of the 'results' of pre-marital sex for poorer or culturally deprived women. On the one hand, a certain preference is being given to the male-breadwinner regime. On the other, the lack of attention to lone mothers, lack of information on contraception, pressure to renounce the right to abortion and advice to abandon babies (as an alternative) would appear again to present the most negative image of the lone, never-married mother: that of a mere procreator, unworthy of bringing up or even nursing her baby.

In its social security system above all, the Italian welfare system retains many cultural features of the earlier patriarchal model (Bettio and Villa 1993). However, at the local level, welfare provisions now seem to be characterised mainly by the importance placed on the family support network. In general, the system is one in which dependence is intergenerational rather than between men and women. Women's presence in the labour market depends on the re-allocation of their care-giving work to older women. Moreover, young people's lack of economic resources relies on the extension of their parents' economic responsibility. However, if we look at the gender gap in respect of the time devoted to paid work and housework, we realise that, far from being in conflict with the gender regime, generational solidarity actually contributes to maintaining it. Financial aid from the family of origin, together with child care by grandmothers supplements the economy of the nuclear family, but weakens male responsibility for caregiving and, if the family breaks up, for maintenance. Italian familism prevails over the male-breadwinner model, but also masks it, at least partially, just as it masks the economic weakness of women, especially lone mothers, in the labour market.

Despite the Northern dual-breadwinner norm (see Table 7.10), women who are professionally less qualified and those who live in the South of the country in areas of high unemployment are more strongly affected by the way in which employment is conceptualised as a full-time activity for adult males despite the declared gender neutrality of Italian labour policies. Women and young people are deterred by the contractual and regulatory obstacles to part-time work and the lack of effective means to enter or re-enter the labour market. Discrimination against women is forbidden by law, but the larger workings of the labour market hinder the increase of female participation in paid work. There has been an increase in the dual breadwinner system in the more developed areas of Northern and Central Italy, where the inclusion of women workers in insurance-based welfare has tended to hide the great build-up of responsibilities for lone mothers. However, most of the country retains the norm of female economic dependence on marriage and the family. Unemployed lone mothers in those areas where there are few jobs even for men can count neither on a marginal position in the labour market, nor on the earnings of their former partner and especially not, as we have seen, on the efficacy of the welfare system. In these areas compulsory familism conceals the effects of a strongly male-breadwinner orientated system.

In conclusion, it can be said that lone mother policies are not defined within the framework of an explicitly male-breadwinner welfare system, although recent national measures would appear to tend in this direction. On the whole, local policies are more influenced by the familist tendency of welfare assistance, which is weak as regards economic intervention, fragmentary in its recognition of rights and ambiguous in its cultural orientation. In particular, social assistance is inextricably linked with and subordinate to labour policy, which in its turn is directed towards keeping children dependent on the family in more developed areas and wives dependent on their husbands in poorer regions.

References

Barbagli, M. (1990) *Provando e riprovando. Matrimonio, famiglia e divorzio in Italia e in altri paesi occidentali.* Bologna: Il Mulino.

Bettio, F. and Villa, P. (1993) 'Strutture familiari e mercati del lavoro nei paesi sviluppati. L'emergere di un percorso mediterraneo per l'integrazione delle donne nel mercato del lavoro.' *Economia e lavoro 2*, 3–25.

Bimbi, F. (1991) 'Parenthood in Italy: asymmetric relationships and family affection.' In U. Bjornberg (ed) *European Parents in the 1990s. Contradiction and Comparisons.* The State University of New Jersey, New Brunswick: Rutgers, Transaction Pub.

Bimbi, F. (1993) 'Gender, "gift relationship" and the welfare state cultures in Italy.' In J. Lewis (ed) *Women and Social Policies in Europe. Work, Family and the State.* Aldershot: Edward Elgar Publishers.

Bimbi, F. (1995a) 'Rappresentazioni e politiche familiari in Italia.' In J. Bradshaw *et al. Politiche per le famiglie. Nuovi modelli familiari e politiche sociali in Europa.* Torino: Edizioni gruppo Abele.

Bimbi, F. (1995b) 'Gender division of labour and Welfare State provisions in Italy.' In W. Tineke, G. Frinking and R. Vogels (eds) *Work and family in Europe: The Role of Policies.* Tilburg: Tilburg University Press.

Bimbi, F. (1995c) *Répresentions et politiques familiales en Italie. Modes de garde des enfants, activité professionnelle des méres et crise politique-institutionelle des années 1980–1990.* Rapport de recherce pour le CNAF, Paris. Padoue: Université de Padoue.

Bimbi, F. (1995d) 'Metafore di genere tra lavoro pagato e lavoro non pagato.' *PolisPolis 3*, 379–401.

Bimbi, F. (ed) (1996a) 'Costo dei figli e disegualianze di genere.' *Inchiesta 111*, special issue.

Bimbi, F. (1996b) Differenze di genere nelle decisioni di procreazione. *Inchiesta 111*, 15–22.

Bimbi, F. (1996c) 'Symbolismes partagés et paradigmes societaux. La construction des questions sociales autour des familles.' In J. Comaille and F. De Singly (eds) *La famille dans la construction de l'Europe politique*, Le cahiers du CEVIPOV, 15, Centre d'étude de la vie politique française, Paris: FNSP, CNR.

Bimbi,F. (forthcoming) 'Le politiche familiari in Italia. Un caso di federalismo mancato?' In F. Bimbi and A. Del Re (eds) *Genere e democrazia. La cittadinanza delle donne a cinquant'anni dal voto.* Torino: Rosemberg and Sellier.

Bimbi, F. and Castellano, G. (eds) (1990) *Madri e padri. Transizioni dal patriarcato e cultura dei servizi*. Milano: Angeli.

Blangiardo, G.C. and Bonarini, F. (1988) 'Abortività e controllo dei concepimenti.' In A. Golini *et al. Secondo Rapporto sulla situazione demografica italiana.* Roma: IRP CNR.

Boccia, M.L. *et al.* (1987) 'Il Movimento Femminista degli anni '70.' *Memoria 19–20*, special issue.

Bock, G. (1992) 'Povertà femminile, maternità e diritti della madre nell'ascesa dello Stato assistenziale 1890–1950.' In F. Thebaud (eds) *Storia delle donne. Il Novecento.* Bari: Laterza.

Bordin, M. (1996) 'Uno, nessuno, centomila welfare. Evidenze empiriche da una ricerca sulle politiche provinciali per le madri sole. Paper for the Conference' *Riflessività e responsabilità. La società italiana in un'epoca di globalizzazione.* Italian Sociological Association. 'Everyday life' Committee, Padua: University of Padua, October 3–5.

Calabrò, A.R. and Grasso, L. (eds) (1985) *Dal Movimento Femminista al Femminismo Diffuso*. Milano: Angeli.

Cappiello, A. *et al.* (1988) *Donne e diritto. Due secoli di legislazione 1796–1986.* Roma: Commissione nazionale Pari Opportunità, Presidenza del Consiglio dei Ministri.

Castiglioni, M. and Dalla Zuanna, G. (1995) 'Some indications on reproductive behaviour of never-married women in Italy.' In M. Castiglioni and G. Dalla Zuanna *et al. European Population Conference, Contributions of Italian Scholars.* Roma: CNR, IRP.

Centro nazionale per la tutela dell'infanzia, Dipartimento Affari sociali (1996) *Rapporto sulla condizione dei minori in Italia 1996.* Roma: Presidenza del Consiglio dei Ministri.

Comitato per l'anno internazionale della famiglia (1994) *Per una politica familiare in Italia.* Roma: Dipartimento Affari sociali, Presidenza del Consiglio dei Ministri.

Commissione d'indagine sulla povertà e sull'emarginazione (1996a) *La povertà in Italia 1980–1994.* Roma: Presidenza del Consiglio dei Ministri.

Commissione d'indagine sulla povertà e sull'emarginazione (1996b) *La povertà in Italia 1995.* Roma: Presidenza del Consiglio dei Ministri.

De Grazia, V. (1992a) 'Il patriarcato fascista: come Mussolini governò le donne italiane 1922–1940.' In F. Thebaud (eds) *Storia delle donne. Il Novecento.* Bari: Laterza.

De Grazia, V. (1992b) *How Fascism ruled women 1922–1943.* Berkeley: University of California Press.

De Sandre, P. (1988) 'Quando i figli lasciano la famiglia.' In E. Scabini and P. Donati (ed) *La famiglia 'lunga' del giovane adulto.* Millano: Vita e Pensiero.

De Sandre, P. (1991) 'Contributo delle generazioni ai cambiamenti recenti nei comportamenti e nelle forme familiari.' In P. Donati (ed) *Secondo rapporto sulla famiglia in Italia.* Paoline: Milano.

De Santis, G. (1992) 'A standardized measure of the years spent in a given conjugal or marital state.' *Genus 1–2*, 19–47.

Del Re, A. (ed) (1996) *Quale cittadinanza per le donne?* Milano: Angeli.

Egidi, V. and Zaccarin, S.(1995) 'Women's condition and reproductive behaviour: a multilevel approach to the analysis of Italian data.' In M. Castiglioni and G. Dalla Zuanna *et al. European Population Conference, Contributions of Italian Scholars.* Roma: CNR, IRP.

European Community Commission (1995) *Employment in Europe.* Brussel: ECC.

Eurostat (1995) *Labour Force Survey. Results 1993.* Luxembourg: ECC.

Gauthier, A. H. (1995) *The State and the Family. A Comparative Analysis of Family Policy in Industrialized Countries.* Oxford: Oxford University Press.

Giacobazzi, D. *et al.* (1989) *I percorsi del cambiamento. Ricerca sui comportamenti contraccettivi in Emilia Romagna.* Torino: Rosemberg & Sellier.

Giullardi, S. (1996) Lone mothers, dependence and poverty. Paper for the Conference *Riflessività e responsabilità. La società italiana in un'epoca di globalizzazione.* Italian Sociological Association. 'Everyday life' Committee, Padua: University of Padua, October 3–5.

Golini, A., Menniti, A. and Palomba, R. (1987) 'Social needs and use of services by one-parent families.' In L. Shamgar-Handelman and R. Palomba (eds) *Alternative Patterns of Family Life in Modern Societies.* Roma: IRP, CNR.

Golini, A. *et al.* (1988) *Secondo Rapporto sulla situazione demografica italiana.* Roma: IRP, CNR.

Golini, A. (1988) 'Profilo demografico della famiglia italiana.' In P. Melograni (ed) *La famiglia Italiana dall'Ottocento a oggi.* Bari: Laterza.

Golini, A. (ed) (1994) *Tendenze demografiche e politiche per la popolazione. Terzo rapporto IRP.* Bologna:Il Mulino.

Gorrieri, E. (ed.) (1983) *Famiglia e reddito.* Commissione nazionale per i problemi della famiglia, Roma: Ministero del lavoro e della previdenza sociale.

Gorrieri, E. and Saraceno, C. (eds) (1986) Rapporto sulla povertà. *Inchiesta 73,* 4–39.

Guizzardi, G. (1976) New Religious Phenomena in Italy. Toward a Post-Catholic Era?. *Archives de Sciences Sociales des Religions 42,* 97–116.

Guizzardi, G. (1982) Famiglia e secolarizzazione. La caduta di due sacralità. *Città e Regione 4,* 72–84.

Ipsen, C. (1993) *Population Policy and Theory in Fascist Italy.* Working paper. Roma: IRP, CNR.

Istituto di Ricerche sulla Popolazione (1985) *Primo rapporto sulla situazione demografica italiana.* Roma: IRP, CNR.

Istituto Nazionale di Statistica (1985) *Indagine sulle strutture ed i comportamenti familiari.* Roma: ISTAT.

Istituto Nazionale di Statistica (1993) *Famiglie, Popolazione, Abitazioni, Indagine Multiscopo sulle Famiglie, vol. 2.* Roma: ISTAT.

Kertzer, D.I. (1993) *Sacrificed for Honor: Italian Infant Abandonment and the Politics of Reproductive Control.* Boston: Bacon Press.

Kyllonen, R. (1996) 'Le 'madri normali' e le 'madri marginali'. I percorsi dell'esclusione e le strategie dell'inclusione sociale delle madri sole nel servizio socio-assistenziale.' Paper for the Conference *Riflessività e responsabilità. La società italiana in un'epoca di globalizzazione.* Italian Sociological Association. 'Everyday life' Committee, Padua: University of Padua, October 3–5.

La Mendola, S. and Neresini F. (1995) *Lone Mothers in Italy. A Small but Differentiated Problem.* London: Working Paper of the Gender and European Welfare Regime research of the Human Capital Mobility Programme of DGXII of the European Commission. Contract n. CHRX CT93 0224 EEC LSE.

Lesthaeghe, R. (1992) *The Second Demographic Transition in Western Countries: An Interpretation.* IPD Working papers, Brussel: Vrije Universiteit.

Livi Bacci, M. (1980) *Donna, fecondità e figli.* Bologna: Il Mulino.

Livi Bacci, M. and Breschi (1992) 'La fecondità.' In M. Barbagli and D. Kertzer (ed) *Storia della famiglia italiana. 1750–1950.* Bologna: Il Mulino.

Menniti, A. and Palomba, R. (1988) *Le famiglie con un solo genitore in Italia.* Roma: IRP, CNR.

Menniti, A. and Palomba, R. (1994) 'Demografia e pianificazione delle nascite.' In A. Golini (ed) *Tendenze demografiche e politiche per la popolazione. Terzo rapporto IRP.* Bologna: Il Mulino.

Menniti, A. (1995) 'Social policy and family policy in Italy.' In M. Castiglioni and G. Dalla Zuanna *et al. European Population Conference, Contributions of Italian scholars.* Roma: CNR, IRP.

Nava 1996 'Il figlio unico. Modelli di doppia presenza e strategie di decisione delle coppie', *Inchiesta 111,* 5–14.

Palomba, R.(1987) *Vita di coppia e figli. Le opinioni degli italiani degli anni Ottanta.* Firenze: La Nuova Italia.

Palomba, R. and Menniti A.(1994) 'Genitori e figli nelle politiche familiari.' In A. Golini (ed) *Tendenze demografiche e politiche per la popolazione. Terzo rapporto IRP.* Bologna: Il Mulino.

Pinnelli, A. and Prati, S. (1994) 'Concepimenti fuori dal matrimonio.' Paper for the Conference *Mutamenti della famiglia nei paesi occidentali.* Bologna, October 6–8.

Pomata, G. (1980) 'Madri illegittime tra Ottocento e Novecento. Storie cliniche e storie di vita.' *Quaderni storici 44,* 497–542.

Pressman, S. (1995) *The Gender Poverty Gap in Developed Countries: Causes and Cures.* Luxembourg: Luxembourg Income Study, working paper series 135.

Rossi Sciumé, G. and Scabini, E. (1991) 'Le famiglie monogenitoriali in Italia.' In P. Donati (ed) *Secondo rapporto sulla famiglia in Italia.* Milano: Paoline.

Rubery, J. and Fagan, C.(1993) *Wage Determination and Sex Segregation in Employment in the European Community.* Network of experts on the situation of women in the labour market. Bruxelles: Equal Opportunity Unit, ECC.

Ruspini, E.(1996) 'Madri sole, povertà e politiche familiari in Europa.' Paper for the Conference *Riflessività e responsabilità. La società italiana in un'epoca di globalizzazione.* Italian Sociological Association. 'Everyday life' Committee, Padua: University of Padua, October 3–5.

Sabbadini, L.L. (1991a) 'Le convivenze prematrimoniali.' In A. Menniti (ed) *Le famiglie Italiane degli anni '80*. Roma: IRP, CNR.

Sabbadini, L.L. (1991b) 'Le libere unioni.; In A. Menniti (ed) *Le famiglie Italiane degli anni '80*. Roma: IRP, CNR.

Sabbadini, L.L. and Palomba, R. (1994) *Tempi diversi. L'uso del tempo di uomini e donne nell'Italia di oggi*. Roma: Commissione nazionale per le pari opportunità, Presidenza del Consiglio dei Ministri, ISTAT.

Santini, A. (1988) 'Natalità e fecondità.' In A. Golini *et al. Secondo rapporto sulla situazione demografica italiana*. Roma: IRP, CNR.

Santini, A. (1995a) 'La fecondità in Emilia Romagna dal dopoguerra: continuità e discontinuità nel comportamento riproduttivo delle donne nate tra il 1920–1962.' In M.G. Porrelli (ed) *La popolazione dell'Emilia-Romagna alle soglie del 2000*. Bologna: Regione Emilia Romagna.

Santini, A. (1995b) *Continuità e discontinuità nel comportamento riproduttivo delle donne italiane nel dopoguerra: tendenze generali della fecondità delle coorti nelle ripartizioni tra il 1952 e il 1991*. Working papers 53. Firenze: Dipartimento Statistico.

Saraceno, C. (1988) 'La famiglia: i paradossi della costruzione del privato.' In P. Ariés and G. Duby (eds) *La vita privata. Il Novecento*. Bari: Laterza.

Saraceno, C. (1991a) 'Redefining maternity and paternity: gender, pronatalism and social policies in Fascist Italy.' In G. Bock and P. Thone (eds) *Maternity and Gender Policies*. London:Routledge.

Saraceno, C. (1991b) 'Dalla istituzionalizzazione alla de-istituzionalizzazione dei corsi di vita femminili e maschili?' *Stato e Mercato 33*, 431–449.

Saraceno, C. (1992) 'Le donne nella famiglia: una complessa costruzione giuridica. 1750–1942.' In M. Barbagli and D. Kertzer (eds) *Storia della famiglia italiana. 1750–1950*. Bologna: Il Mulino.

Saraceno, C. (1994) 'The ambivalent familism of the Italian Welfare State.' *Social Politics 1*, 60–82.

Simoni, S. (forthcoming) 'Lone mothers in Italy: an invisible subject.' In O. Hufton and Y. Kravaritou (eds) *Gender and the Use of Time*. London: Kluwer Law International.

Stiglitz, J.E. (1993) *Economics*. New York: W.W. Norton & Company.

Sutter, R. (1996) 'Politiche sociali per le madri sole. L'osservatorio del servizio sociale di Ravenna.' Paper for the Conference *Riflessività e responsabilità. La società italiana in un'epoca di globalizzazione*. Italian Sociological Association. 'Everyday life' Committee, Padua: University of Padua, October 3–5.

Terragni, L. (1996) 'Madri nubili e loro figli illegittimi: segretezza, controllo sociale, carità assistenza. Una valutazione del sistema normativo e assitenziale dall'Ottocento ad oggi.' Paper for the Conference *Riflessività e responsabilità. La società italiana in un'epoca di globalizzazione*. Italian Sociological Association. 'Everyday life' Committee, Padua: University of Padua, October 3–5.

Trifiletti, R. (1995) *Defining Family Obligations in Europe: The Case of Italy*. Research Report, Bath: University of Bath.

Trifiletti, R. (1996) 'Pratiche sociali e costruzione identitaria. Primi orientamenti e note dal campo di una ricerca in corso in Toscana.' Paper for the Conference

Riflessività e responsabilità. La società italiana in un'epoca di globalizzazione. Italian Sociological Association. 'Everyday life' Committee, Padua: University of Padua, October 3–5.

Zanatta, A.L. (1996) 'Famiglie con un solo genitore e rischio di povertà.' *PolisPolis X* *1*, 63–79.

The Contributors

Franca Bimbi is Associate Professor of Family Sociology in the Department of Sociology at the University of Padova. She is the founder of the 'Elvira Badaracco Foundation Research Centre on Women's Liberation Movements in Italy and a member of the ESA (European Sociological Association). She is also a Consultant to the Italian Minister of Social Solidarity and to the Italian Minister of Equal Opportunity. Her current areas of research and publication include the welfare state and women's citizenship, local welfare in Italy, the ethics of care, the gender division of labour and the social construction of assisted fertilisation.

Jet Bussemaker is Assistant Professor at the Department of Political Science and Public Administration, Free University in Amsterdam. During the first half of 1997 she was a visiting scholar at the Center for European Studies, Harvard University, Cambridge (Ma). Her current research focuses on gender, citizenship and welfare state reform in European countries.

Pauline Conroy was previously a Research Fellow with the European University Institute, Florence and the Council of Europe, Strasbourg and is currently a Research Fellow for the Social Science Research Centre (UCD) where she is a guest Lecturer in European Social Policy at the Department of European Social Policy and Social Work. She is also currently the Technical Editor of the European Commission's Annual Report on equal opportunities. She has undertaken research and been published on women's employment and poverty in Europe, women's reproductive rights in Ireland, the status of mothers and the phenomena of social exclusion in Europe.

Annemieke van Drenth is Assistant Professor at the Department of Women's Studies of Leiden University. During the last few years she has been a Research Fellow for the National Science Foundation on a programme on gender and care and is currently preparing a book on 'caring power'. She has published work on the history of girls' education ,and welfare state policies on girls and women.

Barbara Hobson is Director of the Advanced Research School in Comparative Gender Studies and Associate Professor of Social Policy in the Sociology Department at Stockholm University. She is also the founding and current

Editor of *Social Policies: International Studies of Gender, State and Society*. She has published articles on gender and welfare states and on the themes of gender and citizenship, women's power resources and welfare state formation, and woman's economic dependency and social citizenship. Some of her publications in these areas include: (with Marika Lindholm) *Women's Collectives, Power Resources and the Making of the Welfare State;* 'Theory and society' in *Thematic Issues on Citizenship*, Summer (1996) and; 'Frauenbewegung fur Staatsburgerrechte-Das Beispiel Schweden' in *Feninisistche Studien*, Fall (1996).

Trudie Knijn is Associate Professor in the Department of General Social Sciences at the University of Utrecht. She is also coordinator of the European Network for Theory and Research on Women, Welfare State and Citizenship. Her current research projects include; the (im)possibilities of caring fatherhood; gender and welfare regimes; and gender, care and welfare states. She has published widely on the topics of gender, parenting and citizenship.

Jane Lewis was formerly Professor of LSE at All Souls College, Oxford where she is currently a Fellow and Director of the Wellcome Unit for the History of Medicine. Her areas of research include; gender and welfare regimes with special reference to one-parent families; effects of the new Community Care Legislation; and the boundaries between the voluntary and statutory sector. She is author of 14 books and some 70 articles including most recently 'The Boundary between Voluntary and Statutory Social Service, 1970-1918' (forthcoming) in *The Historical Journal* and (with P.Bernstock, V.Bovell and K.Wookey) 'The Purchase/Provider Split in Social Care: is it Working?' in *Social Policy and Administration 30*, 1.

Ilona Ostner is a Professor of Social Policy at the University of Göttingen.

Janneke Plantenga is Assistant Professor at the Economic Institute of the University of Utrecht. She has a Ph.D. in Economics from the University of Groningen. Her main fields of interest are the history of women's work, changing working time patterns and social policy. She is the Dutch Member of the European Network of experts on 'Gender and Employment'. Together with A. Geske Dijkstra she edited *Gender and Economics: A European Perspective* (1997).

Birte Siim is Associate Professor at the Department of Development and Planning at Aalborg University. She is a coordinator of the EC project 'Gender and Citizenship: Social Integration and Social Exclusion in European Welfare States (1969–1999)'. Her current areas of research include: comparative studies of welfare states; democracy and political culture; political participation and political identities; and gender and citizenship. Among her latest publications in English are: 'Engendering democracy : The interplay between women's citizenship and political participation in Scandinavia' in *Social Politics: Interna-*

tional Studies in Gender, State and Society, 1, 3 (1994) and 'Gender, Citizenship and Empowerment' in *CID Studies 12* (1996). She is presently the co-ordinator of the national Danish research project 'Gender, Democracy and Welfare States – In Transition (1996–2000)'.

Mieko Takahashi is a doctoral student in the Department of Sociology at Stockholm University. Her research focuses on gender dimensions of family life in Sweden and Japan. Some of her recent publications include: 'Solo parent families in Sweden: family policies and tendencies' (translated from the Japanese), *Household Economy Quarterly,* Summer (1997) and; with Barbara Hobson, 'Gendered dimensions of social citizenship: The case of solo mothers in Sweden' (translated from the Swedish) in *General Welfare: Threats and Possibilities,* Welfare Project Report 3 (1996).

Subject Index

abortions
  Britain 53
  Ireland 80, 82
  Italy 173
adoptions
  Ireland 79–80
  Netherlands 114
allowances
  Britain 7, 57, 58
  Ireland 81
Annual Report of the
  National Assistance
  Board (1949) 58
autonomy
  Caribbean women 100–1
  dual-breadwinner model
    143–6
  fight for, Ireland 78–9
  issue of 16–17
  rights to, Sweden 129–30

behaviour, attempts to
  change 51, 67–8
benefits 1, 5–6
  Britain 61, 63
  Denmark 142, 154–5,
    156f, 159
  Germany 27–8
  Ireland 89–90, 91
  Netherlands 107t, 108
  Sweden 130–1
Beveridge, William 7, 57–8
birth rates
  Denmark 146
  Ireland 80
  Italy 189
births, out-of-wedlock
  Britain 52–4, 55t
  Denmark 146

Germany 23, 24, 26t,
  33–4
Ireland 77, 79
Italy 173, 174t, 178
Netherlands 100
BOM-mothers 115
breadwinner–caretaker
  regime, Netherlands
  97–8

care provision
  never-married mothers,
    Netherlands 113–14
  unmarried mothers,
    Ireland 76
care work
  recognition of 2, 13–16
  Scandinavia 144
  see also child care
Caregiver Social Wage
  Model 15–16
categorisation, of women
  Britain 65
  Ireland 88–90
  Italy 182
  Sweden 121, 127
Catholicism, Italy 182,
  183, 184, 185–6, 194
child care
  Britain 58–9, 63–4
  Denmark 155, 157–63,
    167
  Italy 177, 187–8
  Netherlands 112–13
  Norway 144–5
  Sweden 131
child poverty, Britain 69
Child Support Act (1991)
  9, 65, 67–8, 71–2, 85
Child Support Agency 85
childlessness, Germany 36
children
  Britain
    allowances 7, 57
    legislation 68–9
  Germany
    best interests 22, 31
    family income 30t

legitimised 26t
status 43
Children Act (1989) 68–9
choice, freedom of
  compensation, Sweden
    128
  employment, Britain 62–3
  welfare dependency 5–6
citizenship see social
  citizenship
Civil Code (1942) 183
cohabitation
  Britain 54–5, 64–5
  Denmark 146, 157
  Germany 35
  Italy 180
  Netherlands 109
  Sweden 133
Commission for
  Constitutional Reform
  38–9
Commission on Family and
  Marriage 129–30
community employment
  schemes 92
Concordat (1929) 183
contraceptives 80, 179, 180
costs, lone parenting,
  Sweden 134–5
crèches, Italy 187–8
crime rates, Britain 67
cultural image, Denmark
  142, 146, 150
cultural norms, Germany
  28, 47
custody rights, Germany
  45–6

Dáil debate 89
daycare see child care
decommodification 2
defamilialism 2
demographic changes,
  Germany 33–6
Denmark 140–67
  autonomy and
    dual-breadwinner
    model 143–6

206

Author Index